REVOLT
AGAINST MODERNITY

SOCIAL, ECONOMIC AND POLITICAL STUDIES OF THE MIDDLE EAST

ÉTUDES SOCIALES, ÉCONOMIQUES ET POLITIQUES DU MOYEN ORIENT

VOLUME XXXIX

MICHAEL YOUSSEF, Ph.D.

REVOLT
AGAINST MODERNITY

LEIDEN
E. J. BRILL
1985

REVOLT
AGAINST MODERNITY

MUSLIM ZEALOTS AND THE WEST

BY

MICHAEL YOUSSEF, Ph.D.

LEIDEN
E. J. BRILL
1985

BP
60
Y 68
1985

ISBN 90 04 07559 3

*Dedicated to the late
Dr. James F. Hopewell (Emory
University, Atlanta, Georgia),
a friend, fellow priest, mentor,
and wise counselor, whose memory
I will always cherish.*

CONTENTS

ACKNOWLEDGEMENTS

The English poet, John Donne, said it well: "No man is an island." Paraphrasing Donne, I might say, "No man (by himself) is an author." Many people have contributed significantly to this book.

I want to thank Emory University professors, Drs. Steven M. Tipton, Earl Brewer, James Hopewell, Robert Paul, and Ken Stein. Dr. Stein, in particular, worked long, hard hours to help make my task easier. His direction and evaluation, especially on the sensitive issues and the historical overview, were extremely valuable.

Also, I greatly appreciate the assistance of John Bachman, Scott Schreffler, Ruth Self, and Brenda Williams in editing, typing and proofing the manuscript.

And I especially want to thank Haggai Institute, and particularly its founder, Dr. John Haggai, for giving me the time and allowing me to write this book.

INTRODUCTION

The Iranian revolution (1978-1979) startled even those who were exceptionally knowledgeable about Iranian events. The revolution perplexed political analysts and sent a shock wave through the oil-dependent world. Questions were feverishly asked about the meaning of the social upheaval in the Middle East. Many asked whether the government of Shah Muhammad Reza Pahlavi would be the last pro-Western government in the area to fall.

Such questions came not only from officialdom, but, increasingly, from the public at large. When a group of Muslim students occupied the U.S. Embassy and held sixty of its American employees hostage month after month, the world began to pay serious attention to Islamic revolutionary movements.

The October 1981 assassination of President Anwar el Sadat of Egypt by so-called "Muslim extremists" further alerted the world, and more particularly the West, to the violent manifestation of Islamic revolutionary movements. And because of the high degree of dependency of Western industry and even Western civilization upon oil from that part of the world, the West was impelled to take notice of the new Islamic fervor in the Middle East.

One fact of major importance is that the Christian West no longer enjoys the multifaceted supremacy and hegemony that it did in the decades immediately after World War II. In the last thirty years, well over one hundred new nation-states, at least formally, have asserted their independence and exposed the West, particularly the United States, to their own distinct cultures.

In the process of asserting and affirming their independence, many of these nations have reached into the reservoir of their past in an attempt to retrieve "archaic" elements of their heritage; often they have displayed these elements in an exaggerated fashion.

This trend is clearly seen in Islamic circles through what has become known as the "resurgence of Islam." For example, the 16 April 1979 cover story of *Time* Magazine described this dynamic emergence in the following terms:

> "Muslims are rediscovering their spiritual roots and reasserting the political power of their Islamic way of life. Repelled by the bitter fruits of modernization and fired by a zealous pride in its ancient heritage the *Ummah* (the community) of Islam is stirring with revival ... the West can no longer afford to ignore or dismiss the living power of the prophet's message."

Two issues, which some Western analysts tend to ignore, however, are of particular relevance to the roots of this East-West conflict.

1. The process of development and modernization engenders certain discrepancies within and between nations, i.e., it creates a gap between the haves and the have-nots.
2. The international capitalist economy has penetrated almost every corner of the Third World; more specifically, the Muslim world as a result of the development of the Middle East oil industry.

Indeed, attentiveness to the full historical context is crucial if one is to correctly decipher the term "Islamic resurgence" and what it connotes. This context, which encompasses at least the past two hundred years, revolves principally around the theme of the Muslim world's disadvantageous encounter with the West. Emerging out of protracted interaction, the indigenous political and ideological response of the subordinated Muslim world to the dominant European world gave the first signals of modern "Islamic resurgence" to the Christian West.

Given such a historical context, a strong anti-West flavor is to be expected in the ideological mix of any Muslim country after independence. In the Middle East, particularly in Egypt, the contribution of the Christian West toward the creation of the Jewish state of Israel is a painful thorn in the side of the Muslim Arabs and has further augmented the anti-Western thrust.

Furthermore, the existing regimes, in most cases, suffer from a lack of legitimacy which is often transferred into a lack of legitimacy of the systems over which they preside. This is the result of the unrepresentative and often oppressive character of most regimes in the Muslim countries—on the left or the right—which operate from a narrow social basis.[1]

The problem of legitimacy of the system becomes more acute when models of development—whether of the "laissez faire" or socialist variety—are imported from abroad and fail to satisfy the moral and material aspiration of the masses.

The radical Islamic alternative then becomes attractive to important segments of the population. Its appeal derives from a combination of authentic aspirations for genuine autonomy that other developmental models have never had or no longer possess.

The antagonism between the Christian West and the Muslim East is sobering when put into its proper historical perspective.

Talking with some members of the self-confessed radical or revolutionary Islamic groups, specifically the "Muslim Brotherhood" in Egypt, one soon discovers a root of resentment deeper than that of mere opposition to colonialism.

---

[1] Having lived in Egypt during the Nasser regime, I watched firsthand what happened to voices of opposition. Some were imprisoned, and some were under house arrest; included in these were journalists and former landowners, etc., such as, Mustafa Amin and Fouad Serag el Dean.

To most of these people, the Crusades were not just events in history that took place nearly eight or nine hundred years ago; instead, the Crusades signify a perpetual desire on the part of the Christian West to dominate them and prove their religion inferior. Thus, it is essential to explore even beyond the Crusades in order to comprehend fully the undercurrents of today's Islamic resurgence.

I. STATEMENT OF PURPOSE

This research will deal with the socio-political manifestation of Islamic resurgence in modern Egypt, focusing primarily on the *al-Jihad* movement, from its inception in 1980 to the execution of its leaders following the assassination of Egyptian President Sadat. The group is one of the three major twentieth-century Islamic socio-political and religious movements that together have affected the nation dramatically.

The thrust of this thesis is that Islamic social movements portray unique characteristics as they express themselves within Egyptian society. Because the change desired by these movements is predicated upon what they perceive to be the ideal Islamic state, under one political unit, the leadership of the Prophet and his immediate four successors (caliphs) or the guided four. And, wherever this socio-political ideal is absent, these Islamic socio-political movements adapt revolutionary tactics to overthrow the existing order and return the nation to the ideal.

A study of this nature would be incomplete unless put in its proper context—i.e., in terms of (1) a historical analysis of the roots of Islamic social movements, current Islamic thought as expressed in *al-Jihad* as a stream flowing out of a peculiar interpretation of Islam. (2) The movement's ideology and *modus operandi* as found in the book *The Missing Religious Precept* (an original translation from Arabic is attached in the appendix). And (3) the comparative analysis of *al-Jihad* with other social movement paradigms to assess that Islamic social movements do possess uncommon manifestations.

II. HISTORICAL OVERVIEW

The evolution of Islamic social movements has been shaped by centuries of friction between the East and the West during which there has been a powerful undertow of religious discord. The historical clashes between the Christian West and the Muslim East have been inevitable largely because of their seemingly irreconcilable religious differences.

Islam's implicit goal of global conscription has further contributed to an already volatile situation. Throughout history use has been made of Qur'anic texts such as:

"O ye who believe! Take not the Jews and Christians for friends. They are friends
one to another. He among you who taketh them for friends is (one) of them. Lo!
Allah guideth not wrong doing folk." (Surah 5:51)

Standing upon this Qur'anic foundation and facing a history of hostile confrontation, the *al-Jihad* group and their counterparts are not isolated factions.
They are links in the chain of this continuous historical tension.

   The polarization of the East and the West can be traced back to divergent
Hellenic and Persian worldviews. Still, we must not depreciate the role of the
Prophet Muhammad, who distinguished Muslims (House of Islam) from non-
Muslims (House of War). Further application of this doctrine by the Proph-
et's second successor Omar as stated in his covenant with the conquered
Christian lands exerted tremendous influence on the stance of modern Islamic
social movements.

   Other historical events are important to an understanding of the East/West
conflict. The Crusades have had an adverse and lasting effect on Muslim
society despite the economic benefits they brought to the Middle East. The
curtailment of the Ottoman Empire, coupled with the geographical and
technological expansion of Europe at the turn of the century, compounded
the dilemma. Furthermore, European intervention in the creation of the state
of Israel aggravated the distrust and animosity of the Arab world towards the
West. The Arabs allege that the West implanted the state of Israel in the Middle East in order to advance its interests.

   Also, internal division has characterized Islam, a religion which often tried
to give the impression of being monolithic. There are four schools of interpretation of the sacred law, in addition to the main denominational division
between the Sunni and the Shi'a/Kharijites. The Kharijites are a prototype for
Muslim revival movements;[2] in particular, their belief in the right to usurp and
even assassinate apostate leaders presages the motivation of the social movement under consideration.

   Egypt, the home of *al-Jihad*, has throughout its history been dominated by
foreign powers, but the Arab conquest was a watershed. The imposition of
Islamic norms and values hereafter created tensions between the Copts (pre-
Islamic Christian residents of Egypt) and the Muslims. Conversely, Egyptian
Christians and Jews have been accused of collaboration with the West.

   Another area of acute tension is the issue of socio-economic advancement.
The founder of modern Egypt, Muhammad Ali, and his successors promoted
Western-style socio-economic development and, at the same time, tried to
align it with Islamic principles. They faced a task complicated by the uneasy
encounter between the Islamic Egyptian conscience and progress, which sup-

---

   [2] The terms *revival*, *social*, *sociopolitical*, *religious*, *revolutionary*, and *millenarian* are used
synonymously throughout this book when referring to Islamic movements.

posedly, as an import from the West, would undermine and corrupt Islam. Recently, Sadat's "open door" policies further antagonized those opposed to an influx of Western values.

Thus, two distinct voices have arisen in Egyptian nationalism, one orthodox and the other progressive. On the shifting ground of this dichotomy, Islamic social movements have crystallized their objectives and implemented their strategies in an attempt to secure for the nation the stability of a doctrinally pure religious system.

III. *Al-Jihad*: Description and Evaluation

Al-Jihad was a group of Egyptian young men who are mainly university graduates or university students who banded together in secret cell groups throughout the country.

Their strongly held belief is that Egypt is in deep social and economic trouble because its leadership has gone astray from the original teaching of the Qur'an.

Jihad according to their manifesto (*The Missing Religious Precept*), is precisely: a religious precept (like fasting and praying) that needs to be implemented and imposed on the populace. They go even further to declare *jihad* not only against "infidels" but even against their fellow Muslims whom they perceive as not living up to the tenets of Islam.

The leadership of the movement at least believed that nothing short of a wholesale, radical change in the society can remedy "the current dismal situation which the country is in."

This change can be affected only by enforcing the *Shari'a*, the strict interpretation of the Qur'an and the Sunnah.

Although *al-Jihad* first developed as a secret, underground movement in 1980, it had a sudden and unexpected emergence into the public arena in Egypt during the late 70's and early 80's. This public manifestation was supported by an extensive network of roots that grounded it in previous Islamic movements.

A careful examination of *al-Jihad* as a revolutionary group exposes deeplying threads of continuity, especially with the Muslim Brotherhood movement which started in the 1920's. At the same time, *al-Jihad* differs sharply from preceding Islamic social movements by its unique emphasis on an ideology of violence, which the founder of the movement, Muhammad abd al-Salam Farag, enshrined in his book *The Missing Religious Precept*. (See Appendix)

The respective governments of Nasser and Sadat provided a backdrop for the development of modern Islamic social movements. Both presidents contributed to the renewal of fundamentalist activity: Nasser suffocated democracy and experimented with socialism, whereas Sadat opened the door to Western influences.

The Muslim Brotherhood arose as a reaction to Western domination and as a bid for Islamic unity. Its first leader, Hasan al-Banna, coalesced the religious and political spheres in his ideology. Later, under Said Kotb, the direction of the movement became more acutely anti-government because of the torture its members experienced in prison. Basically, however, the Muslim Brotherhood was a reformative movement that operated within the existing socio-political framework and appealed to a wide cross-section of the populace.

The precise link between the Muslim Brotherhood and *al-Jihad* is *al-Takfier wa al Hijrah* group, which advocated complete dissociation from society until its collapse, when members of the group would return to construct a new Islamic society. The escapist approach of this group was simply not tenable, although the intensity of its aversion to a secularized Islamic society was distilled in the *al-Jihad* movement.

Instead of collective retreat, *al-Jihad* strove to assume power and install their own system of government; they planned to accomplish this change through violent measures.

Like the Muslim Brotherhood, *al-Jihad* advocated strict adherence to the sacred law and the complete amalgamation of politics and religion. The majority of its members were young university students without theological training; yet they were unyielding in their commitment to Islam.

It is important to underline that *al-Jihad* was a highly organized movement at both the structural and operational levels, with widespread overseas contacts. The degree of organization evident in the assassination of Sadat and the plans for seizing power demand that we seriously and carefully evaluate this potent social movement. *Al-Jihad* was not in the least a random and discrete venture.

The impetus behind *al-Jihad* has been preserved in the pages of Farag's book *The Missing Religious Precept*. Farag, the catalyst and real leader of the movement, refined the ideology of *jihad* into its purest form: it involves the killing of those deemed infidels—in particular, leaders who have betrayed Islamic principles. The book offers a detailed prescription for implementing *jihad*.

Hence, we observe in the evolution of Islamic social movements, such as the Muslim Brotherhood and *al-Jihad*, a subtle ebb and flow in which an essential current of reformative zeal and religious fervour remains.

Significantly, too, we note that in spite of the execution of the key leaders for the assassination of Sadat, *al-Jihad* is a formidable, albeit submerged, force in Egypt today.

IV. COMPARATIVE ANALYSIS

Classical definitions of social movements have provided an inadequate expression for the impetus behind Islamic social movements. While most definitions center on comprehensive change in the social order, they often fail to indicate the peculiar nature of the change which Islamic social movements have sought to implement. The marriage of religious and social elements is the crucial distinctive in Islamic social movements.

A precise treatment of an Islamic social movement requires an original definition which will encompass both the social and the religious dimensions of its motivation: that is, its desire to purify and integrate society on the basis of a literal interpretation of Islamic law and in response to a certain socio-political encironment environment.

This study will explore from several angles the nature of the change that *al-Jihad* tried to launch. We will enumerate conditions which, according to *al-Jihad*, contributed to the need for radical social surgery and the correlative rise of social movements; in this case, political dislocation, the reversal of diplomatic relations, economic discrepancies coupled with moral decadence, and social heterogeneity all combined to produce severe cultural stress in the nation of Egypt where *al-Jihad* was born.

Further, we will attempt to ascertain the relative position of *al-Jihad* viz a number of social movement paradigms. While *al-Jihad* eludes the typical delineation between secular and religious movements and makes the task of classification difficult, we will define *al-Jihad* in the Egyptian context by applying to it the developmental structure of Wallace's revitalization-movement theory. We will examine the stages in the evolution of *al-Jihad* and account for its past failures and current regrouping. We will raise the question of whether new leadership will arise to revive *al-Jihad's* attempts to achieve its goals.

When we contemplate the ultimate implications of the rise of a social movement like *al-Jihad*, we are compelled to conclude that though violence of itself as a vehicle of change can seldom be justified, *al-Jihad* may serve as a catalyst for positive changes to the social order in the future. *Al-Jihad* has prompted Egyptian society to entertain the possibility of a shift in direction and forced it to confront the conflicts inherent in comprehensive change, whether reactionary or progressive. Significantly, *al-Jihad* introduced the possibility of change, just as the Protestant Reformation indirectly opened the mind of medieval Europe to progress and new ideas by reclaiming and restoring its heritage of first-century Christianity.

SECTION ONE

HISTORICAL ANALYSIS

CHAPTER ONE

THE ROOT OF THE EAST/WEST DISPUTE

The history of the controversy, one even ventures to say enmity, between the Christian West[1] and the Muslim East goes beyond Charles Martel's victory at the battle of Tours in 732 by which the Muslims were prevented from entering the heart of Europe; it goes beyond the Crusades, which were fought because both Muslims and Christians believed they were liberating their holy places from the "infidels"; it goes beyond these two events, as important as they may be. While the Crusades form a major preliminary chapter in the book of the East versus West quarrel, and chapters on Colonialism and what can be called "neo-Colonialism" are bound to follow, the very first chapter must uncover the root of the dispute, which lies deep within Hellenistic culture.

The miracle of the Greek mind imparted a rich heritage to the West. Hence, Europe merely asserted what it deemed a spiritual and cultural prerogative when it sought to defend and even extend its borders eastward into adjacent territories. Naturally, the European assumption of superiority and will to dominate caused friction.

The war between the Greeks and the Persians over the frontiers of Hellenistic culture constituted the first interval, then, in the struggle between the East and the West. The initial clashes between these two cultures, or two world powers occurred on the field of Marathon in the year 490 B.C. and at Salamis in 480 B.C. By the fifth century B.C., two distinct cultures had formed: on the one hand, there was the way of life and thought of the Hellenistic civilization, while, on the other hand, there was the cultural pattern of the Persian Empire, with which Asia was identified. Eventually, however, the Greek victory over the Persians led to the expansion of Hellenistic frontiers throughout the ancient world; this process culminated in the dazzling rule of Alexander the Great (356-323 B.C.).

Until then, the conflict between the East and the West had been a matter of race and culture. A religious element was added under the Romans, though, because of both the Christianization of Rome and the rise of Islam in the East.

---

[1] I prefer to use the "Christian West" rather than just the "West" because that is how it is viewed by the Muslims themselves. In fact, the fashionable term among Muslim Fundamentalists to describe the West is "The Crusaders."

Islam Marching on Christian Lands

The struggle between Muslims and non-Muslims, shaped by the tension between the East and West in general, began during the lifetime of the Prophet.
Although Muhammad directed most of his wars against the pagans of Arabia,
he made enemies of the Jews when some Jewish tribes in Medina refused to
accept his prophetic authority. Meanwhile, Christians remained potential
allies and converts. Later on, when Muhammad was expanding his influence
in the Arabian peninsula, he collided with Christian tribes and turned against
them. Like the Jews, they now needed to be humiliated and subjugated.[2]

The Islamic campaign against unbelievers acquired a new intensity, which
impelled the Muslims to cross the Red Sea to Egypt and North Africa and
north to Palestine and Syria, lands long dominated by the Christian Byzantine
branch of the Roman Empire. The Muslims also marched to the East, conquering the pagan Persians (Zoroastrians). However, the Islamization of the
Christian lands, such as Egypt and Syria, was slower than the Islamization of
Persia.

In the West, Islam was forced to recognize a rival; here Muslims encountered another revealed religion and universal state, with a strong sense of
mission and a message for all mankind. Far from needing conversion
themselves, Christians were actively converting others, and with no small success. Hence, the Muslims soon realized that the conquest of the Christian
West would be much more difficult than the assimilation of the pagan Persians.[3] They confronted a religious and political system which was not only
different, but hostile, and which denied the very basis of the Islamic world
order. The irreconcilable nature of the differences between Islam and Christianity prompted the Muslims to solidify their commitment to world conquest.

This world view stems from the division of their world into two abodes—
the House of Islam (meaning all the Muslims) and the House of War (all non-
Muslims) and this is a pivotal foundation of the Islamic ideology. Muslim
jurists very cleverly interpreted this law to state that a limited truce can be affected with the House of War and that this truce could be renewed as often
as necessary.

The goal of world domination through *jihad* has embarrassed moderate and
secular Muslims, yet today it is precisely the language of the modern Islamic
revivalists. For example, Engineer Mohammad Abd al-Salam Farag, the
founder of the movement under consideration, reiterated the concept of
jJihad or "holy war" in a book entitled *The Missing Religious Precept*. He

---

[2] Edited by the Late Joseph Schacht with C. E. Bosworth, *The Legacy of Islam*, (London W.I.:
Oxford University Press, Second Edition, 1974), pp. 179-180.

[3] J. J. Saunders, *A History of Medieval Islam*, (London, Henley and Boston: Routledge and
Kegan Paul, 1975).

argued that religious leaders who ignore *jihad* are denying a fundamental Islamic duty as important as the other pillars of Islam.

This is by no means the common or monolithic interpretation of the meaning of *jihad*. Throughout the history of Islam the concept of *ijtihad* or interpreting the Qur'an and the *Sunna* in accordance with the current needs and circumstances of the Muslim community has developed. In modern times a number of Muslim modernists have interpreted *jihad* in spiritual terms, such as one's fight against the flesh and the Devil.

The law of *jihad*, like other Muslim jurisprudence, received its basic shape during the first century and a half of Islamic history when Islamic legions were advancing into Spain and other parts of the world. There seemed to be no reason then to doubt that the final triumph of Islam over the world was not only inevitable but very near. But when the Islamic Empire fragmented into small states, the fervor of *jihad* became dormant and the relationship of mutual tolerance between Muslims and non-Muslims became the order of the day. Even today modern apologists such as Seyyed Hossein Nasr in his book (*Ideals and Realities of Islam*) try to water down the classical interpretation of *jihad* and interpret *jihad* as a purely defensive obligation, but even go so far as to say that *jihad* is a moral struggle of the conscience. (See Chapter 2.) Not until the past few decades has *jihad* been universally revived. In the present post-colonial era, Shaykh al-Azhar, the highest Islamic authority in Egypt, revived the practice of calling the non-Muslims who live in Muslim lands Ahl al-Dhimmah (Dhimmi), i.e. the "protected of the state," in his message to Christians on 7 January 1983 as reported by the major Egyptian newspaper.[4]

At the height of his success, when Muhammad approached the end of his life, he sent letters from Medina to Caesar and Chosroes II, the respective Roman and Persian Emperors, and informed them of his mission, summoning them to accept Islam or suffer the penalties of unbelief.[5] Notably, this state of mind categorized and later inspired the Islamic invasion of lands that were long dominated by Christendom. It is imperative that one encapsulates the life of the Prophet, particularly his relations with non-Muslims, in order to provide the background necessary for this study.

---

[4] *Al-Ahram*, (7 January 1983).

[5] *Sahih Al-Bukhari* (The Early Years of Islam), Translated and explained by Muhammad Asad, (Great Britain: Dar Al-Andalus, 1981), pp. 248-251.

CHAPTER TWO

MUHAMMAD, THE PROPHET OF ALLAH

Mecca, the religious center of pagan Arabia, was also the birthplace of Muhammad, the prophet of Islam. The vast, hot, sparsely populated Arabian peninsula was an unlikely birthplace for one of the world's great religions. Until the seventh century when the Muslim conquerors drew aside the veil of obscurity, Arabia was, to the rest of the world virtually an unknown land, although a great stream of caravan traders constantly passed over the Arabian peninsula and made it the commercial land link between the Mediterranean and the Far East. Yet, from this peninsula, in the span of a single century, arose one of the most extraordinary marvels of history, the vast Arab empire that stretched from Spain to India.

The swiftness, magnitude, extent and permanence of the Islamic conquests are incredible when examined from a historical perspective. Few conquerors or exporters of revolutions have ever lasted as long, or matched the Islamic conquest in magnitude. The great Persian empire is defunct. The spiritual supremacy of the Hellenes is no more. Yet Islam continues to command loyalty, with eight hundred million adherents worldwide at present.

Muhammad was born in the autumn of A.D. 570 into the tribe of "Quraysh," which consisted of two main clans, the Hashemites and their Omayyad cousins, the aristocracy of Mecca. Muhammad belonged to the poorer Hashemites. Thus, it is no surprise that Muhammad revolted against wealth by asking his rich cousins to share with the poor, the orphans, and the widows.

Before Muhammad began preaching, the existing religion in Mecca was a synthesis of local natural religion and Jewish legend or what W. Montgomery Watt calls "tribal humanism."[6] Even though Muhammad travelled with his uncle to Syria and encountered Christians with their churches and religious artifacts, he showed far more familiarity with Judaism than with the tenets of Christianity. Later on, Muhammad used Jewish legends to claim that Islam was equal to Judaism and Christianity by virtue of its relationship to Abraham. However, toward the end of his life, Muhammad revised this claim, stating that this revelation superseded both Judaism and Christianity and had become, in essence, the final revelation of God.[7]

---

[6] W. Montgomery Watt, *Muhammad Prophet and Stateman*, (London, Oxford, New York: Oxford University Press, 1961), p. 51.

[7] Muir, Sir William, *The Life of Mohammed*. (Edinburgh: John Grant, 1923), p. 366.

It is of immense importance to note that Muhammad's mission (A.D. 611-630) coincided with the Christological controversies that threatened the Christian church between the council of Nicaea in 325 and that of Constantinople in 680.

The variant theological conceptions of the divinity of Christ and his incarnation in human flesh divided the church and created many schisms as a result of these divisions. Arius taught that Jesus was human until the time of His baptism when God adopted Him as His son. Nestorius argued that Mary was not the mother of God, but only the mother of the man Jesus, who received His divinity later in life. The Monophysites declared that the human nature of Christ was totally absorbed in His divine nature. The Monothelites insisted that Jesus was the possessor of the one divine will.

Numerous church councils classified these diverse teachings as heresies and condemned their followers, forcing them to take refuge in Arabia. The implications are significant. Muhammad, confronted with the controversies that divided the church, naturally denounced the divinity of Christ. His view that the miraculous virgin birth of Jesus was really no different from the miraculous creation of Adam was predicated upon his response to the schisms rampant in the church.

Muhammad's first vision was allegedly communicated to him by the angel Gabriel at the cave where he meditated. At first, he was doubtful, but with the encouragement of Khadijah, his wife and first convert, he continued to listen to the angel. A small band of his friends trusted the authority of his claim and became his first disciples. Abu Bakr, the second believer, was the direct successor of the Prophet.

The majority of Meccans, however, held aloof and scoffed at Muhammad's preaching. The Qurayshites became sworn foes of Muhammad, whose position in Mecca deteriorated so much that he began to look beyond Mecca, primarily to Medina, about 250 miles away. By the time of Muhammad, the three Jewish clans—the Nadir, the Kuraiza and the Kainuqa—that had previously dominated Medina were overshadowed by eight Arab clans of the tribes of Aus and Khazraj. Feuds between these two tribes kept the city in a constant state of tension and disorder. A golden opportunity awaited Muhammad, for there seemed no better arbitrator than the man from Mecca who called himself the Prophet of God!

It is noteworthy that in this major breakthrough for Muhammad's mission he made use of two cultural phenomena that were peculiar to tribal Arabian society. *First*, the most common method of resolving disputes in Arabia was to bring in an arbitrator from outside who could act as judge and keep the peace. *Second*, the Jewish population of Medina lived in a state of Messianic expectation. Thus, they were open and receptive to the idea of a prophet who would save them from their Arab oppressors. Even their pagan neighbors welcomed such a prophet because of the constant Jewish threat of vindication at the time of the Messiah's coming.[8]

Soon after his arrival at Medina, Muhammad drew up a treaty which is recognized as the earliest sketch of Islamic theocracy. This treaty was later on to become the platform of many Islamic movements. (*Al-Jihad* is no exception) in which the leader would insist that he who is not in the House of Islam is in the House of War. All Muslims, whether from Mecca or Medina, were to form one community (the "Ummah"). They were to stand together and fight against unbelievers. Disputes among them were to be referred to the Apostle of God. Since these were common grounds in forming a new clan, such a confederacy was not unknown in Arabia, but it was the first to be forged on the basis of religion.

The basis of distinction now was not to what tribe or what clan one belonged, but rather whether one belonged to the *Ummah* of Islam or not. As it has been pointed out earlier, the distinction between the House of Islam ("Dar al-Islam")—those who believe in Allah and His Prophet—and the House of War ("Dar al-Harb")—those who either do not belong to Allah and His Apostle or refuse to join—became the pivotal foundation upon which Islam was built, and remains today as the cornerstone of Islam's world view. This distinction is often highlighted during the rise of Islamic social movements. The one under consideration here is no exception; in fact, it emphasizes this division more than most groups.

With varying degrees of success, Muhammad and his *Ummah* persuaded the Jews of Medina[9] to receive him as the last of the three major messengers of Allah (namely Moses & Jesus). Moreover, Muhammad claimed to have completed and superseded the messages of both Moses and Jesus by bringing to mankind a more perfected revelation of God. In the attempt to win favor with the Jews, Muhammad commanded his followers to face Jerusalem when they prayed and insisted on the observance of the Jewish Day of Atonement as a solemn fast. When the Jewish religious leaders ridiculed him, Muhammad realized that these and other similar measures had failed to secure Jewish support. Thus, understandably, the Prophet's attitude became bitterly hostile toward the Jews, an attitude expressed later by changing the direction of prayer from facing Jerusalem to facing Mecca. In addition, instead of fasting on the Day of Atonement, Muhammad decreed that during the entire month of Ramadan the community must fast from sunrise to sunset.

By 624, after establishing his community (*Ummah*) in Medina, the Prophet turned his attention toward the idolaters of Mecca and began to attack their caravans. A Qur'anic revelation made jihad (holy war) against the pagans a

---

[8] Ibid., p. 116.
[9] *Sahih al-Bukhari*, p. 246.

duty for every Muslim. The sign of God's hand of approval was behind Muhammad and his *Ummah* when they defeated the pagans at the war of Badr. Exhilarated with victory, Muhammad focused on his Jewish critics who were relatively easy to defeat. The victory over Banu Kainuqa, the first Jewish group defeated, brought the *Ummah* much desired and needed spoils and booty.

It was not all triumph, however, for the Prophet and his *Ummah*. In March of 625, the Muslims suffered a crashing defeat at the hands of Quraysh (the dominant tribe in the war of Mecca ... Muhammad's own tribe who fought him hard, disbelieving in his mission) in the war of Uhud; many died and the Prophet himself was wounded. Some interpreted this to mean that God was no longer on their side; but Muhammad, a shrewd strategist and statesman, assured the community, through a divine revelation, that Uhud was God's punishment for their sins as well as a test for their faith and steadfastness. In order to divert their attention, the Prophet concentrated the energy of the warriors on striking the Jews afresh, mainly the remaining clans of Nadir and Kuraiza. Having predicted victory, the Prophet convinced his *Ummah* once again of God's favour and gained prestige among the Bedouin tribes.

Early in 630, an army of ten thousand men of the Muslim *Ummah* marched into Mecca, and the Prophet triumphantly took possession of his birthplace. He destroyed the idols and dedicated the Kaaba anew to the worship of the one true God. The spread of the news of Muhammad's victory brought an avalanche of delegates from neighboring countries and nearby territories in recognition of the Prophet as the new conquering hero of Arabia.

During the pilgrimage of 631, the Prophet proclaimed that in the future no pagan would be permitted to approach the Kaaba, and in his last speech he included the Jews, Christians, and all non-Muslims among those prohibited; he also forbade their entry into the holy city and commanded the faithful to "fight against them (non-Muslims)" (Qur'an 9:29). By that time Muhammad had become a dominant power in Arabia; and whereas the tribes who fully accepted Islam were well treated, the Christians and Jews who refused to submit, though given special exemption, were not deemed equal to Muslims. This inequality manifested itself in their designation as the "protected" of the state (Dhimmi), on the condition that they were to pay a tribute tax (*jizya*). For example, the Christians of Najran had to pay 2,000 cloth garments annually.

Most likely, Muhammad was aware of the power of the Persians and the aversion of his neighbors, such as Syria and Egypt, to the Byzantines. Thus, his strategy was to continue with raids and expeditions toward Syria. By now he was sixty years of age and in failing health. On 8 June 632, he died requesting that Abu Bakr, his first convert and father-in-law, lead the prayer in his place. Abu Bakr was a man of great wisdom and fortitude. He managed to cement the *Ummah* together, despite the threat of a great civil war.

There is no denying that the Prophet of Islam had a stately and commanding figure. In the world's history, he disclaimed all pretention to sinlessness
and miracle working; and when asked for a sign he pointed to the Qur'an as
the greatest miracle. Yet, it would be wrong to deny the fact that the Prophet
of Islam was viewed unsympathetically by both Jews and Christians
throughout all generations. Fanciful stories and accusations such as
"impostor" or "liar" have lasted as long as Islam itself. Yet, his religious
system can be described as a pure and uncompromising monotheism which
rests upon five pillars: *shahada*, the profession of faith; *salat*, the five daily
prayers; *sowm*, the fast during the month of Ramadan; *zakat*, alms giving;
and *hajj*, the pilgrimage to Mecca (only if it is affordable).

Any study of Islamic social movements forfeits its acuity when it lacks an
adequate portrayal of Muhammad, if for nothing else, for its nationalistic
equalitarian thought. By severing ties with the established social order and
creating a new one, Muhammad became the model that has inspired generations of Islamic revolutionaries, most of whom purport to be the enforcers of
his true teaching. On this thought Bellah explains that "the effort of modern
Muslims to depict the early community as a very type of equalitarian partici-
pant nationalism is by no means entirely an unhistorical ideological fabrica-
tion."[10] The influence of the life and teachings of Muhammad on the ideology
of *al-Jihad* can be seen by reading *The Missing Religious Precept* included as
an appendix to this study.

The Concept of Jihad

Like most of the Islamic tenants, *jihad*—or literally "struggle" (commonly
translated Holy War)—took its first meaning in Islam under the leadership of
the Prophet Muhammad. He started his expansionist and missionary career
as a revolutionary warrior. When his calls for turning to Allah from paganism
were not heeded, he issued a call to arms to his band of believers, thus beginning a military operation in a guerrilla fashion, attacking the Meccan traders.

These guerrilla attacks took on the form of a more organized battle, during
which Muhammad widened his base until he fully entered Mecca and ruled it
on his terms.

In the course of these wars, revolutionary tenets such as *jihad* became
institutionalized. Thus many of these tenets came back to haunt the established Islam throughout its history. There are, for example, many Qur'anic texts
that command the believers to fight (*jihad*) in the way of God.

Contextually these struggles were against the unbelievers of Arabia, but
Islamic revolutionary movements throughout Islamic history thought it

---

[10] Robert N. Bellah, *Beyond Belief*, (New York: Harper & Row, 1970), p. 151.

logical to assume that it was also necessary to wage these struggles against corrupt Muslims who followed in the way of unbelievers (as it will be shown
clearly in the case of *al-Jihad's* views of Sadat and hence the rationalization
of assassinating him).

Jihad was invoked by Muslim groups thoughout the history of Islam, but
more specifically during the early five centuries, with movements such as
Kharijism and Shi'ism and others who sought to overthrow the existing
political system in order to restore what they perceived to be the true teaching
of Islam.

CHAPTER THREE

THE ISLAMIC CONQUEST AND THE CRUSADES

The First Threat to Unity

The death of Muhammad threatened the dissolution of the Muslim *Ummah*. The bedouin tribes initially had submitted to Muhammad out of fear, but once they heard of his death they retracted their submisson to the *Ummah*, one after the other. They considered their earlier consent to be more to the person of Muhammad than his successors. This retraction of allegiance is known in Islamic history as *ridda* or "apostasy."

By sheer leadership ability, Abu Bakr won them back; he exercised a clever strategy when he appealed to their passion for war. He called all able-bodied men to quell the sedition and bind the disgruntled Bedouin to Islam, then directed their attention to other lands. Thus, in the middle of 633, the Muslims decided to raid their northern neighbor on an expedition in the name of Allah. Early in 634, Abu Bakr declared holy war, divided the army into three groups under the respective commands of Amr ibn al-As, Shurahbi ibn Hasanah, and Yazid (the son of Abu Sufyan), and sent them to Syria. Abu Bakr dispatched another force under Khalid to raid lower Iraq.

The news of victory in Syria and Iraq cheered the last few days of the life of Abu Bakr, who died in August 634, at the age of 63. Abu Bakr, learning from the mistakes of his master (who had not clearly nominated a successor), named Omar to be his successor. Omar's ascension to power appears to have been unchallenged. Not unlike St. Paul, Omar was a persecutor of Islam turned to its zealot. He gave his daughter to the Prophet as a wife.

Most historians seem to describe him as a shrewd and forceful politician. On assuming the succession, he referred to himself as Amir al-Mu'minin, "commander of the faithful," and he ruled the decade (634-644) which is often described as the most glorious in the annals of Arabic Islamic history. During this period in the life of the Islamic *Ummah*, Egypt and Syria (including Palestine) were brought under the territorial control of the new Islamic community.

In addition to collating the Qur'an, Omar's most significant contribution, particularly pertinent here, has become known as "the pact of Omar." This pact came to regulate Muslim relations with non-Muslim communities. It is a clear example of how Omar put into practice the Prophet's revelation and visions. Several versions of this pact are summarized below. Allegedly, the Christians in Syria imposed upon themselves the following:

1. We will pay tribute out of hand and be humiliated.
2. We will not hinder any Muslim from stopping in our churches by night or day.
3. We will beat the nakus (bells) only gently in our churches and not raise our voices in our chanting.
4. We will not shelter in any of our homes a spy of an enemy of the Muslims.
5. We will not build a church, convent, hermitage nor repair those that are dilapidated.
6. We will not assemble in any church that is in a Muslim quarter, nor in their presence.[11]
7. We will not display idolatry, nor show a cross on our churches, nor in any of the roads or markets of the Muslims.
8. We will not prevent any of our relatives from converting to Islam if they wish.
9. We will not make our houses higher than those of the Muslims.
10. We will not keep weapons or swords, nor wear them in a town or on a journey to Muslim lands.
11. We will not sell wine or display it.
12. We will not strike a Muslim or keep a slave who has been the property of Muslims.[12]

Tritton questions the authenticity of such a covenant because conquered people do not normally decide the terms of submission to their victor. Also, it is strange that Omar ratified this treaty, which deals with an anonymous town. Thus it is not unreasonable to assume that Omar was the author of that covenant and not the Christians themselves. In any case, most fundamentalist Muslims view this pact as a guide to the pursuit of relations with non-Muslims who live in Muslim lands. The terms of this Covenant were in fact amplified and applied during the rule of the Ottoman Empire, even as recently as the beginning of this century. It is noteworthy that Omar was stabbed to death by a Persian Christian, Abu Lu'lu'a, on 4 November 644. Before his death, he appointed a *Shura* (consultative council) of six men, including Ali and Uthman, to choose his successor. Omar was the man who put flesh and blood to Muhammad's vision and expanded the Islamic Empire. The disorders which followed his death indicate the loss which Islam suffered by his untimely death.[13]

---

[11] Today it is illegal to build a church that is within 1000 meters of a mosque. No new churches are to be built or old ones renovated without the permission of the president of the nation.

[12] A. S. Tritton, *The Caliphs and Their Non-Muslim Subjects*, (London: Frank Cass & Co., Ltd., 1970).

[13] J. J. Saunders, *A History of Medieval Islam*, (London, Henly and Boston: Routledge and Kegan Paul, 1965), p. 57.

The Second Threat to Unity (Khawarjas and Shi'ats)

The first threat of the "Khawarjas," which immediately followed the death of Muhammad, was handled with fortitude on the part of Abu Bakr; still, division was not avoided altogether. At the death of Omar, many anticipated that Ali, Muhammad's young cousin, son-in-law and the father of the only two grandsons of the Prophet, would be the logical successor. Ali was not selected; Uthman Ibn Afan was chosen instead. On the surface this event appears harmless, yet it was a crack that widened and developed from 632 on to be Islam's largest division before or since.

The third caliph, Uthman a distant cousin of the Prophet, who succeeded Omar in A.D. 644, came from the clan of Umayya, one of the old ruling families of Mecca. He was looked upon as an outsider. Even worse, he antagonized many of his soldiers by appointing relatives to provincial governorships, reserving for them a share in war spoils, and for the first time attempting to impose religious uniformity on the Muslim community. In A.D. 656, he was killed by disgruntled soldiers.

Muhammad's cousin Ali, who had been passed over for a second time when Uthman was elected, was then acclaimed as caliph by Muslims in Medina. Two elements here contributed to the division that followed. *First*: Ali failed to take action against those responsible for Uthman's death; some of whom were Ali's supporters. *Second*: He did not replace Uthman's relatives with his own in appointments to the governorship.

Thus, revolt started both in Medina and the conquered territories, especially Syria. Because Syria's governor Mu'awiyyah (Uthman's relative) refused to acknowledge Ali as caliph, a civil war erupted in A.D. 658 between the supporters of Ali, who became known as Shi'at Ali (party of Ali), and the rest of the Muslim community under the leadership of the Syrian governor Mu'awiyyah. To end the war Ali agreed to an arbitration by two judges. But a group of Ali's fanatical supporters rejected this compromise and refused to accept the pronouncement of the judges, declaring that there is no judgment but God's (The implication was that Uthman's murder had been a just punishment for his errors).[14]

Ali's ascension to the office of Caliph annoyed a number of Muslims, including Muhammad's beloved wife, Aisha, and two of Muhammad's friends, Talha and Zubeir. They marched into Basra, where Ali set up his headquarters, and demanded that Ali step down from the office of Caliph. The result was a bloody confrontation in which both Talha and Zubeir lost their lives and Aisha was sent back to Medina.

---

[14] Edward Mortimer, *Faith and Power: The Politics of Islam*, (New York: Vintage Books, 1982), p. 41.

Mu'awiyyah, the governor of Syria (from the clan of Umayyads, as opposed to the clan of Hashim, the Prophet's own clan; both belong to the Quraysh tribe) did not approve of Ali's egalitarian policies and opposed him in a war that took place on the plain of Siffin, near Raqqa. After this war, which ended by Mu'awiyyah's soldiers hoisting the Qur'an at the tips of their swords, a group of Ali's supporters deserted him and became what is known as *khawarja*.

Both Ali and Mu'awiyyah agreed to arbitration to settle the issue, but when no consensus was reached, both Ali and Mu'awiyyah declared themselves to be the legitimate Caliph. Mu'awiyyah assumed power in the Syrian region and his armies began to overrun Arab territories as far as Yemen. Ali's power became confined to Iraq with Kufa as his capital. However, on the 28th of January 661, he was assassinated by one of the *khawarja*, Abd al-Rahman Ibn Muljam al-Moradi. Many *Shi'ites* believe that he was hired by Mu'awiyyah to assassinate Ali. Ali, however, was buried near Kufa which grew into a holy site and a center of *Shi'ite* learning. The elite of Kufa elected Ali's son Hussein to be the Caliph but, because of lack of support for Hussein's leadership, he abdicated to Mu'awiyyah. When Hussein died, the *Shi'ites* claimed that he had been poisoned by Mu'awiyyah's men.

This is the background of how the minority Muslims who followed Ali formed the group called *Shi'a* (sect). There are, however, some theological differences as well as political and tribal differences. Most prominent is the *Shi'ite* insistence that the descendants of Ali are the Imams (all of whom were considered virtually infallible leaders of all spheres of life, including politics) and that these Imams were able to interpret and reinterpret the Qu'ranic text. To put it in Christian terminology, they believe in "continuous revelation," but mainly through the Imams. To be sure, the Qu'ran is the word of Allah; nonetheless, its application can be open to the Imam's interpretation.

It is important to point out here that Shi'ism became the state religion in Iran only in 1501 with the establishment of the Safavid dynasty. Previously the religious situation in Iran was one of multiple Islamic groups.

Twelver Shi'ite

The Twelver Shi'ite teaches that the infant Twelfth Imam went into hiding on earth in the 9th century and will remain hidden until the end of time, when he will return to earth as Mahdi (Messiah) in order to establish the millennium of perfect equality.

The Safavids (1501-1722) were able to control the *Ulama's* agitation and their intense expectation of the Mahdi by importing Arabic-speaking theologians (*Ulama*) who were naturally favorable toward the Safavids. These *Ulama* also depended financially upon the rulers, whereas the financial independence of the Iranian *Ulama* posed a threat to the Safavids.

By the 17th century, however, we hear of leading *Ulama Mujtahids* who claimed that they had more right to set policy than impious wine-bibbing shahs. This claim seemed to have gathered some strength by the 18th century when the leading *Ulama* moved to Iraq away from the reach of the Iranian rulers. Iraq remained the center of Shi'ism until replaced by Qom in 1950. In fact, by the end of the 18th century the doctrine which says that believers should follow the rulings of a *Mujtahid* became dominant.

Among other things that helped in the promotion of this doctrine was the economic power of the *Ulama* which grew as a result of donations and religious taxes taken chiefly from the Bazaaris. This relationship between the Bazaaris and the *Ulama* developed out of mutual interest stemming not only from their similar beliefs but also from the intense desire to combat Western penetration, which meant economic loss and dislocation for many Bazaaris.

In any event, the institution of Mujtahids who could interpret certain aspects of Shi'ite law developed gradually, beginning considerably after the twelfth Imam disappeared. Some Mujtahids began to claim superior political legitimacy to the shahs, as already mentioned. The most powerful manifestation of the Mujtahids' claim appeared in the tobacco protest of 1891-92 which formed the background of the constitutional revolution of 1905-1911.

The Kharijites

Some of the fanatical supporters of Ali have become known as Kharijites, an Arabic word meaning *to go out*. They were the first distinctive dissenters in Islam. The Kharijites asserted that all those who did not follow them were unbelievers (*kafir*), whereas the mainstream of Muslims (the Sunni), who followed the tradition of the Prophet, were satisfied with the minimum elements of the faith, i.e., the oneness of God and the finality of the revelation to Muhammad.

It follows then that those who differed with the Kharijites were infidels, according to those who remain in the main stream, and *jihad* was declared against them. Moreover, the Kharijites authorized assassination as a means of political change. They were absolute and uncompromising egalitarians, and later on would not accept any notion that the family of the Prophet should have the privilege of ruling. The true believers were given all instructions necessary in the Qur'an to command good and evil. Thus they gave themselves the right to overthrow an unjust caliph and in his place to choose anyone who was morally and religiously irreproachable.[15] This kind of belief has lingered on, and it can be seen clearly in the teaching of *al-Jihad* (see appendix).

Accordingly, they founded a form of primitive democracy with an equitable distribution of wealth. This group survived intact throughout the Ummayyad

---

[15] Ibid., p. 42.

period (661-750), and a less radical remnant still exists in Oman and East and North Africa. They, in this way, have been the prototype of all subsequent Muslim revival movements.

It is sobering to find that the main document of *al-Jihad*, written by its leader Abdel Salam Farag, reflects this teaching, as we shall see later on. In the writings of Farag, the government leader was made to be a *kafir* and, therefore, the murder of Sadat was carried out in accordance with the constitution of the group.

The Shi'a

The Kharijites have continued to be smaller in number than the other great sect, the *Shi'a*. As mentioned before, *Shi'a* became the official religion of Iran in the year 1501. The *Shi'a* division also represents about 45 percent of the Iraqi population and a smaller percentage of the population in Lebanon, Syria, and Palestine. The *Shi'ite* division is a further indication that Islam is far from the monolithic religion that some proclaim it to be.

When Ali died in A.D. 661, Shi'at Ali or the party of Ali supported both his right to the caliphate and that of his descendants. The argument is that Ali was not only Muhammad's cousin and son-in-law but was almost like an adopted son. (Muhammad had no surviving sons.) Moreover, Ali was the father of the Prophet's two favorite grandsons.[16] The *Shi'a* points out numerous traditions, namely, that Muhammad asked his followers to take both the Qur'an and Ali as their authorities and to be loyal to both.[17]

After Ali's death, this school of thought was naturally passed on to his sons, the Prophet's grandsons, Hasan and Hussain. While they were not strong enough to fight the coming of the well-established Ummayad dynasty, they became an important focus of opposition to the Umayyad dynasty. The notion that the descendant of the Prophet would be *al-Mahdi*, a leader directly guided by God, intensified their resistance. The Umayyad period was punctuated by frequent revolts based on these ideas.

Muhammad's uncle, Abbas, led a revolt which eventually succeeded, resulting in the Abbasid control of the Islamic Empire. Only after the Abbasids had repudiated *Shi'a* ideas and made themselves the new establishment did the *Shi'a* take on the form of a sect, distinct from the mainstream of the Muslim *Ummah*.[18]

If the Umayyad age was one of military conquest, (ending in 750), then the Abbasid era was one of wealth and culture and lasted for over half a half a

---

[16] Ibid., p. 43.

[17] Michael M. J. Fischer, *Iran—From Religious Dispute to Revolution*, (Cambridge, Massachusetts and London, England: Harvard University Press, 1980), pp. 13-14.

[18] Dwight M. Donaldson, *The Shi'ite Religion*, (London: Luzac & Company, (Luzac's Oriental Religions Series, vol. VI), 1933), pp. 5-7.

millennium (750-1258). However, as has happened with every empire in history, wealth and power resulted in decadence and dislike of military service.

The Crusades

The Crusades are not merely a chapter in the history of the tension between the Christian West and Muslim East. They have become a major continuing theme in the history of that conflict.

An examination of the larger historical context not only puts in proper perspective the motivation of the Crusaders, but also helps one appreciate more the Islamic revival in the postcolonial or, as some Muslims prefer, the neo-colonial era.

A number of complex issues arose during the Crusades, in addition to Christendom versus Islam. They included the West versus Arabian and the theological dispute between the Orthodox and the Roman Church. Their controversy saw the Eastern Orthodox Church profoundly resent the attempts of the Western Church to dominate them theologically and culturally. This became more apparent in Egypt in the seventh century.

As the Islamic empire fragmented, however, the Mediterranean picture began to change. By A.D. 945 John Curcouas had won for the Romans some towns and districts in upper Mesopotamia that had not seen a Christian army for three centuries.[19] By 974, John marched all the way into Baghdad. At that time the emperor celebrated his triumph and the choir sang, "Glory be to God who has conquered the Saracens."[20] Nicephorus, who saw himself as the champion of Christianity, even threatened to march into Mecca and establish the throne of Christ.

In retaliation, the Fatimid Caliph Hakim burned 30,000 churches between the year 1004 and 1014, and in 1009 he burned the church of the Holy Sepulchre itself. It is interesting to note that despite the fact that Caliph Al Hakim claimed divinity and is considered by most Muslims to be a heretic, some modern Egyptian Muslim zealots admire his courage to "burn the shrine of idols," as one of them exclaimed.

The waves of the Crusades, which lasted for nearly four hundred years, began to accelerate at that point. Suffice it to say that Pope Urban II's fervent speech in France on 27 November 1095, called for Holy War against the infidels in order to give credence to the pending war. His speech can be summarized in three points: (1) the brethren in the East needed assistance; (2) Eastern Christendom had appealed for help because the Turkish army was

---

[19] Stephen Runciman, *A History of the Crusade*, Vol. 3, (Cambridge: Cambridge University Press, 1951-1954), pp. 29-30.

[20] Ibid., p. 32.

advancing into the land of the Christians; (3) the holiness of Jerusalem was at stake.[21]

None of this was ever accepted by Muslims; nor did it help them to understand the reasons behind the Crusades ... the Crusades were an aggression against Muslims pure and simple. Thus antagonism toward the Christian West cannot be easily forgiven or quickly forgotten.

The Ultimate Failure of the Crusaders

The economy flourished under the Crusaders even after their defeat, and the Muslim authorities believed this was to their advantage. Still, with the exception of the economic legacy in the Levantine trading colonies, the Crusaders left behind little of a positive nature in the Middle East.

Indeed, the Crusades have had a lasting adverse effect on Muslim society. The Muslims had been fairly tolerant of Christians and Jews (*dhimmis*) before the Crusades. However, because the Crusaders inflicted such brutal treatment on the Muslims during the three centuries of their occupation, the Muslim leaders (especially the Mamluk Sultans and later the Ottoman Sultans) afterwards demonstrated much harsher attitudes toward Christians and Jews, whom they automatically associated with the infidel invaders.

In many ways the Crusades reopened the wound of Muslim-Christian conflict which, as shown previously, began in Arabia and expanded with Islamic conquests of the Middle East in the later part of the 600's. The Crusades left a deep psychological scar that showed itself over and over during the Colonial era which was seen as a modern-day Crusade.

Today, Middle Easterners, particularly active Islamic groups, believe that the Crusades are not over. Seldom in personal discussions do they refer to the U.S. or Western Europe as the "West" or even Christendom; instead, they refer to them as the "Crusaders." In fact, there is a basic threefold formula in the mind of these Islamic groups regarding the status of their enemies: Communists (*al-Shuyou'iyya*), Crusaders (*al-Saliebiyya*), and Zionists (*al-Sahyouniyya*). In Egypt, because of her close ties with the West—specifically the United States and the signing of the Camp David Peace Treaty—the Muslim Brotherhood and the other Islamic groups rank the elimination of these enemies in order of priority: the Zionists first, the Crusaders next, and the Communists last. The following quotation exemplifies this: "The Muslims are coming, despite Jewish cunning, Christian hatred, and Communist storm."[22]

---

[21] Thomas Patrick Murphy, ed., *The Holy War*, (Columbus, Ohio: Ohio State University Press, 1974), pp. 11-13.

[22] *Al-Da'wah* (The Call Magazine), 21 March 1979 (This magazine was published by the Muslim Brotherhood in Egypt and was closed down by President Sadat in September 1981.)

CHAPTER FOUR

THE RISE AND FALL OF THE OTTOMAN EMPIRE

The declared purpose of the Ottoman thrust against the Crusaders (in the later part of the 1400's) was to reestablish and further extend the power and the glory of Islam. No sooner had the Ottomans achieved this goal than they turned their attention toward other weak Muslim areas including Egypt. "The Turkish counter crusade launched in the first instance against European Christians soon was destined to be an unremitting war of conquest of Muslim territories in the sixteenth century and the Arab world sank into servitude under the Ottoman yoke."[23]

Until modern times, Turks have retained the image of Europe trembling with fear at the prospect of a Turkish invasion. "The Ottomans, in the words of William Harborn 'became fearful and terrible to the whole world.'"[24] Indeed, the Turkish conquest gave Muslims unprecedented military power over Christian Europe, creating another link in the chain of animosity between the Arab Muslim world and the Christian West.

During the sixteenth century, three major changes, mainly of external origin, affected virtually the entire life of the Ottoman Empire. The first was the halt of the Ottoman advance into Europe. The frontier had provided work and reward to the warriors of the Ottoman state; in the meantime, failure on the part of Ottoman leaders and armies in spreading the faith of Islam by the sword to new lands, thinking they were bringing civilization and true faith to the infidels, resulted in discouragement and loss of zeal.

Secondly, the Ottoman system of military organization, civil administration, taxation, and land tenure was geared to the needs of a society expanding by conquest and colonization into the lands of the infidels. When the Ottoman advance was halted in the plains of Hungary, the system began to crumble because it was not designed for a static situation.

The third change ensued from the exploratory voyages of the Western maritime peoples that in effect turned the whole Eastern Mediterranean area, where the Ottoman Empire was situated, into a backwater. Thus, on a very great scale, the growth of the Ottoman Empire was curtailed, and for some time it neither continued forward, nor retreated. Consequently the demise of the Ottoman Empire became inevitable. With the shrinking economy and the

---

[23] Aziz S. Atiya, *Crudade, Commerce and Culture*, (Bloomington: Indiana University Press, 1962), p. 252.

[24] Norman Daniel, *Islam, Europe and Empire*, (Edinburgh: Edinburgh University Press, 1966), page 11.

escalating cost of supporting its super-structure—which included a splendid palace, the bureauracy, the religious hierarchy, and the army (which were overly large and anachronistic in a world of rapidly modernizing states)—gave the Ottoman Empire little chance for survival.

The Ottoman Empire began to disintegrate in the latter part of the 1800s. The bureaucratic government grew fat and lethargic. The Ottoman armed forces declined dramatically, even though they once stood in the forefront of military science. Great technical and logistic developments in seventeen-century European armies were followed tardily and inefficiently by the Ottomans. "The decline in the alertness, in readiness to accept new techniques, is an aspect ... perhaps was the most dangerous ... of what became a general deterioration in professional and moral standards in the armed forces, parallel to that in the bureaucratic and religious classes."[25]

The European Comeback

Within the sprawling Ottoman Empire lived a diversity of religious, national and ethnic groups: Turks, Tartars, Arabs, Kurds, Turkomans, Berbers, Mameluks, Bosnians, Albanians, Greeks, Bulgarians, Hungarians, Slavs, Romanians, Armenians, Copts, Georgians, and Jews. The elaborate hierarchy of the imperial Ottoman government presided over this amalgam of people. But in the midst of all these various religions and cultures, the Christians and the Jews were a category unto themselves, called the *dhimmis*. The Ottomans viewed the *dhimmis* in more or less the same way many modern Muslim activists would view them: persons who occupy a half-way house to the truth, because they had accepted only the initial revelations and not the final manifestations of God's truth to Muhammad.

In accordance with Muslim perceptions, the *dhimmis* clearly had intelligence inferior to Muslims. Their inferiority was not innate since any *dhimmi* could obtain superiority by converting to Islam. If a *dhimmi* converted to Islam, then he left his previous *millet* (religious groupings) and immediately entered the Muslim *millet*. In the Ottoman Empire there were four major *millets*: Muslims, Jews, Greek Orthodox and Armenians. Later on the fifth *millet* was recognized and it consisted mainly of Roman Catholics. In Egypt, the Copts, the Jews, and the Muslims were the major *millets*.

The Roman Catholic *millet* was made up of non-Osmanli citizens who emerged as the fifth *millet* after the first treaty of capitulations was signed between Suleiman I and Francis I of France in 1536. These capitulations generated reciprocity of treatment between French and Ottoman merchants selling goods and establishing residence in either area. French citizens residing

---

[25] Bernard Lewis, *The Emergence of Modern Turkey*, (London, Oxford, New York: Oxford University Press, 1961), p. 26.

in the Ottoman Empire for the purpose of commerce would be tax exempt and would not be subject to the *shari'a* or to the law of any of the other three Ottoman *millets*. Consequently, the French ambassador was looked upon as the head of the fifth *millet*, along with the chief rabbi and the patriarchs. By the end of the sixteenth century, England and Holland were also granted capitulary treaties.

However, the Western nations took greater advantage of these treaties than the Ottomans. For example, European countries granted citizenships to Ottomans who were employed in European consulates and businesses while the Ottomans did not grant similar privileges to Europeans, thus failing to gain equal influence upon Europeans.When the Ottoman Empire began to manifest its weakness, European countries declared themselves to be protectors of the various groups within the empire. Among others, Russia claimed the Greek Orthodox, France claimed the Catholics, and the United States claimed the Armenian Protestants. These supposed protectors, however, were prompted more by a desire to interfere in the Middle East than a genuine desire to protect these groups.

The general decay of the Ottoman administrative institutions coincided with the rise of more powerful European nations and states. By the end of the seventeenth century, the Ottoman Empire was under constant military attack by Europeans. It is believed, however, that the primary reason the Ottoman Empire survived much longer than expected was the vested interest of rival European states in not allowing the division of territorial spoils that would occur once the Ottoman Empire fell.[26]

The Russian Connection

Russia was the third great European nation to stake out Middle Eastern claims in the pre-Napoleonic era. Russia's success in becoming a major European power was partly at the expense of the declining Iranian and Ottoman Empires. Relentless Russian pressure pushed both Shah and Sultan further and further south into Asia. When the Safavid dynasty collapsed in Iran in 1722, a sharp diplomatic struggle ensued between the Russians and the Ottomans for Iranian territory. French mediation persuaded the Tsar and Sultan to prevent an immediate outbreak of war, and furnished Russia with the Iranian Transcaucasian and Western provinces.

However, the French intervention did not aid the Ottomans in the same way it helped the Iranians to benefit from the Russian expansion. The Czars were determined to establish themselves on the Black Sea and to dominate access to the rivers that flow into it. For the next century and a half Russia's

[26] Don Peretz, *The Middle East Today*, (New York, Chicago, San Francisco, Dallas, Montreal, Toronto, London, Sydney: Holt, Rinehard and Winston, 1963), p. 63.

endeavor to topple the Ottomans was a dominant concern of European diplomacy.

Russia now not only shared the shores of the Black Sea but also was assured of all unrestricted commercial navigation through it and through the straits leading into the Mediterranean. Henceforth, a major drive of Russian foreign policy was complete domination of the straits in order to gain unequivocal entrance into the Mediterranean. Not only are the Russians today disliked for their atheism, but their policy of aggressive expansion is hated by modern Islamic movements and adds the Russians to their list of enemies.

In 1774, a six-year-old war waged between the Russians and the Ottomans, terminated by what came to be known as the *Kuchuk Kainarji Treaty.* This gave the Russians the same capitulatory privileges previously acquired by other European powers, and extended transit protection to all Greek Orthodox Christians in the Ottoman Empire.

England, whose Indian Empire was expanding rapidly in the 1770s, interpreted the treaty as a warning of growing Russian might in the Middle East. For the first time, Russian penetration of the region seemed to threaten the Western overland approaches to India, particularly by way of Iran. The British used this excuse, more than anything else, to expand the British Colonial power around the world. In addition to the Russian expansion, the French invasion of Egypt by Napoleon provided the British with a prerequisite for action. Britain moved swiftly in order to curtail both the French and the Russian movements, which, according to the British, threatened to hinder its trade with India.

CHAPTER FIVE

EUROPE AND COLONIAL RULE

The technological advance of Western Europe in manufacturing and management was an obvious source of the strong sense of cultural superiority which marked the period from the 17th to the 19th century. Accumulating wealth and power not only raised the standard of living, but also increased the firepower of arms, improved professional military skills and civilian administration methods. The Europeans traveled the world, fought colonial wars and established imperial governments in order to stabilize the best conditions for their economy. But the classic surge for raw materials and manufacturing markets as technology expanded and accelerated was only part of the process; all this overseas activity far exceeded the necessities of trade and commerce.

Eventually, the Europeans believed that they alone could command the technological process; it became proof of their right to rule. The nations under European control insisted upon independence yet, at the same time, sought progress and Western style modernization.

In applying the imperial rule to the Muslim world, one cannot escape the moral superciliousness of the Europeans. Three aspects of the European disposition manifested themselves:
1. The historic hostility between Christianity and Islam
2. The disapproval of Muslim polygamy, apparent sensuality, and the inferior position of Muslim women with the attendant "evil social consequences"
3. The tradition of treating Islamic things as exotic, a tradition which maintained symbiotic relationship with imperialism

Despite a degree of camaraderie with Islam as an old imperial power, the European attitude of superiority was enacted in policy. As well, it was reinforced by the failure of Muslims to appropriate the technologies of the West, even though the imperial powers deliberately witheld the opportunity from them.

In the light of this blatant discrimination, which Sadat called "modern slavery," it is understandable that the forces of nationalist movements have directed its hatred and wrath toward the West, even though today Colonialism, as it was in the latter part of the nineteenth century and early part of the twentieth, no longer exists.

Members of *al-Jihad* reiterated repeatedly that America is "the new master" and now they are "buying Sadat and his cronies. How can a true

Muslim lower himself as to deal with those Crusaders who only seek to humiliate our religion?''

Psychologically, Muslim nationalists have never recovered from their sense of distrust of Western powers. With the Crusades and the blatant occupation of their countries by the British and the French, they ask, ''How can we ever trust people who feel superior to us and who feel that their religion is superior to ours?''

The fact that there are secular governments in the West that are not necessarily concerned with which religion is superior, is no convincing argument to the zealot Muslim nationalists.

America to them is carrying the mantle of the British. When the argument points to how friendly the United States is to Egypt, they are quick to say, ''If they really are friendly to Egypt, how come they still support Israel?''

You can't be a friend of two enemies in the Middle East. You must choose sides for this is the only way one can find his identity. Being an independent individualist is no virtue in Middle East culture.

Imperialism And The Middle East Prior To World War I

Throughout the nineteenth century, Great Britain pursued a policy of preventing any nation from becoming strong enough to dominate the dying Ottoman Empire, lest this foothold endanger British positions in India and the East. In support of this policy, the British acquired outposts from Malta all the way to the borders of India. No other power had such an elaborate and extensive defense system or controlled such a vast territory between the Mediterranean and India. Russia no longer seemed to be a great threat, and differences with France had been settled amicably. Germany now represented the sole potential menace to not only Great Britain but also France and Russia.

At the time, extensive German economic and political penetration seemed to be undermining British policy in the British Empire. Young Turks, admirers of Prussian militantism, formed an alliance with the Kaiser causing Russia to fear that their dream of controlling the straits and absorbing Northern Iran would never be realized. France resented its loss of predominant cultural and commercial influence over the Ottoman Empire, while the British were concerned about their network between the Mediterranean and India.

Only a few months before the outbreak of World War I, an awareness of the impending doom grew. The British and the Germans made efforts to compromise their commercial conflict in the Ottoman Empire, but the truce came too late to have any effect on the general worldwide political situation, and within a few weeks war broke out.

The international conflict found the Middle East divided into four principal areas:

1. The Ottoman Empire, with the exception of Egypt, had shifted into the German sphere of influence.
2. Egypt was theoretically still an autonomous province of the Ottoman Empire, but in reality was a British protectorate.
3. The Sudan and the Persian Gulf coast of the Arabian peninsula were completely dominated by Great Britain.
4. Iran was divided between British and Russian zones of influence.[27]

For our purposes, the secret political arrangements made to divide the Ottoman territories among the victorious Allies are more significant than any military activity. Great Britain, France, Russia, and Italy schemed to carve up the Ottoman Empire in four principal sets of agreements. The Sykes-Picot agreement is of the most importance to our study.

This agreement between the British and the French was the key to the future of the Ottoman Arab lands. France would obtain outright possession of the Syrian coastal strip north of the city of Tierra, the Ottoman province of Adana, a large part of Cilicia, Syria, and Northern Iraq, including Mosule's fields, which had become an independent Arab zone under French protection; Iraq and the Persian Gulf would become British spheres. Russia insisted on the internationalization of Palestine west of the Jordan River, between the cities of Gaza and Tierra, excluding the British enclave around Acre because of its many Orthodox religious establishments.

In addition to the various secret agreements among the Allies, there were conflicting British commitments to the Zionist and the Arab nationalists. Ambiguities in British policy were created by discord between the British-Indian government and the foreign office. The former was primarily concerned with interests in the Persian Gulf and Iraq, while the latter concentrated on making fruitful contacts with Arab nationalists in the Arabia Hijaz and the Levant.[28] A good example of this occurred when the representatives of the foreign office in Cairo schemed to involve a notable Hashemite family in the British cause with the enticement of an independent Arab state. Negotiations were carried on through correspondence between Sherif Hussein, Keeper of the Holy Places in Mecca, and Sir Henry McMahon, British High Commissioner in Egypt. Although Britain's promises to the Arabs were somewhat vague, they prompted nationalists to actively support the Allies. The following factors contributed to the aura of uncertainty created by the substance of the Hussein-McMahon correspondence:

1. The apparent conflict with other British commitments, such as the British-Indian office support of Hussein's antagonist, Ibn Saud

---

[27] Ibid., pp. 98-101.
[28] George Antonius, *The Arab Awakening*, (New York, New York: Paragon Books, 1979), pp. 244-245.

2. The Sykes-Picot agreement
3. The Zionist claim to part of the Holy Land on the basis of the Balfour Declaration of November 1917

Again, this kind of maneuvering behind the scene, and manipulating of events, only seemed to confirm to the Muslim nationalist movements that the Westerners, in this case the British, were not trustworthy.

In the Middle East it is all right to lie to or manipulate those who are inferior to oneself. For example, covenants with infidels are not binding upon the Muslim's conscience. These covenants can be entered into only when the Muslim is in a disadvantaged position.

Here again it is understandable that Muslims do not read these events as "British diplomacy." These are manipulations of the inferior by the superior. Therefore, the degree of hatred toward the West can only become greater.

Until World War II, the history of the Arab world was determined less by the wishes of the native populations than by the decisions of Western politicians. The only foreign voice that spoke for the Arabs against the British occupation was that of President Wilson in 1919 at the Paris Peace Conference, where he tried to modify the Allied wartime agreements. He argued that they violated publicized war aims, stating that future governments in the area would be based on the self-determination of the local populations.

Wilson sent two members of his American Inter-Allied Commission to the Middle East to investigate the wishes of the local inhabitants. The two American commissioners, Charles R. Crane and Henry C. King, reported that independence was most fervently desired, but if political restrictions were required, then the population would prefer an American mandate.

Wilson's illness forced him to withdraw from the Paris Conference and led to complete American non-involvement. Since Great Britain and France utterly disagreed with Wilson, they disregarded his recommendations and divided the Arab East to suit their own mutual convenience in April 1920 at San Remo, where various modifications of the Sykes-Picot agreement were settled upon.[29]

Immediately after victory, the British appointed Amir Faisal, the son of Sherif Hussein, the military governor of Damascus. This was another confirmation to Muslims that opportunities for leadership of nations were made by their foreign-occupying masters, and they were not the master of their destiny. They had previously promised to compensate him for cooperation with the British. But when France took over Syria, they were not content to have a British-controlled governor in Syria. Thus, Faisal was constrained to leave Syria. Meanwhile, in 1921, at a meeting in Cairo, Sir Winston Churchill, then

---

[29] P. M. Holt, *Egypt and the Fertile Crescent 1516-1922*, (Ithaca and London; Cornell University Press, 1966), pp. 271-277.

the Colonial Secretary, decided to compensate Faisal for his loss of the Syrian kingdom by offering him the crown of the new kingdom of Iraq. However, since the British had promised Iraq to Abdullah, Faisal's brother, they separated the area of Transjordan from the Palestinian mandate and converted it into an emirate—a status somewhat lower than a kingdom—presented it to Abdullah, the great-grandfather of the present King Hussein of Jordan and the first *amir* or prince of that province. During this time, the British tightly controlled Egypt. In fact, Egypt never was at the negotiating table with the French; the British clearly indicated to the French that everything was negotiable except Egypt.

Antonius describes the Sykes-Picot agreement as "a shocking document. It is not only the product of greed at its worst, that is to say, of greed allied to suspicion and so leading to stupidity: it also stands out as a startling piece of double-dealing."[30] Antonius suggests that the "breach of faith" is more serious than all the misjudgments and errors in the agreement. The agreement had been negotiated and concluded without the knowledge of Sherif Hussein, and it contained provisions which were in direct conflict with the terms of Sir Henry McMahon's compact with him. Worse still, the fact of its conclusion was concealed from him because many feared that he would unhesitatingly denounce his alliance with Great Britain. He only heard of the existence of the agreement some eighteen months later.[31]

These historical manœuverings on the part of the Western Imperalist powers created no small sense of frustration and humiliation that embattled the hearts and souls of Muslims for generations. It is difficult to predict whether the future can bring a change in this attitude. However, as we concern ourselves with the present, it is evident that this sense of frustration is manifesting itself in many Muslim lands in an anti-Western fervor which has led some to suicide missions against Western buildings and Western personnel in the Middle East whose presence is perceived as a symbol of Western imperialism.

To be anti-West, to modern Muslim Zealots, is perceived to be a true Muslim. As some of them have explained, "true Islam cannot be found anywhere in the world unless it is built upon the ruins of an immoral, corrupt Western civilization that served to pervert the Muslim world."

---

[30] Antonius, *The Arab Awakening*, p. 248.
[31] Ibid., pp. 249-250.

CHAPTER SIX

THE STATE OF ISRAEL AND THE DEEPENING
OF THE TENSION BETWEEN ISLAM AND THE WEST

The Balfour Declaration was proclaimed in order to win worldwide Jewish backing for the war effort at a time when Great Britain urgently needed every possible source of support. Russia had dropped out of the war because of the 1917 revolution. Since many leaders of the new anti-war leftist Soviet government were Jewish, it was feared that their coreligionists would support the revolutionary cause rather than the Czarist regime whom the Allies backed. Some British leaders even hoped to win German-Jewish support away from the Kaiser. Late in 1936, wartime Prime Minister David Lloyd George revealed that the Zionists had promised to rally Jewish pro-Allied sentiment if they received a commitment for establishing a Jewish national home in Palestine. "They were helpful," he commented in the House of Commons.[32] The declaration took the form of a public letter from Lord Balfour, the British Foreign Minister, to Lord Rothschild, a prominent English leader in Jewish causes. It stated:

> "His Majesty's government views with favor the establishment in Palestine of a national home for the Jewish people and would use their best endeavors to facilitate the achievement of this object. It being clearly understood that nothing shall be done which may prejudice the civil and religious rights of existing non-Jewish communities in Palestine, or the rights and political status enjoyed by Jews in any other country."[33]

To mollify Arab concern about this statement, Great Britain sent Commander D. G. Hogarth to reassure Sherif Hussein that its promise to the Zionists would be implemented only insofar as it did not conflict with the freedom of the population in Palestine.

Palestine

Palestine was an anomaly. Its Jewish and Arab populations were among the most politically sophisticated and culturally developed in the area. Conflict between Jewish and Arab nationalism, however, frustrated all British attempts to encourage local self-government. Arab nationalists considered Palestine part of the Arab heartland and refused to surrender any of their rights or claims. Zionists, on the other hand, envisioned Palestine as a Jewish

---

[32] Don Peretz, *The Middle East Today*, p. 101.
[33] Ibid., p. 101.

national home and were determined to realize their aspiration. The devious dealings and duplicity of the British operation did not help the situation very much. The promise of the officer at the foreign office in Cairo would be diametrically opposed to that of the foreign secretary in London; this kept the Arabs and the Zionists guessing all the time.

To illustrate, the British tried to stop the Zionists from expansion when the Arab nationalists pressured them; similarly, when the Jewish lobby in Britain counter-pressured the British, they, in turn, leaned on the Arabs.

Britain came to feel what they called the "dual obligation." On the one hand, they tried to accommodate the pressure of Zionists whose power in England showed at the ballot box and, on the other hand, they tried to appease the Arabs, whose satisfaction the British felt obligated to ensure.

The details of the British dealings under this "dual obligation" are horrific.

Zionism: *The European Beginning*

Modern Zionism, inspired by the ancient land of Israel of the Old Testament is the movement that calls for a Jewish return to the homeland. Zionism was a direct product of the economic, political, and social conditions of the nineteenth-century European Jews. Indirectly, Zionism was the culmination of the many centuries of Jewish history that followed the dispersion of the Palestinian Jewish community after the Roman conquest during the first century A.D. From the Holy Land, Jews emigrated or were transported to Europe, for the most part, where they usually lived together in communities separate from the Europeans and practiced the laws, traditions, and customs of ancient Israel.

Despite the many generations over which they lived in the various countries, they remained, in essence, foreigners. It is no surprise, therefore, that when the idea of a homeland became a reality, thousands of them flocked to Israel from most European countries. The Jews, then, were isolated from the community at large and, frequently, expelled en masse. Nearly every major European nation—Spain, France, England, Poland, Romania, and Germany—exiled its Jewish community at one time or another.

"The Jews," Herzl wrote, "... would always be persecuted no matter how useful or patriotic they were. Nowhere was their integration into national life possible; the Jewish problem, the hatred of the Jewish minority by non-Jewish majority, existed wherever there were Jews. Even immigration to hopefully safe places did not exempt Jews from eventual anti-Semitism."[34]

In 1914, there were some 600 thousand Arabs and 85 thousand Jews in Palestine. The Arabs had not as yet developed any nationalistic feeling, because the Islamic or Christian *millet* claimed their loyalty, not the state. A

---

[34] Ibid., p. 259.

distinctive Arab and later Palestinian common nationalist movement did not emerge until World War I. Osmanlis exercised only a shadow of control over many parts of Palestine. The Bedouin still roamed and periodically raided the settled villages in the hill country on the northern plains.

Immediately after the outbreak of World War I, the Osmanlis (the Ottomans) clamped rigid restrictions on Palestine and the surrounding area. In addition to the harsh treatment, widespread drought and a locust plague caused a famine. Foreign minorities fared worse than others at the hand of the Ottoman government because they had lost the protection of capitulations, which had been abolished by the Osmanlis in 1914.

The unrest of Arab nationalists within and beyond the borders of Palestine forced the British to clarify their position in Winston Churchill's white paper of July 1922. It maintained that Arab fears were caused by "exaggerated interpretations" of the Balfour Declaration and "unauthorized statements" that Palestine would become wholly Jewish. Churchill's address drew attention to the fact that the Balfour Declaration did not acknowledge "that Palestine as a whole should be converted into a Jewish national home, but that such a home should be found in Palestine." All citizens of the country were Palestinian, and none were entitled to any special judicial status.

On the other hand, to allay Jewish apprehensions, Churchill affirmed that the Balfour promises would not be abandoned. He explained that the Balfour Declaration did not entail an imposition of Jewish nationality on all the country's inhabitants, but simply the continued political and economic development of the existing Jewish community with the help of world Jewry.

Great Britain's *de jure* position in Palestine was confirmed by the Lausanne Peace Treaty with Turkey in 1923, although the League of Nations had already assigned the Palestinian mandate in July 1922. It differed from the other Middle East mandates that called for progressive development of independent states. In Palestine, the British were vested with "full powers of legislation and of administration save as they may be limited by the terms of this mandate."[35] The mandate did not mention the Arab community.

The mandate also authorized Jewish immigration and "closed settlement" on the land. Jews who decided to establish permanent residence would be assisted in obtaining Palestinian citizenship. Jewish community leaders were authorized to construct and operate public works, services, and utilities not directly undertaken by mandatory administration.

Both Jewish and Arab communities complained that the British mandatory authorities discriminated against them. Both protested any measure intended to lead toward self-government: the Arabs because the measures were not drastic enough; the Jews because the measures appeared to favor the Arabs.

---

[35] Holt, *Egypt and the Fertile Crescent 1516-1922*, p. 292.

Torn between Arab and Jewish demands, the mandatory officials attempted to balance one side against the other. Some British thought that the implementation of the mandate would jeopardize Great Britain's friendship with other Muslim nations by antagonizing the Arabs and would thus be impossible. Others regarded the Jewish community as a progressive element that could serve as an example to revitalize the whole Middle East. Thus, policy fluctuated on all levels according to whims and prejudices of local officials.

In this kind of environment, the antagonists became increasingly bitter toward one another and toward the mandatory power, until the gaps became unbridgeable. Each community went its own way, developing its separate institutions in violent conflict with those of the other.

Despite the formal existence of Palestinian citizenship, Palestinian government and Palestinian officialdom, there was really no Palestinian community. Instead, on the one side, the British official life operated in its own framework of military and administrative organization, while, on the other side, the Arab community, with its growing national movement, fused the Muslim and various Christian *millets* under the control of the Muslim leading families. The Arab self-governing institutions often supplemented the functions of British mandatory government.

The British role in creating the state of Israel and, later on, America's recognition of that state have left a deep scar in the body of the Arab world. That is the reason this particular period of history has received a careful and thorough consideration. Arabs and, in particular, Muslim activists are certain that the Christian West has implanted Israel in their midst in order to keep control of the area. This thought interwoven with four hundred years of Crusades has convinced them that the Christian West has never respected their dignity.

The Arabs, unlike the Westerners, cannot forget the past very easily. To them the Crusades happened yesterday. To them colonialism still exists in the form of the state of Israel and, thus, the United States and Western Europe are to be blamed for every conceivable problem that has arisen in the Middle East. These are not just wild accusations, but deeply felt convictions. Therefore, today, most Muslim activists are mindful of the duplicity of the British and the French in the Sykes-Picot agreement and also that of the British in Palestine, Egypt, and Iraq. They are aware of the false declarations of independence for Algiers and the Levant.

The thought of "the House of War," namely Israel, occupying a land that belongs to the House of Islam is no small matter to Muslim revolutionaries. For it smacks at the heart of their religious ideologies.

Al-Jihad now and the Muslim brethren before them have repeatedly sworn that there can be no peace with Israel. "It is (they say) a constant reminder of the Westerner's humiliation to Muslims." They planted their own base in a Muslim land, and Islam cannot rest until the Jews either leave "Palestine" or accept rulership by a Muslim government. The entire Lebanese Civil War (1974-present) is another example of an "Imperialist Western power (in this case France) creating an environment in which a national Christian is the president of a Muslim land, an intolerable state of affairs," one of the leaders exclaimed.

Having considered the broad strokes of this Christian West versus Islamic conflict, it is appropriate now to set apart Egypt, in order to focus attention on its history and its role in the rise of Islamic militant groups.

CHAPTER SEVEN

EGYPT—FROM ANTIQUITY TO THE ISLAMIC CONQUEST

The mainstream of Islamic ideological thought, in relation to non-Muslims, is concentrated upon the idea of the "House of Islam" versus The "House of War" and its ramifications in East/West relations. The role of this ideology has been no less significant in the Egyptian context than in the wider context.

Most modern scholars who have written about Egypt, be they historians or social scientists, have tended to ignore altogether an important element in Egyptian society which played a key role in the visible manifestation of the activity of *al-Jihad*. This element is the Coptic Christian minority in Egypt.[36] The visible signs of the growth and expansion of *al-Jihad* included the stoning of churches, the attacking of priests, and sporadic skirmishes between student members of the movement and Christian students, especially at the universities of Assiut and Alexandria.

Two basic elements comprise Egypt today—the Arabic and the Islamic elements, which form the basis of common culture. It is interesting to note that while Iran was once conquered by the Arabs and shared this culture, it did not belong to the great block of Arabic-speaking populations, as did Egypt. This, I believe, is due to the Coptic Christians' docile nature and willingness to submit, while the Zoroastrians in Iran accepted Islam as a religion, but rejected the Arabic cultural wrapping that accompanied it.

To try to explain away this vital social movement without taking these important events into account is tantamount to recounting American history during the sixties without reference to the civil rights marches or the Vietnam War. A very brief historical analysis of Egyptian Coptic and Muslim relations will be recounted in order to provide a crisper and clearer explanation of the movement under study.

The history of Egypt is described perfectly in the words of Butcher who states that it "... is inextricably interwoven with that of the successive masters—Roman, Byzantine, Arab, Kurd, Circassian, and Turk—who have verily made the land of Egypt a house of bondage for her own children."[37,38]

---

[36] Mohamed Heikal's book, *Autumn of Fury: The Assassination of Sadat*, (New York: Random House, 1983), is an exception.

[37] E. L. Butscher, *The Story of the Church of Egypt*, (London: Smith, Elder and Company, 1897), p. VII.

[38] Since Butcher is British, and keeping in mind the date of the book (1897), one certainly has to add to the list the British who have ruled Egypt directly or indirectly from 1885-1954. Also the Greeks and the Persians should be added to the list.

It is painfully obvious to Egyptian specialists that for over two millenniums Egypt has passed from one foreign domination to another. The late President Sadat frequently referred to this in his speeches, deploring the fact that from the end of Pharaonic rule until 1952, Egypt had not been ruled by the Egyptians.[39]

What was mentioned in the previous chapter regarding the East/West controversy is best illustrated by the case of Egypt because of its Western (mainly Hellenic), as well as Christian heritage, and its direct confrontation with Islam in the middle of the 600s. The rule of the Persian Empire over many ethnic and religious groups in the Middle East area stretched from the Indus to the Nile between 550-330 B.C. Thus, when Alexander the Great humbled the Persians and tried to absorb much of its territory into his own, Egypt became the theater on which the Hellenistic-Zoroastrian (Persian) wars were played.

The inhabitants of Egypt at that time were divided, roughly speaking, into three groups: Greeks, Jews, and Egyptians, the latter being the larger and more dominant group. While each of these three groups still held to their own religion, in name, the Greeks, by this time, were practically atheists and thought as little of their gods as they did of their emperors.[40]

One of the most glaring manifestations of the Egyptian enslavement at the time of Augustus Caesar was the right of two foreign groups—the Greeks and the Jews—to possess citizenship, which was denied to the Egyptians in their own country.

Egypt after Christ

Most non-Biblical traditions indicate that Mark, one of Christ's disciples, brought Christianity into Egypt, though the exact year is uncertain. Mark's first convert in Alexandria was a man by the name of Annianus, a shoemaker who later became the second Bishop of the church (the first being Mark himself).

The Egyptian church of today (Coptic Orthodox) prides itself on the fact that it does not differ now from the time of its founder! "We are the only Orthodox Church in existence today," said one of its leaders. "By Orthodox I mean no change, whatsoever, from the first teachings of Mark."[41]

Another leader commented that "the three orders of Bishop, Priest and Deacon have continued from Mark until today without a break."[42]

Yet, it is obvious that clinging to the celibacy for bishops and the chief bishop (patriarch) is the result of later teachings in the Egyptian church, which

---

[39] July 1952 was the date of the Egyptian revoltion against what was considered a foreign (Albanian) monarchy and the British occupation.
[40] Butcher, *The Story of the Church of Egypt*, p. 3.
[41] A personal interview, July 2, 1982.
[42] A personal interview, July 2, 1982.

is the leading church in the Monastic movement. The Egyptian priesthood, like that of the Greek and unlike the Roman, is emphatically a married priesthood. In addition to this, a host of rituals, fasts, and religious laws developed later.

Such is the church which was founded in the first century and which endured for two millenniums the stormy waves of persecution by Roman and Byzantine Christians who sought to dominate the church and the country ecclesiastically as well as politically. This tension between the Coptic church and the Byzantine church regarding the nature of Christ as well as its political ramifications have helped in aiding and speeding the success of the Arab invasion. Finally, the Arabic invasion brought Arabic and Islamic influences into Egypt.

A Brief Persian Attempt

By A.D. 603 Byzantine rule in Egypt was on the verge of collapse, while, at the same time, the Egyptians' impatience with Byzantine domination was growing in the same proportion as its national independent spirit.

The days of Byzantine rule over Egypt were numbered. For a new and energetic power was rising up from the dust of the Arabian peninsula. Early in 640, when Omar became Caliph, he sent the strong and able General Amr ibn al-As who, having overrun Syria, turned his eyes upon the far more valuable prize of Egypt.

From Arabia Into the Mediterranean

From 639 until 640 Amr ibn al-As attacked Babylon unsuccessfully. After seven months of failure, he attacked Egypt on three fronts; and in a major battle between two alien armies, namely the Byzantines and the Arabs, Egypt stood still and watched itself being destroyed. Eventually Amr concentrated his forces in Alexandria, which held out against the Muslims for more than a year.[43]

It its reported that Amr urged the Copts to side with him against the Byzantines on the grounds of kinship between the Copts and Arabs through Hagar. The Copts, however, argued that this relationship was tenuous, whereupon Amr granted them four days to consider the matter.[44]

---

[43] Butcher, *The Story of the Church of Egypt*, p. 367.

[44] Alfred J. Butler, *The Arab Conquest of Egypt*, (Oxford: The Clarendon Press, 1902), p. 215.
Butler explains that when Amr became victorious over the Romans in Egypt, in order to align with the Copts and discourage them from taking up arms against the Muslims, "... he invited some of the leaders among them to dinner. He had a camel slaughtered, and the flesh boiled in salt water and set before a mixed company of Copts and Arabs. The Arabs ate of the meat, but the Copts only turned away in disgust, and went home dinnerless. Next day Amr ordered his

It is important to note that there are conflicting accounts of the Arab conquest of Egypt. The Arab historians indicate that the Egyptians welcomed Arabs with open arms in order to free themselves from Byzantine domination. Yet, Coptic historians recount in detail many instances of persecution by Muslims and many burdens which were put upon the Copts for their faith, especially the *jizya*. The details of these conflicting accounts cannot be discussed in the limited scope of this chapter or in this book in general.

Nonetheless, these arguments are not simply in history books. Rather, both Muslim and Christian preachers have recorded them for posterity on tapes, which are on sale today or are secretly circulated. The Muslim revivalists insist that since the faith of Islam came to Egypt there is no need for Christianity to exist, at least in its present form. Instead of Christians sharing equality with Muslims, they think that the *shari'a* should be implemented so that Christians once again become *ahl al-dhimmah* or the protected of the state.

The Copts, on the other hand, insist that Islam is a foreign intrusion and should be treated as such, even now! "The only true Egyptians are the Copts. If we are willing to live in this disguised, subservient position ... why do they want to impose the rigid *shari'a* where we shall become legally second-class citizens?",[45] asked a Coptic leader.

Thus, this tension between the Copts and the Muslims in Egypt is at the heart of the *Jihad* movement, just as it was and still is at the heart of the Muslim Brotherhood movement. Yet, the *Jihad* group has gone a step further in condemning Muslims who follow the pattern of a Western lifestyle, which they consider identical to a Christian lifestyle. The educated Muslims who accept this lifestyle according to Farag in his book, are "compromisers and should be killed, for they are worse than the infidels themselves ..."[46]

The rest of Egypt's history is a cycle of tension and calm, of persecution and pressure by various Muslim rulers upon the Copts, who became a minority within 1000 years of the Arab invasion.

---

cooks to search the town of Misr for every dainty and delicate dish it could provide to dress a banquet. This was done, and the same company sat down to a sumptuous repast. When dinner was over, Amu spoke to the Copts as follows: 'I must have for you all the regard which our kinship imposes. But I understand that you are plotting to take up arms once more against me. Now aforetime the Arabs ate camel's meat, as you saw yesterday; but now when they have discovered all this dainty fare that you see before you, do you think that they will surrender this city? I tell you they will give their lives first; they will fight to the death. Do not therefore hurl yourselves to destruction. Either embrace the religion of Islam, or pay your tribute, and go your ways to your villages'."

Meanwhile, when Alexandria finally fell, Amr concluded a treaty with the Egyptians on 8 November 641, which is in essence similar to the previous treaty of Amr i.e., "a general security was given for the life, property, and churches of the Egyptians, ... for the payment of tribute and taxes constituted them a protected people (ahl al-dhimmah)."

[45] Personal interview, July, 1982.

[46] Muhammad Abd al-Salam Farag, *The Missing Religious Precept*, Michael A. Youssef, trans.

The Umayyads

The Umayyad dynasty intensified not only the process of Islamization but also Arabization of Egypt. Caliph Abd al-Malik bore down even harder. The "Muslims burnt the crops, pillaged the monasteries, and dragged the nuns to be dealt with at Merwan's (Caliph) pleasure."[47]

The Umayyads were overthrown by the Abbasids, the descendants not only of the Quraysh of Mecca, like the Umayyads, but also of the Prophet's own clan (Banu Hashim).

The Abbasid rule was better for Egypt than that of the Umayyad in that the Egyptians were able to develop the intellectual and cultural characteristics of Islam, mingling them with the best of the old Greek-Byzantine-Coptic heritage.[48] The lesson which may be learned here is, "unless Muslim revivalists of today allow themselves the freedom to borrow and learn from the evolutionary process and progress of the West, they will find it difficult if not impossible to progress and develop in what could be a truly Islamic progress."[49]

The Abbasid caliph began to crumble, however, into gubernatorial dynasties, each of which was short-lived. The first Ottoman dynasty in Egypt, established by Ahmad Ibn Tulun, represented a new ethnic element, which, for a millennium to come, would play a dominant part in the Eastern and central lands of Islam.

The Fatimids

In the year 893, a strong body of Shi'ite Arabs, known as the Fatimid party (because their head claimed descent from Fatima, the daughter of the Prophet Muhammad), made themselves masters of Pentapolis and the surrounding districts. Sixteen years later their leader assumed the title of caliph in opposition to the Abbasid caliph.

The emergence of the Fatimid caliphate is a major event in Egypt's Islamic history. It was the first time a large part of "Dar al Islam" had passed under the control of a sect, which not only rejected the spiritual claims of the Abbasids, but also resolved to replace them by a new universalist Imamate. The progeny of Ali were to govern the whole Muslim world, not as civil magistrates but as sinless and infallible spokesmen of God, which is the main claim of the Shi'ite division. To the Fatimids, Egypt was only a base of opera-

[47] Butcher, *The Story of the Church of Egypt*, p. 414.
[48] Joseph Schacht, ed., with C. E. Bosworth, *The Legacy of Islam*, (Oxford: The Clarendon Press, 1974), p. 4.
[49] A personal interview with a well-known Egyptian intellectual who was promised anonymity, July 1982.

tions from which to conquer all Sunni Islamic nations. The Abbasid started out from Khurasan in 747 and proceeded to put their plans into action with all convenient speed.

The period of the Fatimid rule in Egypt was the only time that Shi'ite Islam held power in Egypt.[50] Generally speaking, the period of 953-975 is known as the calm and reconciliatory period for Egypt's Copts. But upon the death of Saladin, who fought the Crusades, his dominions split up into a loose dynastic empire, controlled by different members of his family, the Ayyubids.

After the death of the last effective Egyptian Ayyubid in 1250, the political control of Egypt passed to the Mamluk guards whose generals seized the Sultanate. Thus, it was the Turkish mamluks who organized the military resistance to the Mongol advance. The decisive battle was fought in 1260 in Palestine.

During most of these conflicts, Egyptian Islam continued to flourish; and Cairo, the Mamluk capital, grew in prestige centered around Muslim power and civilization, especially when the light from Baghdad flickered into extinction.

Islam made forward strides in Egypt, not only through the continuing conversion of the Copts of Egypt, a process which had been going on since the Arab conquest, but also through the penetration of the Christian Numibia by Arab tribesmen from upper Egypt, as well as the conquest, Arabization, and Islamization of what is now called Northern Sudan.[51]

The Ottoman Empire

From the early sixteenth to the early twentieth century, Egypt was part of the Ottoman Empire. Its history during these four centuries can only be properly understood within the Ottoman context as explained above. The Ottomans were only interested in Egypt as a source of income, in the form of taxes, that kept the imperial machine operating. With the decline of the Ottoman Empire, in general, came the decline of Ottoman Egypt.

---

[50] J. J. Saunders, *A History of Medieval Islam*, (London, Henley and Boston: Routledge and Kegan Paul, 1965), p. 132.

[51] Butcher, *The Story of the Church of Egypt*, pp. 440-448.

CHAPTER EIGHT

EGYPT IN MODERN TIMES

Modern Egypt 1800-1928

By the close of the eighteenth century, the rival worlds of Christian Europe and Islam, which had never ceased in their antagonisms toward each other, began to enter a new political era. Europe emerged as the aggressor, whereas the Muslim East, with its grand old days of astounding military conquest past, appeared as the victim.

This was a result of the previous two centuries in which Christian Europe embarked upon great discoveries in the Renaissance and the Reformation, while Egypt settled down to one of the longest periods of isolation and cultural stagnation since its conquest by Islam.[52]

The British, Dutch, and Portuguese navies commanded the sea, but among all the Muslim countries, Egypt suffered the greatest isolation as a result of the discovery of the Cape of Good Hope route, which diverted trade from its land and made it virtually the backwater province of the Ottoman Empire. It was not until 1798 when Napoleon Bonaparte marched his armies into Egypt and toppled the Mamluk powers that Egypt had its first encounter with the modern world.

The threat to Islam at that time became very real, and no match for the traditional enemy, viz the Christian West with its technological advancement and weaponry. The confrontation was one between Europe, which believed in the power of man's will to change the present and determine his future, and Islam, which conceded all knowledge as given and the process of learning as accumulation of the known rather than a process of discovery.[53]

It is true that as a result of Bonaparte's invasion of Egypt a certain degree of transformation and development took place there. This change was in lifestyle, moral values, cultural dress, food, and work ethics. The entire economic and social government structures moved rapidly forward in a relatively short time. Nonetheless, such rapid change presented a problem in that progress did not occur like that of the Europeans, i.e., gradually, organically, and indigenously.

------

[52] Nadav Safran, *Egypt in Search of Political Community*, (Cambridge, Massachusetts; London, England: Harvard University Press, 1961), p. 26.

[53] Even in the sixties, when I was a high school student in Egypt, the best student was judged not by his creative ability but by his ability to memorize facts precisely and restate them.

It was an imposed change rather than a natural change. Thus, the structural change was not accompanied by an intellectual awareness. For example, the existing education system in Egypt was no more than memorizing the Qur'anic texts and simple farming knowledge, while the Europeans came with marketing and technical know-how.

Moreover, this change was induced by foreign powers which eventually dominated Egypt; thus, it was suspect in its intent. This matter of foreign occupation sapped the energy of the subsequent Egyptian intelligentsia which, instead of looking into development and technology on their own merits, became preoccupied with the subject of foreign domination and, in turn, rejected Western progress altogether. This rejection was by no means a unanimous decision on the part of the society, but rather was decided upon after considerable debate. This rejection, however, was not total. They rejected Westernization, but not modernization.

Accepted by some and rejected by others, the change took place and dramatically influenced all social institutions without exception. Just as the case is today, there was a great deal of reluctance about the process of development. The debate continues today in the Egyptian press, in government institutions, and in all Islamic revivalist groups including the group under study here.[54]

The French invasion of Egypt aroused the wrath of the local Muslims toward, not only the Christian French invaders, but also the Egyptian Christians and Jews. Both of these two native Egyptian groups were the object of mob fury. *Jihad* was declared against Christians because they were viewed as collaborators with the French on the grounds of their common Christian heritage, an accusation which was not altogether accurate. In September and October of 1798, the mob attacked Christian men, ravaged Christian women, and brought the heads of the slain Christians to their Mamluk Muslim leaders for a financial reward. Wendell argues that the fact that Bonaparte used Copts and Jews in his administration of the country should not be conceded as the prime reason for resentment by the Muslim majority. "This indeed added an element of impotent rage and necessarily repressed resentment to the normal attitude ..."[55]

---

[54] The author of the book *The Missing Religious Precept* was the leader and founder of the "Al-Jihad" group. He recited the example of Bonaparte's invasion of Egypt and the desecration of al-Azhar University and mosque to prove his case against Muslims who say that education is a weapon which must be acquired. He said, "Education did not stop Bonaparte from trampling Al Azhar University with his horses and troops. Had the Muslims been strong militarily, they would have fought and killed this infidel and kept him from humiliating Islam." (Translated by Michael Youssef from the Arabic version.)

[55] Charles Wendell, *The Evolution of the Egyptian National Image—From its Origins to Ahmad Lutfi al-Sayyid*, (Berkeley, Los Angeles, London: University of California Press, 1972), pp. 96-100.

One does not have to look far in history to find a repetition of hostile acts, one of which is the riot between Christians and Muslims which took place at al-Zawiyah al-Hamrah in January of 1981 when hundreds lost their lives and houses were burned.[56]

Muhammad Ali

As has been mentioned, under the Ottoman rule Egypt remained in stagnation. On the socio-economic level there was a sharp division between *rulers* and *ruled*. The rulers corresponded to their European feudal counterparts, and the ruled, who resembled the peasants, were organized into clusters of religious, social, and economic groups. The contact between the rulers and the ruled occurred mainly through the *shaykhs* who were responsible for the policing of public life and gathering taxes. The *shaykhs*, who served as the linchpin between the ruler and the ruled, ensured that the extent of relationship between the two was minimal. On a social level the different orders of *shaykhs* (shaykh al-Tariqa) were the true leaders. They were religious leaders as well as teachers (educators). They were financially secure and independent. They applied the *shari'a* and kept the *dhimmis* at a distance; their leadership satisfied the craving of the masses for a true Islamic society.

A secular government with its bureaucratic organization would serve to undermine the authority of the religious leaders and, indirectly, the role of religion in society, which is precisely what happened to Egypt under the leadership of Muhammad Ali.

It is no surprise, therefore, that religious Zealots, be they in the *Ulama* ranks or the devout lay members of society, have been protesting the form of a secular government, as well as the use of European code of law, in most of the civil courts ever since.

Both the forms of government and the civil law were bitterly attacked by *al-Jihad* who aimed at changing both once their plans of overthrowing the government succeeded.

The French expedition drew the veil of isolation from Egypt and revealed it to world powers that were trying to destroy each other's kingdoms, especially the French and the British. Muhammad Ali, the head of an Albanian garrison, learned from his European masters to maneuver for power and managed to set the French, the Mamluks, and the Ottomans against each other until he took power in Egypt, thus ending the four years of chaos and

---

[56] Today this seems to be the testimony of both Muslims and Christians who were interviewed for the purpose of this book. For example, a Coptic official explained that natural resentment of Copts on the part of Muslims is far deeper than any one thing ... it is like smoldering fire ready to ignite once it has the chance.

confusion which followed the withdrawal of the French expedition in the early part of the 1800's.[57]

On 13 May 1805, Muhammad Ali was formally declared Pasha of Egypt in the courthouse. Ali is often described as the founder of modern Egypt, yet it must be pointed out that in building modern Egypt, he tore down the traditional political, social, and economic structures. To begin with, he centralized power in himself and in most of his new schools, factories, commercial enterprises, army, navy, etc., which were all created in haste. Ali and his family monopolized agriculture as well as industry. Foreigners enjoyed special privileges under Ali's rule. In all, Ali's administration conformed to Max Weber's description of "the modern state bureaucracy."[58] Again all these changes have sown the seed of resentment and protest which are culminating in "Islamic movements" such as al-Jihad.

The development crusade that was initiated by Ali created the need for a large number of educated personnel to man the new enterprises. In addition to importing more foreign personnel, he sent Egyptian students to Europe in order to learn new skills. Whether intentional or otherwise, this desire for educated Egyptians created a separation between religious schools (kuttabs) on the one hand, and secular schools on the other which were opened by Muhammad Ali. Moreover, this created a new educated elite in the society. This of course had an enormous impact upon the traditional belief system. Ali started to tax the waqfs (religious endowment) and established the tradition of appointing the rector of Al Azhar University instead of letting the man's ulama (colleagues) elect him. Some interpreted these steps as an assault upon Islam, and Ali's way of breaking the hold of the religious leaders upon society at large, so that he acquired sole and absolute power.[59]

As it was pointed out earlier, Muhammad Ali's assault against the established religious institutions caused resentment by Muslim leaders and an eventual Muslim backlash against the secular ruler. To add insult to injury, Muhammad Ali improved the lot of the Copts and opened the door to eventual equality between Muslims and Copts (Christians).

By the mid 1800's, toward the end of his rule, Ali's drive for development began to dwindle, and the last years of his reign were categorized as lethargic. His son Abbas took over the reign, but he reacted against his father's policies and rejected anything that was European. Then, under Sai'id and Ismail the drive toward modernization gained its fullest acceleration, particularly under

---

[57] Jamal Mohammed Ahmed, *The Intellectual Origins of Egypt Nationalism*, (London, New York, Toronto: Oxford University Press, 1960), p. 6.

[58] Max Weber, *On Charisma and Institution Building*, (Chicago and London: The University of Chicago Press, 1968), pp. 66-67.

[59] Abd al-Rahma al-Rafi'i, *Tarikh al-Haraka al-Qawmia fi Misr* (the History of the nationalist movement in Egypt), (Cairo, 1929), vol. 3.

Ismail. Because he was educated in France, he wanted to turn Egypt into a European country when he took power in 1863.[60] He adopted the French language and built opera houses and palaces and, above all, during his reign directed construction of the Suez Canal. He encouraged Western style private enterprise, which was seen as oppressive Western Capitalism, and expanded the railroad system. By 1875 the number of Egyptian students attending schools had vastly expanded since the days of Muhammad Ali, because of the establishment of numerous new government schools, Catholic, Presbyterian and Anglican mission schools, and the first school for girls, built under the auspices of his wife. In all, over two hundred mission schools were opened, and 52 percent of the students were Egyptians.[61]

However, Ismail's most monumental performance, which had far-reaching social, political, and religious effects, was his reinterpretation of the *Shari'a* and reformation of it into a modern European secular code. For the past one hundred years Muslim Zealots have been fighting the government tooth and nail to restore the orthodox Islamic interpretation of the *Shari'a* as the major source of legislation. As it will be shown later on, by 1977 the Egyptian parliament voted the *Shari'a* as the source of legislation.

Ismail's drive for development was implemented by taxing landlords six years in advance, as well as foreign credits, which toward the end of his rule were exhausted. Thus foreign creditors appointed foreign controllers, which was a source of embarrassment to the Khidewi Ismail. These foreign creditor controllers were mainly British and French. It is clear by now that all these "foreign" influences in Egyptian history played a dominant role in the form of the ideology of "Islamic social movements" such as *al-Jihad*. They can point out to all this foreign intervention in their nation's history and show that Westerners "desired nothing but our destruction."

Close contact with European Western ideas created a new class of Egyptians who for the first time were able to understand their country's history and were able to articulate their political and social needs. At the heart of this was the apparent contradiction between the Islamic world view and Western liberal views and philosophies. One can simply say that at this point of history the Egyptian national struggle had begun in earnest.

The Egyptian National Struggle from 1882-1928

The crux of the all-encompassing social problem in Egypt from the late 1800s until today has been the vacuum created when reforms of a mainly

---

[60] M. A. Haykel, *Tarajim Misriyyah Wa-Gharbiyyah* (Egyptia and Western Biographies), (Cairo, 1929), pp. 59-80.

[61] J. Heyworth-Dunn, *Introduction to the History of Education in Modern Egypt*, (Totowa, New Jersey: Biblio Distribution Centre, 1968), p. 436.

Western nature were not interpreted for or, more accurately, were not presented in an Islamic format.

As far as the traditional Muslim masses were concerned, no matter how many benefits they were reaping from progress, especially in the area of agriculture, irrigation, railroad, etc., these ideas were still brought over by infidels and did not have the blessing of the Qur'an upon them. Thus, foreign ideas, whether in education or technology, were suspect, and those who cooperated with foreigners were suspect, even if they were Muslims. For example, the British, after their invasion of Egypt in 1882, not only relied heavily upon the Coptic community to run their banks, companies, etc., but also involved a large number of educated Muslims, who were called by the purists as *Munafiqoun* (hyprocrites).[62]

To aggravate the conflict, since the Muslims firmly believed that all power comes from God, they could never comprehend, let alone admit, that God gave to the Christian infidels the power to rule over the chosen people.

The elements of conflict between the Christian West and Islam came face to face in Egypt, and have not yet been nor ever will be resolved as long as the West is perceived as more powerful than the Muslims and keeps on developing.[63] The question of power, above all else, became the central question. It was natural for Orthodox Muslims to ask whether they could absolve God of responsibility for their subjugation by infidels. This question could not be answered in the affirmative without modifying Islamic views of absolutes and determinism. In fact, it would almost bring the whole Islamic dogma into question which is again unthinkable. Muslim thinkers, such as al-Afghani and his students after him, have struggled with questions of this nature.

Al-Afghani 1838-1897

Al-Afghani came to Egypt from Afghanistan via Iran, filled with a preacher-like zeal, and claimed that the European power of science and technology, methods of organization and diplomacy endangered Islam.[64] The way to repel this onslaught on Islam by the Europeans is by "learning." For a religious leader to give sanction to education and science and the whole idea of development was unique. Al Afghani knew well the implications of his views and the possibility for these views to come in conflict with some dogmatic teaching regarding "causality." He advocated a return to the concept of *Ijtihad*, which is textual exegesis on the basis of current events

---

[62] See article by Shaykh Sharawee in the al-Liwaa' al-Islami (a weekly Islamic newspaper), 1 July 1982, pp. 11-14.

[63] W. C. Smith, *Islam and Modern History*, (Princeton University Press, 1957), Ch. 1.

[64] Albert Hourani, *Arabic Thought in the Liberal Age 1798-1939*, (London, New York, Toronto: Oxford University Press, 1962).

rather than blind acceptance of the traditional Islamic schools of law interpretations. Above all, al-Afghani was motivated to see Islam's progress not
as individual countries but as one nation; in short, he promoted
"pan-Islamism."

The significance of al-Afghani was that his ideas did not depart with him
when he was finally expelled from the country. His charismatic appeal drew
some very able disciples, the best known among them being Shaykh Muhammad Abduh.

At the time of al-Afghani's championship of the cause of Islamic unity in
the face of the threat of the Christian West, there was another group whose
members referred to themselves as the "constitutionalists" and were the
Western educated elite of Egyptian society. Most of their ideas were liberal
European ideas. However, the group's demise came quickly because of an
association with the Urabi revolution; the group collapsed with the failure of
the Urabi uprising.

Muhammad Abduh 1849-1905

The army uprising under the leadership of Colonel Urabi threatened the administration of the khedive. The British wasted no time in landing their troops
in Egypt in 1882 with the declared purpose of restoring the authority of the
khedive and eliminating what they felt to be a threat of disruption to communication between the British and Indian Empire. This action on the part
of the British intensified the nationalist-conscious resistance to Britain. Chief
among them was al-Afghani's student Shaykh Muhammed Abduh.

After a time in France, where he collaborated with his master al-Afghani
in 1884 in publishing the short-lived pan-Islamic revolutionary review, *Al-
Urwah al Wuthqa* (The Firm Bond), Abduh was reconciled to the British and
returned to Egypt via Beirut to hold a high position which ultimately led him
to become the *Grand-Mufti* of Egypt.[65]

When Abduh assumed rulership, he, like Afghani, faced the dilemma of the
inner decay and the need for inner revival in Egypt.[66] However, the contribution of Abduh to the debate of how one brings about the revival is *highly
significant*, not only in terms of the theological controversy but also in relation to the current study.

Fundamentalist Muslims believe that the Prophet Muhammad did not just
preach individual salvation, but that he also founded a virtuous *Ummah* or
society in order that salvation may be found within that society. Thus, the
Prophet and his first *Ummah* were to be used as an example of what a virtuous society ought to be like. This was the declared aim of not only

---

[65] Sufran, *Egypt in Search of Political Community*, p. 66.
[66] Albrt Hourani, *Arabic Thought in the liberal Age*, p. 136.

movements such as *al-Jihad* and the two preceding movements, namely the Muslim Brotherhood and *Takfir wa al-Hijra*.

Abduh, on the other hand, advocated changes in the way Muslims should act in this society in relation to the prophetic time. Abduh explained that circumstances do change and some of the present circumstances were not foreseen by the prophetic message. But by the time Abduh began to formulate his views in order to bridge the gap between what Islamic society should be and what it had become, changes had already taken place under the leadership of Ismail, the *shari'a* was being reformed, and many European codes were being introduced into the Egyptian courts. The main fear of Abduh was the secularization by Ali and his successor of a society fundamentally religious.[67]

Abduh believed that what was required to bridge the gap in Islamic society was not a return to the past by stopping the progress already begun by Muhammad Ali, but rather the acceptance of the need for change and the linking of that change with the principles of Islam. This meant proving that Islam could accommodate a principle of change and exercise salutary control over it. In all this, it appears that Abduh's thinking was influenced by Comte's thoughts of the French Revolution.[68] Like his master, Abduh firmly believed that the Muslim *Ummah* could not become strong and prosperous again until they acquired from Europe the sciences which were the product of its activity of mind, and he believed that they could do this without abandoning Islam.

Like many reformers, Abduh stood in the middle of the road; thus, he was criticized by the Orthodox Muslims for what they perceived to be his liberal views, and he was attacked by the liberals for not going far enough. From the Orthodox Muslim's point of view, Abduh was not really a believer at all.

Out of these two groups rose two distinct voices in Egyptian twentieth-century nationalism. On the one side stands Islamic Orthodoxy, which claims to implement God's will in a society, on the model of the Prophet; and on the other side stands an irreversible movement, which claims that European modernity is invincible in its sweep of the world, and Egyptian society has no alternative but to follow the march toward progress.

Bellah's conclusion regarding Abduh must be the one to adopt here for its incisiveness and perceptiveness, "... neither Muhammad Abduh nor his various disciples have produced anything that warrants the name modernism or anything which can be called reform except in the restricted sense of return to the past, as the term *Salafiyya* indeed implies."[69] Had either Abduh or any of his disciples produced something that was worthy to be called "modern" many of the ensuing events may have been written differently.

---

[67] Ibid.
[68] Ibid.
[69] Bellah, *Beyond Belief*, p. 165.

CHAPTER NINE

EGYPTIAN NATIONALISM AT THE DAWN OF
THE TWENTIETH CENTURY

Abduh's ideology gained acceptance among a small group of reformers, yet the influence of his thought was greater than his opponents would credit. After his death, Abduh's disciples and followers went in different directions. Some insisted that Abduh's real intention was to promote the unchanged and absolute nature of Islam and thus moved more and more in a fundamentalist direction.[70] Others expounded and built upon Abduh's theory of the legitimacy of social change within Islam and their efforts were concentrated upon marrying faith to reason. As it will be shown later on, these two divisions in the thinking of Egyptian society were instrumental in the chain of events that followed during the first thirty years of the twentieth century, and they are prominent today in the debate between the fundamentalists and the liberals.

Among the disciples of Abduh who advocated change was Qasim Amin (1865-1908). He advocated the emancipation of women. Amin's assessment of the cause of decay in Islamic society was ignorance of the true sciences from which alone can be derived the laws of human happiness. Amin contended that this ignorance begins in the main fiber of society, the family, and since women play dominant parts in society as wives and mothers, women must have the freedom and the necessary status to fulfill their role. Furthermore, he held that this could only come through education.[71] Amin, like others in his tradition, got into trouble with Muslim fundamentalists but still insisted that Islam provides equality between men and women (except in regard to polygamy). Amin was not alone, though, and by early 1900 a political party was organized under the name *Hizb al-Imam* (Imam's party) with political principles drawn from Abduh's teaching. By 1907, when more political parties began to form, they changed their name to *Hizb al-Ummah* (National Party). Like all political parties, the *Ummah* party produced its own journal, *al-Jarida*, until the first world war when publications were restricted, and then it folded.

---

[70] The text books used in the curriculum in the educational system of the sixties explained that Abduh is a great Egyptian hero and that students must imitate him in their pursuit of academic excellence. This in no way contradicted Islam, i.e. faith and reason go hand in hand. The problem was and still is in Islam, as it is in Christianity, that there are theological presuppositions that do not stand up to reason. On these issues Muslim reformers begin to waffle.

[71] Hourani, *Arabic Thought in the Liberal Age*, pp. 138-140.

Muhammad Rashid Rida

Muhammad Rashid Rida, Abduh's leading disciple, emphasized orthodoxy more than progress and change. Born in Syria and a resident of Egypt, he was a writer and Abduh's biographer. Rida, however, interpreted Abduh differently. He headed the *Salafiyya Movement* which began as a vehicle for the propagation of Islamic views of Abduh.

The *Salafiyya* called for the solidarity of the Islamic block of nations. It urged reforms yet became increasingly associated with the fanatical Islamic paper *al-Mu'ayyad* and, above all, *Salafiyya*, like the *Wahhabis* of Arabia, advocated a return to Islam's purest origins, the Qur'an and the Sunnah.[72]

Ultimately, *Salafiyya* provided the major opposition to secularism in the 1920s and 1930s, not only in social but also political reforms. They opposed any thought of secularism and nationalism, and they opposed the nationalist political leader Sa'd Zaghlul between 1919 and 1923.

Rida and his *Salafiyya Movement* founded the YMMA (Young Muslim Mens Assocation) in order to develop a social, athletic, and cultural counter part to the YMCA that would be consistent with their emphasis on Islam in its pure origin as the way forward. As well, Muslim youth printed stinging attacks on Westernized Egyptians in their journal. In short, the *Salafiyya Movement* provided fertile ground for Hasan al-Banna and the formation of the society of Muslim Brothers in 1928-29.

The problem that faced the Egyptians during that turbulent time from the end of the nineteenth century to the first half of the twentieth century was the question of the relationship between Islam and society. Because of the French Revolution and the European influence, most nationalists saw Egypt as an independent nation with a unique heritage rather than a part of the Islamic *Ummah*.

Primarily, the nationalists viewed themselves as Egyptians and then as Muslims. Thus, Egyptian Muslims maintained two loyalties, and problems arose when they conflicted. One of the most prolific writers on this subject was Ahmad Lutfi al-Sayyid (1872-1964), a disciple of Abduh who was educated in law and, like other educated Egyptians, read Rousseau, Comte, Mill, and Spencer. He was a founding member of the *Ummah* party, and later became involved with the newly formed *Wafd* party. He served as a professor of philosophy at the University of Cairo, of which he was co-founder and ultimately president.

Lutfi al-Sayyid held the position of Minister of Education twice between 1928-29 and again between 1931-35, became an appointed member of the Senate in 1941, and after 1952 retired from public life.

---

[72] P. J. Vatikiotis, *The Modern History of Egypt*, (New York, Washington: Frederick A. Praeger, 1969), p. 187.

Lutfi's hopes for Egypt and his perception of its progress is of the utmost importance. He translated the works of Aristotle, primarily from the French, so that Egypt's renaissance, like that of the West, was founded on the spread and assimilation of the classics.[73]

The inspiration of Aristotle, Rousseau, Locke and Spencer, which Lutfi had in common with other nationalistic thinkers, manifested itself in his desire to found a base for nationalist doctrine within the scope of liberal, sociopolitical philosophy. Lutfi was critical of Islamic laws, because they had allowed society to accept despotism as the foundation for government. The right government according to him was a constitutionalist government.[74]

Lutfi Sayyid stood in an antithetical position to that of the Islamic Revivalist groups. While Hasan el-Banna and Farag, leaders of the Muslim Brothers and *al-Jihad* respectively, advocated a return to the first *Ummah* of the Prophet in order to achieve justice in society, Lutfi rejected all notions of progress founded on religion.[75]

Depotism, Lutfi insisted, destroys the individual human being as well as the community, because it destroys the element of trust within a nation. Further, despotism creates slavery. Therefore, political freedom is a necessary condition for any kind of freedom. This rejection of absolute government by Lutfi was reiterated in his writings.

Lutfi was first and foremost an Egyptian, and to him Egypt and its existence was the only bond that the people needed, even above religion or any other condition. What makes an Egyptian is the willingness to take Egypt as his first and only mother country.[76] He did not include Egypt among the Arab nations or accept the pan-Islamism which al-Afghani and Abduh advocated very strongly.

One of Lutfi's colleagues and the best known modern thinker in Egypt, Taha Hussein, went further in saying that Egypt belongs to the Mediterranean and not to the Arab world: "We must become Europeans in every sense of the word, acknowledging both its good and its evil! We must follow in the way of the Europeans so that we become equal with them in civilization in its good and in its bad, its sweet and its bitter ..."[77] Taha Hussein's thinking received a million ayes from the Copts who have no time for nationalism based upon Islam.

---

[73] Sufran, *Egypt in Search of Political Community*, p. 92.

[74] Muhammad Lutfi al-Sayyid, *Ta'ammulaat fi 'l-Falsafa wa 'l-Adab, wa 'l-Siyaasah wa 'l-Igtimaa'* (Reflection on Philosophy, Literature, Politics and Society), Articles from al-Jaridah 1912-1914 printed in a book, (Cairo, 1946), pp. 49-50.

[75] Safran, *Egypt in Search of Political Community*, p. 95.

[76] al Sayyid, *Ta'amullaat fi 'l-Falsafa wa 'l-Adab, wa 'l-Siyaasah wa 'l-Igtimaa'* (Reflection on Philosophy, Literature, Politics and Society), pp. 63-66.

[77] Taha Hussein, *Mustaqbil al-Thaqaafa fi Misr*, (The Future of Culture in Egypt), (Cairo, 1938), pp. 4-44.

Hussein believed that Egyptians could adopt the European civilization without adopting its religion.[78] In fact, throughout his writings Hussein tended to ignore the religious differences between the Europeans and the Egyptian Muslims. This subject was left for Ali Abd al-Raziq to expound in his major published work on Islam and its relation to political authority, called *al-Islam wa Usool al-Hukm*, Cairo, 1925.[79] He was very much a student of Abduh, yet the issues of his day were different from those of Muhammad Abduh twenty years earlier.

In 1924 the Turkish reformers abolished the Caliphate as a political institution altogether and provoked debates across the entire Muslim world on whether or not this decision aligned with Islamic tradition. This occasion prompted Abd al-Raziq to write *Islam and the Origin of Rule*, in which he argued that Muhammad was a prophet whose role as a political leader was necessary only in the early stages of Islamic infancy. Because Muhammad's mission was primarily spiritual,[80] he did not appoint a successor; the very idea of a successor came about as a result of a misunderstanding when those who refused to submit to the political leadership of Abu Bakr were accused of rejecting Islam itself.[81]

Obviously, this is more in keeping with Christian thinking about Christ than it is with Islamic traditional thinking. Thus, the book met with violent opposition by the fundamentalists, understandably because Raziq reinterpreted the very history in which religious dogma was embedded.

Generally, the liberal advocates in Egyptian thought undermined Islam in regard to the social institutions, such as family education and the media, etc. Furthermore, they helped to establish, though not very successfully, the foundation for an Egyptian identity free from pan-Islamism. Despite the weak identity, a nationalist revolution finally took place in July of 1952. Initially, the Muslim Brothers were involved in the revolution. Soon after the revolutionary leaders took power, they built on the secular ideas of their predecessors and displaced and crushed the fanatical Islamic groups. The tension between the demand for a government and the outcry for a restoration of Islamic government in its purest form continues to be the debate of today.

The Power Triangle

In the first half of the twentieth century, three elements comprised Egypt's political arena: the British, the palace, and parliament (which normally consisted of one major political party and one or two small opposition parties).

---

[78] Ibid., p. 54.
[79] Abd al-Raziq, *Al-Islam wa Usul al-Hukm*, (Cairo, 1925), p 11.
[80] Ibid., p. 67.
[81] Ibid., pp. 102-103.

The *Wafd* constituted the most dominant party and played a significant role, particularly in the three decades from the twenties until the fifties; it was headed by the well-known nationalist, Sa'd Zaghlul. The *Wafd* represented the secular ideals and de-emphasized the role of religion in government. Thus, it was a popular party through which the Copts became involved in the political process.

The year 1919 witnessed the most turbulent events in the relationships between the British and the Egyptian nationalists. Strikes in all major sectors, looting, violence, and attacks upon British personnel were rampant. The United States' recognition of the British Protectorate over Egypt in that year added to the nationalist agitation. General Allenby, who succeeded Wingate in March of 1919 as the British High Commissioner, began to apply a firm hand on the Egyptians as soon as he arrived in Cairo.

It was not until 28 February 1922 that the British declared the sovereignty of the Egyptian state. The British insisted, however, on certain exemptions that considerably weakened the declaration of independence and created numerous conflicts with successive government. The political atmosphere that followed was utter confusion. Zaghlul led a vigorous attack on what he referred to as an unacceptable formula for an independent state.[82]

By 1924, Zaghlul had become a charismatic leader, *Za'im* of Egypt, but he was unable to resolve the issues around British conditional declaration, and he was undermined by divisions within his own party and constantly attacked by opposition parties.

After the British conditional declaration, the first election was held and the *Wafd* party won 188 of 215 seats in the House of Deputies. This clearly indicated the broad popularity of the *Wafd*; and under its banner Muslims and Christians (Copts) were united, probably as never before in Egypt's history. Copts held key cabinet posts, such as Minister of Foreign Affairs and Minister of Finance; and another cabinet post was held by a Jew. The Wafd also embraced poor and rich, educated and illiterate. In fact, both Zaghlul and Mustafa Nahas, who succeeded Zaghlul after his death in 1927, were *fellaheen* or of peasant background. The personalities of both leaders were attuned to the Egyptian masses.

The tragedy is that the *Wafd* held power for only nineteen months during the three decades after 1922, mainly because of British and Palace meddling in government affairs, each trying to ensure that their interests were assured. When the *Wafd* acted independently, either or both tried to force it out of power.

---

[82] Vatikiotis, *The Modern History of Egypt.*

Socio-Economic Background

After World War II there was a growing resentment by the middle class toward, not only the British and the Palace, but also the small group of land owners who had extensive land holdings and dominated the socio-economic and political life in Egypt. Nasser later called this small group *al-Iqta'iyeen*, which represented less than one-half of one percent of the population (some 1200) yet dominated the scene. Although, as mentioned above, while some leaders of the *Wafd* party, such as Zaghlul, were of a middle class origin, they acquired enough property to be among the upper half of one percent in this respect.

Post-revolution school textbooks have tended to overemphasize the fact that 95 percent of the land was controlled by 5 percent of the population. The revolutionary government stressed social injustice and inequality in Egyptian society and, of course, highlighted the revolution's mission to rectify conditions, in an attempt to justify its position in nationalizing factories, banks, and lands, as well as limiting land ownership first to two hundred *fedan* (a fedan is about an acre), and then to one hundred *fedan* per family.

The majority of the population in post World War II Egypt lived in dire poverty:

> To speak of housing conditions is to exaggerate ... The fellaheen inhabit mud huts, built by making a framework of sticks, usually cotton sticks, and plastering it with mud. The hut is a small enclosed yard, where the family and the buffalo live together, with a small inner room with a roof but no window and a sleeping roof where chickens, rabbits and goats are kept.[83]

The unskilled workers worked from sunrise to sunset for about five cents per day.[84] During all this, the population was increasing by half a million per year, while the limited natural resources were not increasing at the same proportion.

Politically, the *Wafd* party lost its vigor and cohesiveness largely because of the death of its charismatic leader, Zaghlul. Also, the educated middle class perceived the *Wafd* as collaborators with the British during the war. The dissatisfaction of the masses with the status quo manifested itself in many ways. In Cairo there were riots in February 1946 which led to the unproductive revision of the 1936 Anglo-Egyptian Treaty; the combination of these riots eventuated in mass protests in Cairo, and on in 26 January 1952, the protests gave way to mob violence in which a large section of the city of Cairo

[83] Doreen Warriner, *Land and Poverty in the Middle East*, (London: Royal Institute of International Affairs, 1948), p. 43.
[84] This situation has improved somewhat for these workers, mainly due to Nasser's crusade to eliminate illiteracy through evening classes and shorter work hours. Yet poverty persists because of the skyrocketing inflation and the acute shortage of housing.

was burned to the ground. The objects of the riots were luxury hotels, casionos, cinemas, pubs, and exclusive department stores.

An investigation of these riots revealed that Communist and Muslim Brotherhood groups were responsible for the burning of Cairo. Conditions became ripe for a revolution. On 23 July 1952, a small band of army officers, who referred to themselves as "the Free Officers," led a bloodless coup d'etat after years of planning and organizing cell groups among their peers.

This group of officers formed what became known as the "Revolutionary Command Council," who ousted King Farouk, then took over the administrative offices of government. After some two years of wavering between a desire to rule and living up to their stated purposes of restoring democracy and civil government, they decided not to go back to their barracks and remained in power. "Revolutionary Command Council" embraced a broad representation from both extremes, including one Communist, some members of the Muslim Brethren, and a majority comprised of middle-class nationalists who had no clear political aims or social vision.

As time passed, they changed the stated aim of the revolution from reviving the constitutional life in Egypt and purging the army of corrupt elements to a complete takeover of all socio-political institutions. By August of 1953, hundreds of army and police generals were appointed to head companies, government institutions, and local governorships.

In 1956 it became clear that the Revolutionary Command Council (R.C.C.) had taken over with the aim of changing the old system, which in Nasser's view did not work because Egyptians were not yet ready for Western-style democracy.[85] Hence, the revolutionary leaders began to refer to their revolution in terms of "social democracy" instead of just plain democracy. This gave them the necessary excuse to destroy the class distinction between the wealthy and the underprivileged.[86] In this kind of political environment, any dissent, let alone political dissent, was outlawed. Freedom of the press was severely curtailed.

While most historians have agreed on the repressive measures which Nasser and his R.C.C. implemented, very few historians, if any, have explored the question of Nasser's natural resentment toward the Copts. This resentment manifested itself in the imprisonment of the rich Copts, for no apparent reason, and the systematic demotion of Copts who held leadership positions

---

[85] Gamel Abdel Nasser, *The Philosophy of the Revolution*, (Cairo: Dar al-Maaref, 1959), pp. 22-26.

[86] As one who lived through all this, I vividly recall the humiliation and mistreatment of the wealthy as the police took over their palaces and companies. In Nasser's long ad-libbing speeches, he would incite the poor masses to hatred and revenge toward what he called "al-Iqtaa'iyoon, wa 'l-Khawana wa Umalaa al-Isti'maar" (the feudals, the traitors and collaborators with imperialism). This was a very popular phrase which was seldom missing from his speeches.

in government, foreign companies, or banks. Most foreign companies and banks were nationalized by Nasser, including the famous Suez Canal nationalization, which provoked the futile French, British, and Israeli troop invasion of the canal area in 1956.

Prior to the 1952 revolution in Egypt, the British made use of Copts by appointing them to the helm of most financial institutions, post offices, utility companies, and other organizations. This may have been due to the Copts high level of education and their acceptance of the Western lifestyle; another possibility is that the Copts provided the British with a buffer against extremist Islamic nationalists. The British had a natural distrust of Muslims, whom they felt could be easily manipulated by the extremists.

Nasser's methodology in changing the status quo involved creating a position in each company above the rank of manager or director. The position of Chairman of the Board (*Rais Majlis al-Idarah*) was normally filled by a Muslim, often from the ranks of Nasser's army. The holder of the new position did not have to possess any knowledge about the particular field; the most important criteria were that he was a Muslim and that the R.C.C. trusted him. The implementation of this policy in most institutions brought young Muslims through the ranks very quickly in order to make at least 95 percent of the leadership Muslim. By 1969, in most companies, banks, and government institutions, this plan became a reality. It was not unusual to see a Muslim who entered into the service of a bank or a company as late as 1962 and worked under a Coptic boss progress within ten years to become his boss's boss. The main reason for the promotion was not performance but the person's name; i.e., he had a Muslim name rather than a Christian name.[87]

Conversely, Nasser soon discovered that the Copts were a stabilizing factor which he could easily dominate and count on for support without too much difficulty. Thus, the Copts enjoyed a period of relative calm, mainly because of their stated support of the revolution. When Nasser gave the Copts a permit to build a new national cathedral in Cairo, he was in effect enforcing the law of not allowing new churches to be built except by permission from the president of the nation. Nasser used this law to constantly restrain the Copts. Moreover, during the first ten years of the rule of the R.C.C., he opened to a Copt only one cabinet post, the Ministry of Domestic Supply, which was occupied by Kamal Ramzi Steno.

Nasser operated a sophisticated dictatorship, eliminating opposition in several ways: those who disagreed with him from among his own ranks were

---

[87] This open discrimination sent thousands of educated Copts in mass exodus immigrating to Europe, the United States, Canada, Australia and elsewhere. It has been estimated that about 250,000 Copts left Egypt between 1952 and 1982.

assigned to foreign diplomatic and other posts; any outside opposition was either suppressed by being put under house arrest or removed by sending the participants to concentration camps, such as the dreaded one in "Torah" outside of Cairo. A case in point is the house arrest of General Najieb whom Nasser had used as a figurehead for the leadership of the revolution, mainly because of his respectability and age.

SECTION TWO

AL-JIHAD: ITS ROOTS AND IDEOLOGY

CHAPTER TEN

THE MUSLIM BROTHERHOOD, NASSER, AND SADAT

As stated earlier, by the late nineteenth century and early twentieth century, two divergent schools of thought had developed from differing interpretations of Muhammad Abduh's philosophy regarding nationalism and progress. In the last chapter, the progressive thinkers were briefly examined. This chapter will look at the orthodox interpretation in depth.

The real inspiration behind the Muslim Brotherhood movement has never been ascertained, except that it contained a reaction to foreign, especially Western, political and cultural domination, as well as the need to find answers that were strictly national, hence Islamic, in nature. The heart of its formation was concern about the disappearance of the Islamic heritage and its replacement by a Western educational and cultural system which had produced a generation of nominal Muslims.[88]

What gave the Muslim Brotherhood movement the necessary energy and dynamism was the success of the *Wahhabi* movement on the Arabian peninsula.[89] The indication here is that while the Muslim Brotherhood movement was an indigenous political-religious movement beginning in the twentieth century, its motivations and religious objectives were an ideological reversion to the nineteenth-century militant *Wahhabism* and later the pan-Islamic ideal of Jamal al-Din al-Afghani.

Professor Harris draws a parallel between Wahhab and al-Banna, the respective founders of the *Wahhabi* and Muslim Brotherhood movements. The fact that both belonged to the strict Hanbal School of Islamic law indicates that both were well versed in the Hanbalite interpretation of Islamic

---

[88] Richard P. Mitchell, *The Society of the Muslim Brothers*, (London: Oxford University Press, 1969), pp. 4-5.

[89] The Wahhabi Movement in Arabia, which emphasized the teaching of the Hanbally School of Islam, had already been well established in Arabia. Mohammed Ibn Abd-Al Wahhab and his followers demanded the return to the pure Islam of its earliest days. They rejected the Ottoman Empire and what it came to represent. Wahhabis especially resented the Ottoman sultan and his government. This included what he called "ungodly inclination toward the devices of the Frankish infidels." This Wahhabi Movement along with other things emphasized a concept which was not dissimilar to that of al-Banna.
In 1806 the Wahhabi forces, led by the Amir Mohammed Al Saud, occupied Mecca and offered prayers in the name of Saud instead of the Ottoman sultan. When the Turkish ruler wanted to discipline the Wahhabis, he called upon Mohammed Ali Pasha of Egypt to carry out the task. Mohammed Ali in turn sent Egyptian troops to Arabia in order to crush the Wahhabi rebellion. Harris points out that "... some individual Egyptians responded to Wahhabi puritanism." There is no doubt that these individuals, as they returned to Egypt, brought with them ideas which flourished and later on produced the Muslim Brotherhood Movement as we know it.

law. Al-Banna, like Wahhab, proclaimed a need for the intensive literal interpretation of the Qur'an and the Sunna as the sole sources of doctrine and
law.[90]

The link, however, in 1806, between the *Wahhabi* revolt and the time of
al-Banna is probably seen in the *Salafiyyah* Movement and the work of
al-Afghani and Abduh, which we briefly examined earlier. Their activities
have fanned the flames of Islamic nationalism.

Hasan al-Banna and the Muslim Brotherhood

Hasan al-Banna was born in October 1906, in the governate of Buhayra,
in the small town of Mahmoudia, about ninety miles northwest of Cairo. His
father, Shaykh Ahmad Abd al-Rahman al-Banna al-Sa'ati, was the local
Ma'zoon (performer of religious rites such as marriages), Imam and teacher
at the mosque, and author of some commentary on the Hadith. Shaykh
Ahmad studied at al-Azhar University at the time of Shaykh Muhammad
Abduh. His title *al-Sa'ati* (literally a watch repairer) comes from his occupation of watch repairing, which he did in addition to performing his religious
duties. Thus, he brought up his son in an atmosphere of traditional Islamic
piety.

Hasan, the eldest of five sons, joined a number of religious societies even
during the years of his primary education. Shortly after joining, he became
the leader of the Society of Moral Behavior, whose purpose was to sensitize
its members to moral offenses, contrary to Islamic law and practice; interwoven with this preoccupation was his fear of the ideological encroachment
of the Christian missionaries in his town. At the age of twelve, he joined the
Hassafiyya Brothers, a *Sufi* mystical order through which he could express his
distrust of foreign Christian missionary activities. By the age of sixteen,
Hasan was fully entrenched in the teaching of *Sufism*, which called for
"other-worldly qualities," even though it emphasized enough learning to
fulfill one's religious duties and earn one's livelihood.

In 1927 Hasan graduated from Cairo's Dar al-Uloom, the main established
institute for training teachers at that time. The most significant major
influences on Hasan's training were classic Islamic learning and the emotional
discipline of *Sufism*. Moral laxity and what he perceived to be decreasing
respect for religion were his concerns during his early years of teaching. Hasan
deplored what he thought to be blind imitation of the infidel Westerners by
middle and upper-class Egyptians.

As al-Banna became aware of the British occupation of Egypt, and as he
watched the dispute over control of Egypt and the feud between the *Wafd* and

---

[90] Christina Phelps Harris, *Nationalism and Revolution in Egypt*: *The Role of the Muslim
Brotherhood*, (Stanford: Mouton & Co., 1964), p. 161.

the "liberal constitutionalist" parties, he began to view such factionalism as a damning disunity that could engulf not only Egypt but the whole Muslim world. He and six like-minded men formed the organization which became known later as the Muslim Brotherhood. This small group of laborers at the British camp near the city of Ismaliyyah, where Hasan was teaching, expressed to him their discontent over the deteriorated condition of Islam. This movement flourished to the point of recruiting, according to some estimates, one million members by the early fifties. Hasan al-Banna became the first supreme guide and mentor of the group; and after his assassination in 1949, an elderly Hassan al-Hudaybi followed in his footsteps.[91]

Al-Banna and Islamic Ideology

The debate continued to rage whether the Prophet Muhammad intended to found a nation, in the modern sense of the term, or just a community for the faithful. (See Chapter 18) Even so, al-Banna's fundamental conviction that Muslims do not accept or even tolerate a separation of "church" and "state," was thoroughly Islamic. The holistic or totalitarian monotheism created by the Prophet Muhammad in Medina as the first Islamic state was al-Banna's unwavering ideal. It is not unreasonable to assume that al-Banna's ideology, before it was Egyptian or Arabic, was Islamic to the core.

Speaking to his brethren in one of his tracts entitled *Between Yesterday and Tomorrow* he said:

> Brethren, you are not a benevolent organization, nor a political party, nor a local association with strictly limited aims. Rather you are a new spirit making its way into the heart of this nation and revivifying it through the Qur'an; ... If some should ask you: To what end is your appeal made?, say: We are calling you to Islam which was brought by Muhammad, government is part of it, and freedom is one of its religious duties. If someone should say to you: This is politics!, say: This is Islam, and we do not recognize such divisions ...[92]

Hasan al-Banna taught that the Qur'an addressed itself to the social, political, ethical, and legislative aspects of life. Therefore, Muslim nations such as Egypt need not borrow ideas and ideals from the West. He attacked the nationalists, claiming that the very idea of nationalism is a foreign and Western idea. There can be no nationalism in the East apart from Islam. In Islam, he declared, one finds a state that is "more complete, more pure, more lofty, and more exalted than anything that can be found in the utterances of Westerners and the books of Europeans."[93]

---

[91] Hasan al-Banna, *Five Tracts of Hasan al-Banna* (*1906-1949*, Charles Wendell, trans., (Berkeley: University of California Press, 1978), pp. 4-5.
[92] Ibid., p. 36.
[93] Ibid., p. 48.

Al-Banna compared his Islamic ideology with that of the nationalists, and explained that the difference is they

> seek for the most part to free their own country, and then afterwards to build up its strength on the material side, just as Europe is doing today. We, on the other hand, believe that the Muslim is duty bound to give of his person, his blood, and his wealth to carry out his trust, namely, to guide mankind by the light of Islam and to lift its banner on high above the regions of the earth ...[94]

Al-Banna accomplished more in this statement than a mere contrast of his Islamic ideas with those of the nationalists or the West; he articulated Islamic world mission. Caliph Omar, who compiled the Qur'an and established most Muslim tradition, developed the concept of world dominance three years after the death of Muhammad.

On Jihad (Holy War)

Hasan al-Banna believed that his ideal of the *shari'a* was to be imposed in any way possible because he deemed it best for people, even if they did not recognize it as such.

> How wise was the man who said: "Force is the surest way of implementing the right, and how beautiful it is that force and right should march side by side." This striving to broadcast the Islamic mission, quite apart from preserving the hallowed precepts of Islam, is another religious duty imposed by God on the Muslims, just as He imposed fasting, prayer, pilgrimage, alms, and the doing of good and abandonment of evil, upon them.[95]

Al-Banna was convinced from the start that Islam was a proselytizing faith. He felt that the major errors of contemporary Islam was that Muslims had gone to sleep, as it were, and had forsaken their God-given destiny, thus failing in the eyes of both man and God. In the language of al-Fagami, al-Banna explained that originally Islam marched throughout the face of the earth, with the Qur'an in their breasts,

> their homes on their saddles and their swords in their hands, and with the clear argument on the tips of their tongues, calling on mankind to accept one of these three: Islam, tribute (*jizya*), or combat,[96]

Muslims ought to awaken once more, shake off their lethargy, fight the British for their independence, and fortify their faltering government. Al-Banna listed what he considered to be the ten principal goals of reforming government in accordance with the spirit of gebuine Islam. They operate mainly in the political, judicial, and administrative areas of life. Also, he noted thirty principles in the area of social and educational life, and ten prin-

---

[94] Ibid., p. 51.
[95] Ibid., p. 80.
[96] Ibid., p. 82.

ciples in the area of economic life. Listed below are some of the political, judicial, and administrative principles:

1. An end to party rivalry, and a channeling of the political forces of the nation into a common front and a single phalanx
2. A reform of the law, so that it will conform to Islamic legislation in every branch
3. A strengthening of the armed forces, and an increase in the number of youth groups, which should be inspired with zeal on the basis of Islamic *jihad*
4. A strengthening of the bonds between all Islamic countries, especially the Arab countries, to prepare for practical and serious consideration of the matter of the departed Caliphate
5. The diffusion of the Islamic spirit throughout all departments of the government, so that all its employees will feel responsible for adhering to Islamic teachings
6. The surveillance of the personal conduct of all its employees, and an end to the dichotomy between the private and professional spheres
7. Setting the hours of work in summer and winter ahead, so that it will be easy to fulfill religious duties, and so the keeping of late hours will come to an end
8. An end to bribery and favoritism, with consideration to be given only to capability and legitimate reasons (for advancement)
9. Weighing all acts of the government in the scales of Islamic wisdom and doctrine; the organization of all celebrations, receptions, official conferences, prisons and hospitals so as not to be incompatible with Islamic teaching; the arranging of work schedules so that they will not conflict with hours of prayer
10. The employment of graduates of al-Azhar in military and administrative positions, and their training[97]

To work out a constitution based on Islamic principles and to replace the existing one at the time of al-Banna constituted no easy task, even if the Egyptians had been willing to accept change of this nature, because some institutions connected with his theory of government (such as the *Imamate*) had collapsed centuries before. According to the prophetic saying, a Muslim who dies without an *Imam* dies a pagan. Did Hasan al-Banna suggest the revival of the concept of *Caliph, Imam, Amir al-Mu'minin* (commander of the faithful), or all three in one, which are now given to the secular head of state? (These are three titles of the same position, namely the successor of the Prophet, but for example, they are known to the *Shi'ite* as *Imam*, and to the *Sunnah* as *Caliph*, etc.)

---

[97] Ibid., p. 126.

Soon after al-Banna's assassination, the people would rally behind a semi-religious army officer. In turn, the Muslim Brotherhood would be completely crushed and its dogmas treated as impractical and culturally impossible to implement.

Back in the years after 1936, however, the Brotherhood gained so much momentum that several leading politicians hoped to use it for their own ends. Wartime conditions gave the movement greater impetus and helped to spread it throughout Egypt. In the post-war era the organization reached the zenith of its power through violence, student demonstrations, political murders, riots and the bombing of public places. So terrorized were Egyptian politicians that they listened seriously to the Brotherhood's demands.

By 1938 the Muslim Brotherhood became heavily involved in Egyptian politics.[98] In May of that year, al-Banna launched a weekly magazine entitled *al-Nadheer*. In the first issue of this publication he wrote:

> Ten years ago the call of the Muslim brethren began solely for God's sake, following the footsteps of the greatest apostle of God, using the Qur'an as its symbols; reading it, chanting it, examining it, and calling people to it, and living by it ... And now brethren, the time of hard work is upon us ... We shall go with our call to the responsible people of the leaders of our nation, to its ministers and to its leaders, to its deputies and to its political parties, we shall call them to our way and we shall put in their hands our programs, if they answer the call and follow our way to the fulfillment of the goal, then we will help them. If they avoid us or cover themselves with excuses, then we are "war" upon every leader (*za'im*) or president of a political party or any organization that does not work for the victory of Islam ...

Al-Banna continued in the same article to explain the feature that distinguished Islam from Christianity and, in his view, had influenced the leadership of Egypt at that time.

> It is not our fault that (in Islam) politics is part of religion and that Islam includes the rulers and the ruled, for its teaching is not: Give to Caesar what is Caesar's and to God what is God's, but rather: Caesar and what is Caesar's are to the one and the only victorious God.

Al-Banna warned his cohorts that by the standing on these principles they would risk prison and persecution; he called upon the Brotherhood to prepare for the battle and reminded them that the cost of *jihad* is not cheap.

Because the Brotherhood's demands were not met, their threat was indeed carried out. By the end of 1948, they became like a nation inside a nation, with their own armies, factories, weaponry, schools, and hospitals; they were set to take over. But on 8 December 1948, Prime Minister Mahmud Fahmi al-Nuqrashi Pasha ordered the dissolution of the organization, jailed its leaders,

---

[98] Dr. Abd al-Azeem Ramadan, *Ikhwaan al-Muslimeen wa 'l-tanzeem al-Sirri*, pp. 29-31.

took over their assets and, thus, ended a chapter of activity of the Muslim Brotherhood.

The man who succeeded Hasan al-Banna to guide the Muslim Brotherhood was less charismatic and inclined to be less revolutionary than some of his co-religionists. This, probably more than any other reason, accounts for the demise of the movement. When Judge Hassan al-Hodabi became the general guide, the "secret apparatus" of the movement continued its underground activities without his full knowledge. Meanwhile, without the full approval of the leading members, he would discuss policy matters with the leaders of the revolutionary "Free Officers," who came to power by July of 1952.[99] The main catalyst behind the "Free Officers," Gamal Abdel Nasser, was later to use this internal division within the Muslim Brotherhood to destroy the movement altogether.[100]

The 23 July 1952 revolution gave the Muslim Brotherhood momentum as never before or since. On that day the Muslim Brotherhood joined the rest of Egypt in celebrating the dawn of a new era,[101] little suspecting that twenty-nine months later six of the top leaders would be executed and the movement almost obliterated.

On the evening of 26 October 1954, President Gamal Abdel Nasser was delivering a speech in Alexandria for the occasion of the withdrawal agreement (the withdrawal of the British troops from the canal area); at exactly 7:55 P.M., and only minutes into his speech, eight bullets were fired at Nasser and the presidential stand, from the gun of Mahmud Abdul Latif, a member of the "Secret Apparatus" of the Muslim Brotherhood. This disaster ended the visible life of the movement.

The obscure details of the incident and the sketchy, unconvincing story behind the shooting prompted some to speculate that it was a well conceived plan to give Nasser the necessary reason to arrest and consequently destroy the Muslim Brotherhood.[102] It is conceivable that Nasser, who would not tolerate any opposition, let alone one as popular as the Muslim Brotherhood, may have used a simulated event to win popularity among the masses, who had begun to support his anti-imperialistic rhetoric.

A Last Blow

"For the third time since its founding in 1928, members of the Muslim Brotherhood movement in 1966 paid the ultimate price—life itself—for the right to challenge organized authority in Egypt."[103]

---

[99] Ibid., p. 97.
[100] Ibid., pp. 147-150.
[101] Mitchell, *The Society of the Muslim Brothers*, p. 96.
[102] Abd al-Azeem Ramadan, pp. 19-21.
[103] Mitchell, *The Society of the Muslim Brothers*, p. vii.

After Nasser solidified his internal power, he gradually began to release members of the Brotherhood in the early sixties. In May 1964, Said Kotb, one of the pillars of the movement, was also released. Many of them were restored to their previous positions and compensated for their imprisonment.

After having missed the radical changes that had taken place in Egypt over the previous ten years, especially the land reforms, the secularization process, and the involvement of the *Fellaheen* (peasants) and the laborers in the one-party system, members of the Brotherhood came out of jail with one aim in mind—"revenge" for what happened in 1954. They wanted revenge, too, for the savage way that they were treated in prison. Moreover, their hostility was exacerbated by the feeling of alienation from the rest of society, which, out of fear and terror of Nasser's secret police organizations, tended to ignore and dissociate themselves from the Muslim Brotherhood.

All these pent-up feelings contributed to the rise of a new Brotherhood under the leadership of Said Kotb. This time, however, Kotb removed any possibility of the group working with or even being recognized as opposition by the existing government by making the new Muslim Brotherhood a totally clandestine operation. His ideology for the reborn movement, a treaty against the status quo, is explained in his book *Ma'alim fi 'l-Tariq*[104] and summarized in the following eight points:

1. The present world lives in *jahiliyah* (pre-Islamic infidelity). All material progress and development have not improved its condition.

2. This modern *jahiliyah* is fundamentally an attack upon God's kingdom on earth and more specifically His divine attributes, which are the ruling attributes in this world. It replaces His rule with that of people so that they became lords over the rest of his creation and are separated from God's plan for life, which God has never permitted. Modern *jahiliah* differs from the primitive, naive form; it is a faked format which makes society with all its legislation, legal codes, laws and systematic administration look as if its members were under God.

3. Jahiliyah or the attack on God's rule must be viewed as an attack upon His people. In contradistinction to the individual man, the man-made systems, such as communism, fascism, capitalism and imperialism, are to blame for the attack because they humiliate and deny to man his God-given dignity.

4. The Islamic way of life differs from all other systems, insofar as in Islam man is free to worship God alone, fear God alone, and obey God alone, rather than fellow men. This is the new element which Muslims have which the rest of mankind does not know about and cannot produce.

---

[104] See also pp. 314-315 of Abd al-Azeem's book.

5. This "new" Islamic way of life must be applied in practical terms and the nation (*ummah*) must live by it. The nation must declare that there is no God but God, who alone governs; it must refuse to acknowledge that any other being rules. The nation (Egypt) must refuse the legitimacy of any political system that lacks this foundation.

An *ummah* (Islamic nation) of this kind ceased to exist when the *shari'a* (Islamic laws) ceased to rule the face of the earth. It is imperative to restore this kind of *ummah*, so that Islam can play its role in leading mankind once again.

6. It follows, then, that "we must return this religion into the souls of men," even if they call themselves Muslims and their birth certificates certify that they are Muslims. They must know that Islam asserts the belief that there is no God but God, which in its real meaning is restoring the rule of God over all those who attack His rule by heralding themselves as rulers.

7. For "Islamic progress" to begin, they must move on the road against *jahiliyah*, which is so widespread on the face of the earth, to move on though they face at once both isolation from and contact with the surrounding *jahiliyah*.

Therefore, the scouts must know the nature of their role, the fact of their function, the strength of their goal, and the first step on the long road. They must also know what their stand is in relation to the *jahiliyah* which is spread over the face of the earth.

8. The old *jahiliyah* society may or may not submit to or even tolerate the new Islamic society; the old may fight the new. And if the followers of *jahiliyah* were to reject the new Islamic society or its scouts before it grows into a full society, their resistance would resemble that evident in the history of the Islamic "call" from the time of Noah to the time of Muhammad without exception.

Naturally, the new Islamic society does not come into existence and grow unless it has already reached the degree of strength needed to face the pressure of the *jahiliyah* society: the strength of believing and perceiving, the strength of character and of the psyche, the strength of organization and growth, and all other kinds of strength that would help it fight or at least firmly resist *jahiliyah*.

It is evident here that Kotb had moved away from the original idea of reforming society into an "Islamic society," that is returning it to what it ought to be. Instead, since society for him has become a *jahiliyah*, a completely new Islamic society must be established. This is *highly significant* because the middle link in the chain between the Muslim Brotherhood and *al-Jihad* has precisely this point as its distinguishing foundation. This will be explored in greater depth in the next chapter.

Al-Takfir wa al-Hijrah (Infidelity and Flight), the aforementioned link in the chain, built its foundation upon the teaching of Kotb. Mainly, the movement asserted that society is a *kafir* or infidel society; one needs to escape from it, then, after its collapse, return to build it anew.

Sociopolitical Considerations

The Six-Day War, in which Egypt, Syria and Jordan were soundly defeated by the Jewish state of Israel, utterly devastated Egypt with regard to its national image, honor and pride. Moreover, it was a blow to Nasser's own confidence in his army machine.[105]

The postwar days involved the government, the press, and the army in a great deal of self-examination and soul-searching, while another segment of the population insisted that the Russians deliberately kept Egypt weak, hence dependent on them, and that they orchestrated the Egyptian defeat. The common explanation which emanated from religious groups, however, was that the nation neglected to seek God but pursued socialistic ideals.

As a result, Islamic groups began to spring up everywhere in the country, visibly manifesting themselves in society by covered heads in the case of women, and traditional kaftans, the white flowing robes, and full beards in the case of men. (The Prophet supposedly had a beard.) These groups became better organized later on, as we shall see in the example of *Al-Takfir wa al-Hijrah* (Repentance and Holy Flight).

What encouraged and added credence to these groups was President Nasser's speech after Egypt's defeat in the Six-Day War. The extreme Islamic religious groups, such as the Muslim Brotherhood, perceived Nasser to be "secular" and "anti-Islamic." However, when Nasser explained that religion must become more dominant in the lives of the Egyptian people, the crowds received his message enthusiastically, and many interpreted it as a sign of his repentance and his return to the fundamentalist Islamic fold.

The feeling of brokenness and humiliation, nonetheless, continued to haunt Egyptian society in the period between 1967 and 1973. For instance, the six months following the defeat of 1967, *Al-Ahram*, the semi-official newspaper carried an editorial entitled "Bi Saraaha" (frankly speaking), where details of the defeats and possible reasons for it were dealt with at length.

The editor, Mr. Muhammad Hassanain Haykel, a close confidant of President Nasser, repeatedly dismissed the claim of the religious Zealot that the defeat was due to Egypt's departure from religious laws, but stated rather that it was due to Egypt's lack of speed in the progress toward modernization. The conviction, particularly in the minds of Muslim extremists, that the defeat in

---

[105] In a press conference immediately prior to the Six Day War, Nasser boasted that he could light a cigarette and by the time he put it out, the Egyptian army would be in Tel Aviv.

1967 was due to an absence of religious commitment was further vindicated when the Egyptian army crossed the canal, successfully attacked Israel, and partially secured a few square miles of the west bank of the Suez Canal in October of 1973. For one thing, the 1973 war was launched during the month of Ramadan, a glorious month in the Muslim calendar. Furthermore, the military operation was coded Badr, the name given to one of the Prophet Muhammad's more successful wars against unbelievers.

By this time, religious fervor had reached a peak in Egyptian society; the call had never been louder for the nation to move in a religious direction and to introduce the *shari'a* as its source of legislation. The argument was made that, "If by being religious, God gives us victory, how much more successful shall we be when we implement God's own law ... God does not make a mistake."[106]

Another ingredient that contributed to the general religious fervor and the revival of militant Islamic groups was Sadat's embarcation upon the "de-Nasserization" of the society. After Nasser died in September 1970, Sadat moved with dizzying speed away from the socialist state to the liberalization of the Egyptian economy, namely his "Open Door Policy" which aimed at attracting Western capitalists. As well, he rejected the strong Soviet (foreign) influence by expelling thousands of Soviet experts from Egypt overnight and moving closer and closer to conservative Islamic oil states.

Sadat initially used the force of Islamic groups in his effort to "de-Nasserize" the country. He often described Nasser's era as "cooperation with the atheist regime of the Soviet Union." This strategy, coupled with the release from jails and concentration camps of dissidents and members of the Muslim Brotherhood groups as mentioned above, created a fertile ground for the regrouping of the former members of the Brotherhood into new Islamic groups.

Although in the early seventies observers doubted the ability of the Muslim Brotherhood to rise to power in Egypt, their influence has already been felt in the subtle changes of a large number of articles, in order to make existing laws conform with the shari'a. In some courts, judges have set precedents by making the witness of a non-Muslim invalid in the court of law.

---

[106] "Al I'taisam," July 1976, pp. 12-13.

CHAPTER ELEVEN

THE LINK BETWEEN THE MUSLIM BROTHERHOOD AND AL-JIHAD

As a result of interaction in jail, new ideas began to emerge in the Muslim Brotherhood. Their ideas regarding Egyptian society became more extreme than before. The original desire of Hasan al-Banna and the co-founders of the Muslim Brotherhood was to correct the deficiencies within Egyptian society, especially its westernization and its departure from Islam.[107]

When the members of the Muslim Brotherhood were released from jail, they harbored even more resentment and bitterness toward the government because the authorities had inflicted torture on them. They could not reconcile their view of the government with their perception of a pure Islamic society. They wondered how government officials could torture their own Muslim brothers, and concluded that Egypt was not simply a Muslim society in need of reform, but rather a *kafir* or infidel society, just as Said Kotb had thought.[108]

Al-Bahnasawi argues that the idea of *takfir*, the diagnosis of the Egyptian society as an infidel society, originated just prior to June of 1967. He links its birth with a specific incident which took place in the military prison: The jailed members of the Muslim Brotherhood refused to cooperate with the secret police (*mabahith*) and refused to submit to brainwashing. This incident was the beginning of their refusal to acknowledge their loyalty to the ruling regime, which had taken away their rights and threatened to execute them.[109]

They argued that the regime is *jahiliyah* (pre-Islamic), and the society which is cooperating with it is also *jahiliyah*. While Kotb and the *Takfir wa al-Hijrah* movement would concur in their perception of Egyptian society as *kafir*, the *Takfir wa al-Hijrah* substantially altered Kotb's approach to changing society from its present status of *jahiliyah* to *islami* or Islamic. Kotb had recommended a slow change through education and information, whereas the *Takfir wa al-Hijrah* advocated radical alternatives.[110]

Al-Takfir wa al-Hijrah

The *Takfir wa al-Hijrah* group insisted that the only way to reform society was through drastic action. Since society is *kafir*, one must abandon it and

---

[107] Ramadan, *Ikhwaan al-Muslimeen wa'l-tanzeem al'Sirri*, p. 26.
[108] Ibid., p. 11.
[109] Ibid., p. 12-24.
[110] Ibid., p. 317.

stay in another place, preferably the desert, until its collapse, then return as *ghazyes* or conquerors to construct a completely new Islamic society.

The Sequence of Events

Bahnasawi summarizes their ideology as follows:

1. A literal interpretation of the two *shahadas* (i.e. There is no God, but God, and Muhammad is his Apostle) demands complete dissociation from the present society and all its institutions: one must not submit to its rulers, but submit to God alone. However, because Muslims in this age do not know the real meaning of "There is no God, but God," they are not true Muslims.

2. One demonstrates genuine belief by belonging to the Muslim groups (*jamaa'at islamlya*). By virtue of adherence to this stipulation, they viewed themselves as the only true Muslims. They considered anybody who belonged to another Islamic group to be an infidel (*kafir*), even if he prayed and fasted. Because he supported the secular leadership which is usurping God's divine rule, he is not a true Muslim.[111]

This belief, they insisted, necessitates (1) the dissolution of marriage vows if one of the partners does not enter into full fellowship with them, and (2) the refusal to pray behind an *imam* (prayer leader) who does not belong to their group.

Although at this time numerous splinter groups were beginning to emerge, one group stands out because it caught government agents by surprise when some of its members kidnapped and later killed the Minister of Religious Endowment. The government referred to it as *Takfir wa al-Hijrah*, which means that *hijrah* (fleeing away) is necessary in a *kafir* (infidel) society. There is no adequate translation of *Takfir wa al-Hijrah*, but "infidelity and flight" will have to suffice.

The group essentially upholds the belief that only the Qur'anic revelation given during Muhammad's time in Mecca has authority over them and it alone should be followed. They call his Mecca sojourn Islam's "stage of weakling," in which there is no *jihad*, no *zakat*, and no pilgrimage.

The leader of this group (*Takfir wa al-hijrah*), Shukri Mustafa, claimed that a secret meaning resides in every word of the Qur'an. He alone knows the secret meaning. In fact, only he knows the secret contained in every letter. Obviously, he found no scriptural evidence from the Qur'anic text to support his claims.[112]

As mentioned above, in July of 1977, some members of the group kidnapped the former Minister of Religious Endowment and demanded the release

---

[111] Ibid., p. 12-24.
[112] Ibid., p. 40.

of fellow detainees, then killed the minister when their colleagues release was not forthcoming. Since the group had been under surveillance for some time, the murder immediately prompted the government to arrest 620 leading members of the group. Shukri Mustafa was hanged and 465 stood trial by military court.[113]

Al-Jihad

About the same time that members of the *Takfir wa al-Hijrah* group were arrested, a new movement was being born. Muhammad Abd el Salam Farag, a young engineer, reached conclusions similar to those of the *Takfir wa al-Hijrah* regarding the infidelity of Egyptian society to "true Islam." He wrote a book which later became the constitution of the *al-Jihad group*. In his book, *The Missing Religious Precept*, Farag categorically declares the Egyptian society and its rulers to be infidels. His methodological approach to the problem, however, differs from the *Takfir wa al-Hijrah*. His solution is not to flee from society and then come back as conqueror; rather, his answer lies in the "missing religious precept ... *jihad* which has been forsaken and forgotten by the religious leaders of the day." This religious duty is probably the most important religious precept in Islam, according to Farag.

First Public Knowledge of the al-Jihad

On the sixth of October 1981, the world's attention was focused once again on the Middle East. This time it was not a war between Israel and its Arab neighbors, but the assassination of a leader who was esteemed as a peacemaker by Western and non-Western leaders alike. The assassination of Sadat led the Egyptian police to yet another underground operation, from among the Islamic groups, which has troubled the nation for the past ten years. The highly organized group, calling itself *al-jihad*, had avoided the public eye and, more importantly, had evaded the state security.

Its leaders were for the most part university graduates, whose efficiency and clarity of thought increased its likelihood of success; they knew what steps were required to attain power in the nation and had a specific plan of action. However, they clearly lacked an alternative political system to the existing one. With the exception of a very vague idea of applying the *shari'a*, political and social issues had rarely occupied their thinking.

In examining this movement, we shall proceed under two major headings: (1) ideology: (a) the stating of their case; (b) the solution of the problem (2) the organizational structure of the movement.

---

[113] Ali E. Hillal Desouki ed., *Islamic Resurgence in the Arab World*, (New York: Praeger Publishers, 1982, p. 107.

Ideology

In studying any social movement, especially an underground movement, it is often difficult to find written material that adequately explains its main doctrines. Fortunately, the founder of this movement summarized his ideology in a book. Although the book is now illegal and banned in Egypt, I received an Arabic copy which I translated and included as a part of this book.

The stating of their case

The founders of *al-Jihad* believe that society has become very corrupt, insofar as it has been influenced by a Western lifestyle which is immoral and blatantly anti-Islamic. Alluding to President Sadat, some have insisted that the behaviour of contemporary Muslims was inconsistent with the precepts of Islam. Above all

> "we found that the government is lagging in its intention to bring the *Shari'a* back to govern the nation. Why don't they want to bring us back to the rule of God, the perfect rule? God's rule is better, much better, than this rule of Satan which they brought to us from the West. We really don't believe that they want it (the *Shari'a*) nor will they do it." [114]

Farag raised the question, "Do we live in an Islamic state? The mark of an Islamic state is an Islamic ruler." He lists three conditions of any state which is not Islamic, i.e. an infidel state:
1. Its laws are the laws of the infidels.
2. The safety of the Muslims is dubious.
3. There is a dangerous proximity between Muslims and infidels. [115]

Farag quotes ancient Islamic authorities and asserts that above all an Islamic state has become an infidel state when the rules governing the society are not Islamic. This is the primary source of the bitter antagonism of the movement toward the regime. Farag writes about a dialogue involving the ancient authority Ibn Taymiyya.

> A man asked Ibn Taymiyya, "When a town called Mar Dien was ruled by Islamic rulers, then taken over by people who ruled it by the rules of infidels, is it *Dar al-Harb* (abode of war) or *Dar al-Islam* (abode of Islam)?" Ibn Taymiyya responded, "It is neither *Dar al-Islam* nor *Dar al-Harb*. It is a third division in which Muslims are treated as they deserve and outsiders are treated as they deserve." [116]

Farag concludes that Egypt is ruled by the laws of infidels despite the fact that the majority of its people are Muslims. *This is the pivotal problem.*

---

[114] Personal interview, April 1983.
[115] Farag, *The Missing Religious Precept*, see Appendix I.
[116] Ibid., see Appendix I.

On a historical note, Farag explained that "the rulers who are in control of Muslims today are rulers of infidels yet Muslims follow them and God says in Surat al-Ma'idah, 'And he who does not rule by that which God has revealed is an infidel (V:44).' After the end of the caliphate in 1924[117] and the uprooting of Islamic laws from the land, the infidels put the infidels' own laws in their place ... and the situation has become like that of the Tatar."[118]

This is indicative of the author's preoccupation with the fact that the rulers are inept and must not retain power. One of the most significant prerequisites to admittance into the movement was the reading of *The Missing Religious Precept* several times,[119] with its incessant reiteration of the idea that the ruler is an infidel who must be removed. Obviously, this played a dominant role in the minds of those who attacked the presidential reviewing stand on 6 October 1981 in order to kill Sadat and other leaders. (Farag was one of the attackers.)

The movement's leadership contended that while the "present ruler," meaning Sadat, was obviously not the originator of the legal code in Egypt, he

"... has increased the ways of infidelity which have caused the society to digress from the Islamic faith to the point that there is no relation between what they (Sadat and other leaders) say they are and the way they rule."[120]

In his testimony, Farag confessed,

"I am the principal conspirator in the operation to assassinate the President of the Republic. By this means I wanted to implement the law of the almighty God, to eradicate the rule of the unbeliever. The aim was to establish an Islamic state."[121]

To Farag, the government leaders are distant from Islam because they grew up under the imperial system, whether that of the Crusaders (the West), Communists, or Zionists. The government leaders are Muslims in name only, even though prayer and fasting are part of their daily life. Since the Sunnah has declared that the punishment of the *murtadd* (backslider) is greater than the punishment of the *kafir* (infidel), the punishment of the *murtadd* must be death.[122]

Farag compared the present laws to those of the Tatars. The Tatars ruled by *al-Yasiq*, a combination of Jewish laws, Christian laws, Islamic *millet*, and other codes that stemmed from their whims. Whereas the *Yasiq* was redeemed

---

[117] This is the date when the Turkish government decided to abandon the concept of the Khalifa and become a pure secular state.
[118] Farag, *The Missing Religious Precept*, see Appendix I.
[119] Personal interview, April 1983.
[120] Farag, *The Missing Religious Precept*, see Appendix I.
[121] "A Moment of Crisis," T.V. program "20/20" transcript, October 1982.
[122] Farag, *The Missing Religious Precept*, see Appendix I.

to some extent by its Islamic element, the present laws governing Egypt have been infiltrated by Western norms and "have no relation to Islam whatsoever."[123] In contrasting the Tarars and modern Egyptian society, Farag points out that the Tatars failed to impose *jizya* upon non-Muslims and gave them positions of leadership in their administrations.[124]

A member of one of these Islamic groups told me,

> "It makes us sick every time we see Butros Ghali's picture in the paper.[125] Can't they find a Muslim to be in this important position? How can Egypt be represented in the foreign arena by a Copt? (Who, by the way, is married to a Jewess.) Egypt is an Islamic nation and must at least give this impression to the world."[126]

One of the major *fatwas* issued by the *Amir* (the leader of the movement) was to legalize the stealing of money and belongings from Christians and the shedding of their blood. (The court later concluded that there was no conclusive evidence that the *Amir* did this.)

Continuing in this vein, Farag directly applies Shaykh al-Islam Ibn Taymiyya's description of the Tatars to modern Egypt. Farag quotes him regarding the time of the Tatars, when the "contemptible leader who was called al-Rashid (the guided one)" ruled; he was partial to the worst of Muslims over the best of the faithful. The qualifications for power appeared to be corruption, uncleanliness, and disbelief in God and "His Apostle." Infidels, including hypocritical Jews and atheists, pretended to accept the *shari'a* and ascended to high positions in the administration of al-Rashid (a caliphate).

A devious minister dared to suggest that the Prophet had accepted the religion of the Jews and the Christians and did not call them to shift their allegiance to Islam. He used a false interpretation of the text that says,

> "Say, O infidel, I do not worship whom you worship and you do not worship whom I worship and I will not worship whom you worship and you will not worship whom I worship. You have your religion and I have mine."

He declared that this text is not *mansukh* (cancelled).[127]

Farag concludes with the following statement:

---

[123] Ibid., see Appendix I.

[124] Ibid., see Appendix I.

[125] Butros Ghali was the state minister of foreign affairs upon who Sadat relied very heavily in his foreign policy, particularly in his dealings with the West and engineering the Camp David agreement. Mubarak relies on him even more and he occupies the same position. He is a Copt and comes from a well-known Coptic family. His grandfather at one time was the prime minister of Egypt.

[126] Personal interview, April 1983.

[127] Farag, *The Missing Religious Precept*, see Appendix I.

"Is not this kind of Tatar the same as what we have today in the attempts at religious brotherhood and the gathering together of all religions?"[128]

Since the heart of *al-Jihad* ideology is the establishment of an Islamic nation by the sword, Farag belittles any religious achievement which comes short of this idea. As far as he is concerned, modern religious efforts amount to no more than the empty declaration, "Egypt is an Islamic state," and the superficial introduction of the *shari'a*; neither of these is sufficient. Farag demands the strict enforcement of the Islamic laws.

"Islam is obedience. If part of the religion is God's and another part is not God's, fighting is a duty till all religion is God's. That is why God said, 'You who believe, fear God, and end what is left of usury.'"[129]

To Farag, this text clearly indicates that if a Muslim prays and fasts, but refuses to forsake usury, he is still fighting against God.[130] Farag carries the argument one step further: since the people who deviate to the slightest degree from any of the precepts of the *shari'a* have, in effect, declared war against God, Muslims are perfectly justified in fighting them on behalf of God.

It is evident here and elsewhere that Farag sees himself and his followers to be the guardians of God's religion (Islam). He claims that all Muslim religious leaders (*ulamas*) have agreed that anyone who disobeys the obvious Islamic duties must be fought. Following this tradition, the members of al-Jihad believe they carry the weight of responsibility in defending and enforcing God's law on earth. Herein is the crux of Islamic fundamentalism.

Those who disobey Islamic laws as follows must be fought until all religion is in accord with the will of God: If they recite the *shahada* but do not pray, fast, give alms, or go on the pilgrimage; if they refuse to obey the rule of the Book (the Qur'an) and the Sunna; if they fail to forbid gambling, usury, debauchery, wine, or having sex with women other than their wives; if they take unfair advantage of people or money to which they do not have the right; and if they fail to fight the infidels or collect the *jizya* from the people of the book (Christians and Jews).

Muslims who omit even a letter of the *shari'a* are not only weak Muslims but corrupt Muslims, and the decree to kill them is fixed in the Sunna and the Ijmaa'.[131] This is the only available option for Muslims who hope to rectify the situation and reestablish God's law in the land of Egypt which has become so corrupt and westernized.

---

[128] The author is referring to Sadat's effort in calling a referendum to affirm what was "national unity," i.e., close relations between Christians and Muslims and Jews, calling the three religions "the heavenly religions." The referendum was held in 1981. Sadat's assurance of a normal referendum results of 99.9% would automatically diffuse the extremists and foil what he used to refer to as the "sedition."

[129] Farag, *The Missing Religious Precept*, see Appendix I.

[130] Ibid., see Appendix I.

[131] Ibid., see Appendix I.

CHAPTER TWELVE

A CONSIDERATION OF ALTERNATIVES TO SECULARISM

Farag, as well as the rank and file of the movement, ridicule their Muslim brothers who are seeking to bring about changes in the existing secular conditions by any means other than revolution, calling them misguided and naive. Farag lists them, indicating in each the deficiency that serves as a hindrance to carrying out the needed radical reforms.

Charitable Associations

Regarding charitable associations which can be formed with the help of the government and will supposedly encourage people to pray, fast, etc., Farag comments,

> "Prayer and 'zakat' and good works are things of God and we must not minimize the importance of these, but if we ask, 'Will all these good works establish an Islamic nation?' the answer has to be an unequivocal, 'No.' Moreover, these associations belong to the present government and they are registered in its records and they follow its rules."[132]

Spiritual Renewal

Farag ridicules those who advocate an enrichment of the spiritual atmosphere and improvement of society through discipline, worship and closer relationship to God. Whoever thinks that wisdom of this nature cancels the duty of *jihad* or delineates good from evil will perish and cause others to perish with him. Whoever yearns to excel in worship and reach the highest form of obedience must begin *jihad* in the way of God. The Apostle of God, who describes *jihad* as the "highest glory of Islam," states, "He who does not invade is dead as if he died in *jahiliyah* (pre-Islamic times)."[133]

Some people contend that involvement in politics diverts attention from the things of God. Farag accuses them of ignoring the saying of the Prophet: "*Jihad* is preferable to living under the rule of a sycophantic ruler."[134] Whoever opposes *jihad* for supposedly higher spiritual purposes either does not understand Islam or is a coward who does not want to stand firm in God's rule.

---

[132] Ibid., see Appendix I.
[133] Ibid., see Appendix I.
[134] Ibid., see Appendix I.

An Islamic Political Party

Farag scoffs at the establishment of an Islamic political party as a paragon of Islamic purity which would attempt, through the election process, to form the government. Farag is totally against an Islamic political party because that makes it equal with other ideologies. The purpose of *jihad* is to destroy the infidel government, and working through a political party would indirectly acknowledge the legitimacy of the system; a thought that cannot be tolerated in Islamic land.[135]

Infiltration of the Government

Farag derides those who advocate the principle of true Muslims effortlessly taking control by reaching high positions in the government, so that eventually a Muslim ruler would wield power: "When one first hears these things, one thinks it to be a mere imagination or a joke, but the truth of the matter is that there are many in the Islamic field whose philosophy is to go along with this kind of thinking despite the fact that it has no support in the Book (the Qur'an) and the *Sunnah*." Hence, this kind of thinking is not substantiated by facts. In any case, Farag observes that a Muslim would have to compromise his faith in order to reach a high ministerial position because holding office necessitates loyalty to the system.[136]

"The Call"

Farag refutes the Muslims who argue that the way to establish an Islamic nation is through the "call" or *al-da'wah*, and an appeal to popular support:[137] "This does not establish the *ummah* (the nation) despite the fact that some made this point to be the basis for their refusal of *jihad*."[138]

For Farag, the establishment of a wide base of popular support is not at all necessary, since God said, "Few are those who worship me with thankfulness."[139]

The author insists that Islam does not place priority on large numbers. God said, "How many times a small group of people defeated large groups of people by the will of God." Also, God said, "The day will come when you become proud of your number and you will not need anything else done and the earth will become small for you." Then he said, "How few of us are followers of God, but God's riches make up for our smallness." Naturally,

---

[135] Ibid., see Appendix I.
[136] Ibid., see Appendix I.
[137] Farag is attacking the Muslim Brotherhood and the idea of the "call."
[138] Farag, *The Missing Religious Precept*, see Appendix I.
[139] Ibid., see Appendix I.

the "call" cannot succeed when infidels control the media and fight the religion of God. Thus, the endeavor is to liberate the media from the hands of corrupt people. Ultimately, God will reverse the situation, for He said, "When the victory of God comes, you will see people enter the religion of God in large numbers."[140]

Farag and his disciples believed that it is erroneous to follow those who say that people have to be Muslims before they will be responsive to Islamic laws. They denounced anyone who unconsciously thinks that Islam is incomplete or incapable of being self-sufficient. Instead, they claim: "This good and wholesome religion is relevant and can be applied at any time and in any place and it is capable of handling anyone ... If people are happy to live under the rules of infidels, how much happier they will be when they find themselves under the rule of Islam which is all justice."[141] In short, Farag does not ridicule the "call," but warns that it must not replace *jihad* in the mind of Muslims.

Flight

Regarding those who advocate fleeing the infidel society for another and later returning as conquerors[142] to establish a new Islamic society, the author admonishes them "to save their efforts and establish the Islamic nation in their own country, then go out of it conquering others ..."[143] With historical and textual support, the author shows the illegality of such action as far as Islamic dogma is concerned, concluding that these notions circumvent the only right and the only legal method of establishing an Islamic nation. He uses quotes to support his contention:

> "Warfare is ordained for you, though it is hateful unto you; but it may happen that you hate a thing which is good for you, and it may happen that you love a thing which is bad for you." (II:216)

"Fight them until there is no more sedition and all religion is God's."[144]

Education

There are Muslims who believe that *jihad* will stagnate if they do not seek knowledge, but Farag questions the singular pursuit of knowledge:

> "Seeking knowledge is a duty, but we don't hear anybody saying we must neglect a legal command or a duty of Islam to pursue knowledge ..."[145]

---

140 Ibid., see Appendix I.
141 Ibid., see Appendix I.
142 Farag is referring to the "Takfier wa'l-Hijrah."
143 Farag, *The Missing Religious Precept*, see Appendix I.
144 Ibid., see Appendix I.
145 Ibid., see Appendix I.

The author notes later that *jihad* is perhaps the most important religious duty, yet it is missing from the list of the so-called "Five Pillars of Islam."

> "For those who don't know what *jihad* is, they need to know that *jihad* is fighting. Because God said, '*Jihad* is appointed to you.'"[146]

He shows the falsehood of the pursuit of knowledge as an alternative, and compares it with his own solution. Farag contends that if Muslim leaders do not advocate that people forsake prayer or fasting for the pursuit of knowledge, they should not advocate that they forsake *jihad* for the pursuit of knowledge. He proceeds to argue that knowledge obligates a Muslim to carry out an action. If a person has knowledge of the injunction to pray, he must pray. The same is true with fasting. He then applies this logic to *jihad*. The knowledge of *jihad* is readily accessible to all who have good intentions in following the way of God, "but to delay *jihad* for the sake of seeking knowledge is a false excuse."[147]

The irony here is that the author himself, as well as the leaders of the movement, are all university graduates. Farag, 27, was an engineer. Abd al-Rahman, the amir of the group, is a doctor. Most likely, the author is here attacking the educators in Al-Azhar University who advocate the pursuit of knowledge and, more specifically, the implementation of the concept in Islamic jurisprudence called *ijtihad* i.e., relating the rules and laws of Islam to the existing cultural and social settings.

In order to give a striking illustration of his point, Farag chose a historic event which most Muslims remember painfully as a great source of humiliation; it occurred when the horses of Napoleon trampled through Al-Azhar University and mosque. Victory was given to the simple people who had little knowledge of the *fiqh* (Islamic jurisprudence) rather than the *ulama* of Al-Azhar who were unable to defeat Napoleon and his cavaliers. Farag poses the following question: "What good was all their knowledge in the presence of this humiliating experience? ... We are not belittling the knowledge or the men of knowledge (ulama). We believe in it, yet we don't use it as an excuse to forsake the duty imposed by God."[148]

By ridiculing some of the alternatives and highlighting the weaknesses of others, the founder of *al-Jihad* brings his followers to the only alternative left in their endeavor to rectify society—fighting.

Jihad

Jihad consists of fighting both the leadership and the system of government through successive elimination, in order to install new leadership, namely *al-*

---

[146] Ibid., see Appendix I.
[147] Ibid., see Appendix I.
[148] Ibid., see Appendix I.

Jihad leadership, and implement what the movement calls "the perfect law of God." It is legitimate here to ask why the leadership of the government, including the president of the nation, must be eliminated. To members of the movement, the answer is simple. They could not fathom the behavior of Sadat, who purported to be a Muslim leader. He called himself a Muslim yet raised his glass of wine to propose a toast with the "infidels," meaning Western leaders and United States President Jimmy Carter, more specifically. They were shocked when he kissed Mrs. Carter in public. They were unable to understand how he could live in extreme wealth and luxury when 70% of the population did not have enough food to survive. If he were a true Muslim, he would not have delayed or refused to introduce the *shari'a*, the perfect law of God.[149]

Farag argues repeatedly that *jihad* is the only way to enforce God's law, and he finds no shortage of ancient authorities to support his claims. *Jihad* or fighting the leadership of the government takes precedence as far as *al-Jihad* is concerned. Farag indicates that fighting "the infidel ruler" is far more important than fighting external enemies. Fighting an external enemy will only enforce and strengthen the infidel regime by diverting attention away from it. Imperialism does not exist because Muslims are weak, but because so-called Muslim rulers allow it to exist. Thus, to fight imperialism while these rulers are still in power is a futile exercise and a waste of time. The rule of God must first be established in the nation and the word of God must be highly exalted. Therefore, the first battlefield of *jihad* is local, and the first battle involves dislodging "infidel" Muslim leaders and exchanging them for leaders of a truly Islamic system.[150]

Fighting (Jihad) is the duty of every Muslim

According to the movement, *Jihad* is the duty of every Muslim, and the founder incisively defines *jihad* so as to dissolve any doubt or confusion about its interpretation. Farag responds to those who try to minimize the importance of full participation in *jihad* when they say, "If I do my duty of the 'call,' I have discharged my obligations, for this is *jihad*. If I seek education, I am fighting in the way of God." Farag directs such individuals to the text of the *Hadith*: "*Jihad is confronting your enemy and spilling his blood.*"[151] Farag crystallizes his definition of *jihad* by attacking any Qur'anic interpretation that renders *jihad* anything less than the spilling of blood.[152]

---

[149] Personal interviews with former members and current supporters of the movement, April-May 1983.
[150] Farag, *The Missing Religious Precept*, see Appendix I.
[151] Ibid., see Appendix I.
[152] For a more moderate and spiritually oriented interpretation of "jihad," see *Ideals and Realities of Islam* by Seyyed Hossein Nasr, (London: George Allen & Unwin Ltd., 1964).

Jihad is not an exercise in self-discipline, nor is it subject to evolutionary stages, as some claim. Those who understand it as such are "either completely ignorant or terrible cowards."[153] In response to this interpretation, Farag at first presents the opposition argument, which names these three stages: (1) *jihad* of oneself; (2) *jihad* of Satan; (3) *jihad* of infidels and hypocrites.

He then demolished the argument of his opponents, reasoning that *jihad* is of necessity divided into degrees and not stages; otherwise, Muslims would not fight Satan until they had finished the stage of fighting themselves. In reality, the three degrees of *jihad* are concurrent. Nonetheless, Farag does not deny "that the strongest in faith among us who fights (evil) in himself is the most firm ... but anyone who studies the life of the Prophet will find that when he called for *jihad* everybody responded in the way of God, even those who sinned and the new converts ..."[154]

As an application of this, Farag explains to young people that since *jihad* is the absolute duty of every Muslim, like prayer and fasting, they need not seek permission from their parents to join the ranks of his movement and advance *jihad*. One needs no permission to perform this duty.[155]

In fact, forsaking *jihad* has its own punishment: the neglect of *jihad* accounts for the humiliation, division and suffering of Muslims at present. Farag quotes the Qur'an:

> O you who believe, what is wrong with you? When I say, 'Go in the way of God,' you drag your feet as if you prefer this life to the next. The joy of this life, compared with the life to come, is very small; if you do not respond God will punish you and He will replace you with others. God is able to do everything. (Surat al-Taubah)[156]

Actually, the punishment exceeds humiliation:

> Heaven will pour its plagues on those who refuse to go and fight in the name of God. These plagues will not stop till they return to their religion.[157]

It is evident that most Muslim fundamentalists, whether they belong to the *jihad* group or even to the larger and more widespread Muslim Brotherhood still believe strongly the reason for the social unrest and economic malaise in Egypt is that they are not strictly adhering to the *shari'a*, the application and fastidious enforcement of which conditions the blessings of God. Some point to their oil-rich brethren and explain that God has blessed them because they follow the law of God, particularly in Saudi Arabia. However, they quickly dismiss the apparent failures of implementing the *shari'a* in Iran and

---

[153] Farag, *The Missing Religious Precept*, see Appendix I.
[154] Ibid., see Appendix I.
[155] Ibid., see Appendix I.
[156] Ibid., see Appendix I.
[157] Ibid., see Appendix I.

Pakistan, protesting that results do not matter. What pleases God is the only valid criterion for evaluation, for after all, the way God assesses results is different from our way.

Farag, in *The Missing Religious Precept*, delves into many details regarding *jihad*: what methods should be followed; whether Muslims should accept the help of non-Muslims; the legality of stealing the money of non-Muslims; etc.

Many of the strategies mentioned in the book were followed very closely. The trial of members of the movement disclosed the fact that they had stolen from jewelry stores owned by Christians.[158] The author's conclusion that the coming of the *Mahdi* (the Messiah) shall fill the earth with peace and justice is noteworthy. It is not clear whether Farag considered himself to be the *Mahdi* or merely the one who would prepare the way for the *Mahdi* to come.

---

[158] *Al-Ahram*, 10 May 1982.

CHAPTER THIRTEEN

ORGANIZATIONAL STRUCTURE AND OPERATION

If the ideology of such a clandestine movement was to a degree kept secret, then the organizational structure, operations, areas of responsibilities, etc. were concealed to an even greater extent. However, after the arrest of over 1,000 Islamic activists (some of whom were released at a later date), the government prosecutor revealed not only the details of how they planned to seize power in Egypt, but also the intricacies of how this highly organized movement functioned.

By 10 May 1982, Mr. Raji'i al-Arabi, Solicitor General, brought forward alleged confessions of the 299 accused in what has become known as "the case of the terrorist organization."[159]

The hierarchy of the movement is summarized in the chart on the next page, but there are details of each position and its function.

Al-Amir Al-Aam (The Commander General)

Dr. Omr Ahmad Abd al-Rahman held the highest title as the chief leader or *al-Amir al-Aam* of the movement, yet he was not the founder. The founder, Farag, invited him to assume this office, presumably because of his respectability among many of the members of Islamic groups. Most of the secret meetings with the leadership of the movement appear to have taken place at Rahman's home in the city of Fayum outside Cairo. His main responsibility was to provide direction and pronounce the *fatwas* (casuistries).

One of his casuistries gave Muslims permission to steal gold from jewelry stores owned by Christians. His pronouncement was carried out. Stealing from jewelry stores belonging to Christians in Nag Hammadi and Shoubra al-Khaima was among the charges brought against the accused. One of the other casuistries legalized, at least from a religious standpoint, attacking and killing police officers and stealing their weapons. The prosecutor alleged that in one meeting, *al-Amir al-Aam* pronounced a casuistry that led to the assassination of President Anwar al-Sadat, because it declared him to be *kafir* and allowed them to kill him.

Next in rank after the Commander General (*al-Amir al-Aam*) was the General Consultative Council or *al-Majlis al-Shouri al-Aam*, which was the highest commanding council and under the leadership of the Commander

---

[159] *Al-Ahram*, 10 & 11 May 1982.

General. It seems evident, however, from reading the writings of the founder, namely *The Missing Religious Precept*, as well as the writings of other leading members, that Farag was the de facto strategist and commander of the movement, even though he deliberately set somebody else in front with the official title. This is a typically Egyptian cultural distinctive. For example, in the public realm, Nasser, the real leader, used Najieb during the 1952 revolution as "window dressing."[160]

The membership of the Consultative Council covered a wide geographical area and represented a diversity of regions. For example, the founder, Muhammad Abd al-Salam Farag, represented Cairo and Gizah. Karam Zohdi, Asem Abd al-Majied, Muhammad Esam Darbalah, Talaat Fouad, Fouad al-Dawalibi, Najih Ibrahim, Ali al-Sharief, and Usamah Hafez represented upper Egypt.

Springing from this seemingly supreme council were three main committees: the economic committee; the preparation committee; and the "call" committee.

In about August of 1981, two main groups formed within *al-Majlis al-Shouri al-Aam*. The division was mainly geographical rather than functional, apparently in order to facilitate and speed decisions and actions, since the members of each council were also members of the supreme council. There was a *Majlis al-Shouri* in Cairo, mainly for the northern part of the country, and a *Majlis al-Shouri* in upper Egypt, headquartered in Assiut. Farag, who headed the Cairo and northern Egypt council, liaised closely with the leader of the upper Egypt council.

Membership in *al-Majlis al-Shouri al-Aam* included the men mentioned above and the *Majlis al-Shouri* in Cairo consisted of: Muhammad Abd al-Salam Farag, *head and liaison*; Aboud al-Zamer; Tariq al-Zamer; Salih Jahien; and Nabiel al-Maghribi. *al-Majlis al-Shouri* in upper Egypt included: Najig Ibrahim, head; Asem Abd al-Majed; Usamah Hazef; Ahmad Abd al-Rahman; Talaat Fouad; Ali al-Sharief; Muhammad Esam Darbalan; and Fouad al-Dawalibi.

Since all the members of the upper Egypt council were members of the General Council, they were most influential in the movement. The group's ideology manifested itself most critically in Assiut, where members intimidated and harrassed people who failed to adhere rigidly to Islamic law.

In interviews conducted in Assiut, there was unanimous agreement from both the Muslim and the Christian communities that the Islamic groups literally exercised far more power over the social life of people than the government or the police. Three examples of this follow:

---

[160] See reference to Najieb, p. 000.

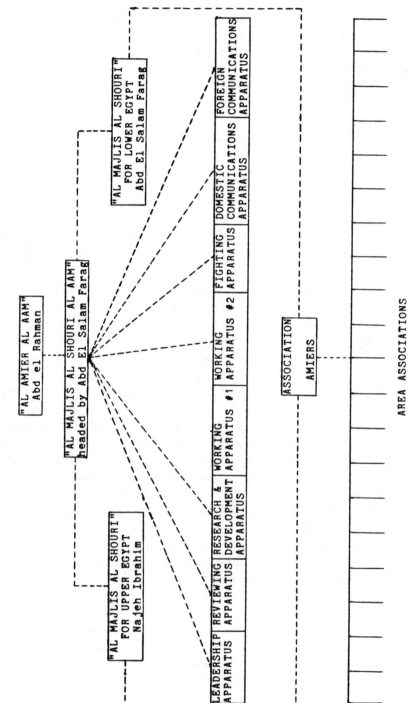

A man and his wife or fiancee or friend would be walking in the street. Members of the Islamic group would approach them as they walked and ask them what relationship they have to each other. If they were not related, the members of the Islamic group would force them to walk on separate sides of the street, and then follow them to their final destination. They would question the woman very angrily as to why she did not wear Islamic dress, take her name, and check the I.D. of both the man and the woman. If the man objected to any of this questioning, he would be beaten. Sometimes the police would be called, but they would merely ask the couple to avoid trouble and comply with the members of the Islamic group. This is not only the word of an eyewitness, but also the testimony of the Chief of Police in Assiut.[161]

A man who was selling liquor was given a warning: unless he closed his business, he would be put out of business ten days later. He continued to sell liquor because it was his only livelihood. Thus, he was still open for business on Christmas Eve. While he and his sons were working in the store, they were attacked and stabbed. He received severe wounds and later died. When the police were called, they politely apologized, saying that they could not do anything about it.

Another man, who owns a shoe store, was playing music loudly on his radio. When the music stopped for the call to prayer, he turned the radio down. A member of the Islamic group gathered five more men; together, they accused him of being anti-Islamic. Since there were five witnesses, he was thrown into jail for forty days. The police later explained to him that if they had not imprisoned him, he would probably be dead, and they themselves would have been the object of attack by Islamic groups. In other words, they jailed him just to satisfy these powerful Islamic groups.

A devout Muslim told me, "They ruled the city and we were all afraid of them... It is no surprise therefore that when finally the decisive hour came, on the two days following the assassination of Sadat (October 7 & 8), the groups battled with policemen for eleven hours in an attempt to take over the city. Eighty-two policemen were killed."

Two of the secrets of the movement's rapid spread were the "cell group" idea and the leadership and organizational ability of Farag. For example, different groups were established all over the greater Cairo area with an *amir* or leader for each. All these *amirs*, in turn, had direct access to the Amir General and *al-Majlis al-Shouri al-Aam*. In fact, most of them appear to have been members of either *al-Majlis al-Shouri al-Aam* or one of the other two later formed *majlises*.

For example, in the vicinity of Cairo there were 23 Islamic associations under *al-Jihad*. Among them were:

---

[161] *Al-Ahram*, 23 February 1983, p. 6, 6 March 1983, p. 6.

District	Amir
Bolaq al-Dakrour	Muhammad Abd al-Salam Farag
Nahia	Tariq al-Zamer
Al-Harm	Tariq al-Zamer
Saft al-Laban	Salih Jahien
Al-Alf Maskan	Nabiel al-Maghribi

The court was provided with an eleven-page document by the police in which details of the movement's organizational structure were revealed. Along with these administrative organizations, there was an executive branch which was responsible to *al-Majlis al-Shouri al-Aam* to follow through on all the decisions made by the organizational leadership.

This structure appears to show eight separate apparatuses. A leader was appointed for each who was in direct communication with *al-Majlis al-Shouri al-Aam*, the decision-making and strategy-planning board.[162]

The Leadership Apparatus

First, the leadership apparatus consisted of *al-Amir al-Aam*, Dr. Abd al-Rahman, and *al-Majlis al-Shouri al-Aam*, the General Consultative Council. The Council's responsibility was planning, decision making, and coordinating the total strategy of the movement. This apparatus surpassed all others; its commands to the other apparatus were not to be doubted, questioned, or disobeyed.

The Reviewing Apparatus

Second, there was the reviewing apparatus (*al-Taqweem*). Its task was reviewing and monitoring all other apparatus and reporting the results directly to the leadership apparatus. Also, they were to make recommendations for ways of dealing with changes and problems.

The Research and Development Apparatus

Third, there was the "Call," the research and development apparatus (*al-Da'wah al-Intizaam wa al-Bahth*). This apparatus was divided into three divisions: (a) mosque preachers, (b) evangelists (*al-do'aah*), and (c) teachers. Its task was teaching the beginners and selecting the best from among them either to join the organization as full-time workers or to assist in research as resource persons and specialists.

---

[162] *Al-Ahram, Al-Akhbar, Al-Jomhouria*, 10 May 1982.

The Working Apparatus #1

Fourth, there was the working apparatus #1 (*al-A'maal*). This apparatus was divided into several divisions: (a) *The physical fitness division* consisted of specialists in karate, judo, and other self-defense and athletic endeavors, who ensured that the main body of the membership was well trained in such physical activities, so that they would never be vulnerable. (b) *The shooting and driving division* was a group of experts who were able to train others how to sharp shoot, shoot from a distance, etc. as well as how to drive all means of transportation, from buses to motorcycles. (c) *The medical division* consisted of doctors who trained the rank and file members of the movement in first aid and military rescue operations. (d) *The military training operation* consisted of army and ex-army officers who imparted their expertise to qualified members of the movement on the use of highly sophisticated weapons and bombs. (It is worth noting here that one of the pending court cases against the movement is the 3 August 1981, bombing of a church in Shubra, a suburb of Cairo, in which three were killed, two of whom were children, and 62 were wounded.)[163] (e) *The communication division* brought together the members of the movement who had communication expertise, particularly in their use of words and their ability to stir crowds into a frenzy.

The Working Apparatus #2

Fifth, there was the working apparatus #2, which operated in tandem with the working apparatus #1. It consisted of six divisions: (a) *The observation section* was responsible to observe and monitor newspapers and magazines and provide accurate descriptions of public plans as well as the plans of particular individuals whose names were provided to them by the hierarchy. It also obtained official documents, maps, etc., and translated from foreign languages. (b) *The propaganda division* mainly printed and distributed or sold all propaganda materials, including booklets and bulletins. Members of this branch had to successfully complete the beginners curriculum as set by *al-Majlis al-Shouri al-Aam*. (c) *The arming division* included members of the movements who were able to contact weapon merchants, both in Egypt and abroad. They were responsible to see that the military division was well armed with weapons. (d) *The chemical division* was comprised of highly specialized chemical engineers who performed experiments and provided the ingredients and formulas for bomb making, etc. (e) *The engineering division* included engineers whose main task was to assist in all engineering questions. (f) *The technical division* included specialists who could falsify and reproduce

---

[163] *Al-Ahram*, 6 May 1983, p. 6.

documents, including ones identical to those issued by the government, and produce copper seals identical to those used by all branches of government.

The Fighting Apparatus

Sixth, the fighting apparatus consisted of those who proved capable through their training; upon them rested the responsibility for the final and decisive battle. All the rules of killing and fighting were to be entrenched in their minds.

The Domestic Communication Apparatus

Seventh, there was the domestic communication apparatus consisting of individuals who were in direct communication with a head of each of the other apparatuses who were surrounded with secrecy.

The Foreign Communication Apparatus

Eighth, the foreign communication apparatus included members who traveled abroad frequently and who had connections with groups overseas that have similar ideologies. They sought both moral and financial support from abroad.

It is important to mention here that the movement had very widespread contact with overseas operations. The court was given itineraries and other evidence regarding contacts made with the Iranian revolutionaries in the hope of closely following the strategy of the Islamic revolution in that country.[164] Moreover, the movement received financial support from the Islamic Center in Aachen, West Germany, and the Islamic Centers in London and elsewhere. Other monetary support came from individuals from Syria, Jordan, Kuwait, Saudi Arabia, and other Islamic countries.[165]

---

[164] *Al-Ahram*, 10 May 1982, p. 6.
[165] Ibid., p. 6-7.

CHAPTER FOURTEEN

STRATEGY FOR SEIZING POWER

Recruitment and the Role of the Private Mosques

At the beginning of the Sadat era (early seventies), many private mosques and *zawiyas* began to arise throughout the nation. Under Nasser's regime, the mosques had been controlled by the government which had exercised veto power over the appointment of the preachers and the Friday sermons. With the spread of privately funded mosques under Sadat, the governmental control activities diminished. In turn, with less intervention by the government, the possibility emerged for the mosques to serve as recruitment centers.

One of the movement's recruiting agents explained that they would watch new faces, especially those who came more than once a day for prayer and showed religious fervor. The best possible prospects were those who attend the *fajir* (dawn) prayers.

> You know that no lazy hypocrites would wake up early to pray. We watch to see if they enjoy hearing a particular sermon. If they express real interest, we ask them to come and attend some of our more constructive teaching sessions. Then we would watch them for about five weeks. If they show more promise and willingness to hear more of our brand of teaching, we ask them whether they would like to attend a special meeting for devout people like themselves. During all this time we mention nothing about our organization, only that we are a concerned group and we are depressed about the state of Islam, but we are not cowards. This is the difference between us and the other Muslims—we want to do something about the situation. We are ready to change things in society. This is the crucial point. If the person would say something to the effect of 'I want to help,' or 'I want to do all I can to see that the law of God will be held high,' then he is a candidate. We then introduce him to one of our *amirs* (group leader).
>
> Depending upon this person's ability and aptitude, we assign him to the right apparatus and by that time he will become a full member. At that point, in the presence of the *amir* of the group, he is to swear allegiance to the group and, above all, swear the oath of secrecy.
>
> Those who prove capable of being recruiters must go through a much deeper level of training and they, in turn, begin to recruit others. One of the tests, sometimes, is whether they are willing to go into a Christian store and pull down the pictures of Jesus and Mary. By this, we would know whether the person is strong enough and willing to take risks. One of the things that is frequently asked of the new member is the reading of the booklet, *The Missing Religious Precept*. Sometimes the best of us would read it many times; even memorize it.[166]

---

[166] Personal interview.

One of the most effective methods of recruiting was the use of printed material and cassettes. A fellow student gave a Christian student (unlike most Christians in Egypt, his name did not readily identify him as a Christian) at the University of Cairo a cassette in which a Muslim preacher explained that Islam was endangered by a *kafir* government; therefore, the leaders must go, in order for Islam to regain its glory. When the young man heard the cassette, he became suspicious. He returned the cassette, whereupon he was asked if he liked what he heard, referring to the preacher; then, the Christian young man was encouraged to join with a group of students to discuss in detail what he had heard on the cassette. At this point, the Christian, out of fear, explained that he was a Christian and could not in good conscience accept the invitation. He was then threatened that if he ever mentioned anything about the tape or the incident, his life would be in danger, for the revolution was imminent.

Funding and the Role of Foreign Money

The funding apparatus used economic ventures to make money and provide necessary funds: first, there were regular membership fees; second, there were regular donations from working members; then there was well-organized fund-raising machinery under the guise of building mosques or sending money to the freedom fighters in Afghanistan. All these funds were used for the operation of the movement. In addition, funds accrued from the stolen gold of the jewelry store robberies mentioned before.

Government investigations revealed that the movement was receiving foreign funds on a regular basis. For example, $ 1,000 was given by Salim Azaam, chairman of the European Islamic Conference in London; 10,400 German Marks came from Esam al Atar, the president of the Islamic Center in Aachen, West Germany; 90,000 Egyptian pounds were donated by some Kuwaitis of Palestinian origin (Omr Ahmad al-Damasi and Hokom Muhammad Nimr Galad); $ 20,000 came from Kuwaiti businessman Muhammad Habib al-Muslim. In addition, many other foreign funds were received.

Another source of funds came from Egyptians who were dispatched abroad, mainly to oil-rich countries, for the purpose of making large sums of money (large by Egyptian standards) and sending one-third of their income to the movement.

Strategy for Gaining Power

All aggressive actions—attacking Christian stores, attacking some police stations, or demanding certain laws be broken simply because they were not in accordance with "the law of God"—were preliminary actions designed to create fear and confusion in the mind of the public-at-large. This was an integral part of their total strategy.[167]

In his testimony in court, the chief of police of Assiut was questioned very closely regarding the events of the eighth of October 1981. The court asked General Muhammad Yusuf Eed, "What, in your opinion, is the reason for the incident?"

Witness: Their purpose was to create a condition of fear, confusion and terror in the city and to get the weapons that belonged to the police by any means and to weaken the resistance of the police in order to fulfill their main purpose which was to completely take over the country. They believed that the masses would rally to their support. In this case, the police would become weak and helpless and could not stop them.

Court. What is your knowledge of the Islamic groups in Assiut?

Witness: I was appointed 'Director of Security' (Chief of Police) in 1980. The first I knew of them was in November of that year. It was the beginning of the academic year and they erected a fence in the university city in order to express their complete control over it. They planned a major demonstration, but I stopped them. There was a government mosque in the university city which they took over. During that operation, some of our officers were wounded. We met with the leadership of these Islamic groups, headed by Najih Ibrahim,[168] so we could reach an agreement regarding the mosque situation, but our negotions failed. Many times I used to call the leadership of the Islamic groups and warn them to keep the peace. While they had freedom to preach in the mosques and religious symposiums and conferences, they must not disturb the peace. In their meetings, they often attacked the government without objection from us.
By the beginning of 1981, there were other disturbing manifestations. For example, they would approach a man who is walking with a woman and ask him, "Who are you? What is your relationship?" and would ask her why she is not wearing the Islamic dress. Many reports came to the police regarding this matter. They began to enter into shops owned by Christians and ask them to take down the pictures of Jesus and Mary. There were many cases like this.

Court: Anything else?

Witness: No . This situation continued until September 1981.[169]

Court: What is the reason for the development of this incident by the Islamic groups?

Witness: To show their power and authority.

Court: Yes, but why?

Witness: So that people begin to fear and respect them.

---

[167] *Al-Ahram*, 23 February 1983, testimony of the Assiut chief of police.

[168] The Amier of Assiut and the head of its "Al-Majlis al-Shouri al-Qibli."

[169] This was the time when Sadat ordered the arrest of many of the Islamic and Christian leaders claiming that they were creating a division (sedition) in the country.

Court: One understands from your words that the policy of the police was one of accommodation to Islamic groups. Was there a government decision for this policy?

Witness: Yes. We had government orders that we should not stop them or interfere with their activities.

Court: Then what prompted you to tamper with them?

Witness: When there was a breakdown of law and order, we felt we had to stop them because they were attacking innocent people in the streets.

The strategy of initiating small skirmishes and creating doubt and confusion in the mind of the public does not differ from prior Egyptian movements and revolutions. In the 1919 revolution, there were similar attacks and assassinations. Before the 1952 revolution, there were murders, bombings, and the burning of the city of Cairo. Thus, *al-Jihad* knew that intimidating actions in rapid succession would create the desirable atmosphere for their final assault. As it happened this time, their plan failed and they were crushed by the power of the state machine which they had intended to destroy.

Evidence provided in the court regarding their plan for taking over political and military power indicates that the general plan for the revolution relied heavily on a small number of individuals who were well trained in the use of sophisticated weaponry. They were to occupy the strategic buildings, not only in the nation's capital, but also in Alexandria and Assiut.

The First Step

As a preamble to this, they would kill the leaders in order to create fear and doubt. On the list of those to be assassinated were President Sadat; his vice-president; the ministers of interior (police, foreign affairs, and defense). The chief of the military staff, the speaker of the parliament, the head of the central security agency, and hosts of others were also slated to be killed. The well-contrived plan called for the simultaneous murder of these people in their homes in the middle of the night, so as not to leave gaps and to exercise an element of surprise.

The Second Step

For the second step of the takeover, the military apparatus of *al-Jihad* worked with the chemical apparatus through one of their contacts, Saber Sowalim, a sergeant in the ministry of defense, who offered candy containing drugs to the guards in the section of the ministry which housed sophisticated weapons. The drugs were provided by a pharmacist, Amen al-Demary. However, the drug lost its effect when it was mixed with the candy and did not have the desired effect upon the soldiers.

Consistent with the general plan, several possibilities before the October 6th assassination of President Sadat were either discounted by the leadership or failed because of error. For example, on the morning of the 25th of September 1981, some of the leaders of *al-Jihad* drove to the presidential home in al-Qanaatir (Barrage) in order to examine gates and fences and assess the possibility of attacking it. They reported to the *majlis* that it would be difficult to reach and there would not be adequate places for hiding. Another aborted plan was to drive a truck full of gas cylinders into the presidential house in Alexandria, then take over the radio station there and announce the revolution.

According to the prosecutor, during this period, they surrounded their operatives with unusually strict secrecy, and employed code names so that the police, if evidence fell into their hands, could not identify the real persons. In Abd al-Rahman's confession, he explained that during September of 1981 his home was searched and he became a suspect of the secret police, so he remained in hiding. On the fourth of October, Muhammad Abd al-Salam Farag came to see him in his hiding place to show him a detailed plan for the assassination of the president of the republic.

Summary of the Plan

First Lieutenant Khaled al-Istamboully (a member of *al-Majlis al-Shouri al-Aam* and a prominent leader of the military apparatus) and three accomplices would attack the presidential reviewing stand during a parade on 6 October. Using guns and hand grenades they would kill the president and all the V.I.P.s in the presidential box.

It was expected that the chaos which would follow the assassination of the leaders of the country would provide an opportunity for *al-Jihad* to take control of the government. Plans were made to mobilize the people to support the revolution. As soon as the assassination took place, a group of members who were experienced guerilla fighters would invade the main radio and T.V. building in Cairo. Their leader, Muhammad Tariq Ibrahim, would then announce to the nation the bulletin of the revolution.

In addition, Farag gave Aboud al-Zamer 800 Egyptian pounds to purchase loudspeakers that would be used to bring crowds into the street following the death of the president. And in Assiut, the leadership of the upper Egypt council would take over the city as soon as they saw the shooting on television.

If necessary to add to general chaos and confusion, there were further plans made to use remote-controlled bombs to attack Sadat's funeral procession containing foreign dignitaries and heads of state.

In the event of a successful revolution, *al-Majlis al-Shouri al-Aam* would serve as Cabinet and all the specific apparatuses would rapidly occupy equivalent government institutions and follow the directions of the leadership. In addition, a *majlis of ulamas* (men of religious learning) would serve as a legislative council.

What Actually Happened

After many possible options had been considered and rejected, the opportunity to assassinate the president was virtually handed to members of *al-Jihad*. On the morning of Wednesday 23 September 1981, First Lieutenant Istamboully was told by his commanding officer that he had been selected to participate in the parade on 6 October, commemorating the start of the 1973 war. Khaled al-Istamboully had already made plans for that holiday weekend and asked to be excused. His request was denied. During the following argument, Istamboully realized that the parade could be the opportunity to attack the key leaders of Egypt who would all be present. With this thought in mind, he finally accepted the order to take part in the parade.

In addition to the standard fundamentalist reasons (Egyptian laws were inconsistent with Islamic law causing social and economic hardship for true Muslims; the Camp David peace agreement with Israel; and government oppression), Khaled had a personal reason for wanting the death of Sadat: his elder brother, Mohamed, was among the members of Muslim groups who had been arrested on 3 September. On the day of his brother's arrest, Khaled had written in his journal a quotation from a book lent to him by Muhammad Abd al-Salam Farag: "The greatest prize for a believer is salvation, and to kill or to be killed in the cause of God."

On Thursday, 24 September, during rehearsal for the parade, Khaled realized that his assassination plan would be possible—if he had assistance. The next evening Khaled visited Abd al-Salam Farag, the spiritual leader of his group, to tell his plan and to ask for assistance. Within twenty-four hours, Farag provided three assistants. The three were two officers and a soldier: First Lieutenant Ata Tayel, Captain Abd al-Hamid Abd al-Salam, and Sergeant Hussein Abbas. All were well-experienced army officers. (Hussein, for seven years champion marksman of the army, was the one who was to fire the first fatal shot at Sadat.)

Farag asked the men if they were ready for certain martyrdom. They all responded affirmatively. Then Khaled explained that he would arrange to have them with him in his truck. When the truck passed the presidential reviewing stand, they would attack. They would need weapons since security for the parade would be tight; no ammunition could be carried by the soldiers, and the firing pins were to be removed from the guns. Farag assured Khaled that he could provide four hand grenades, a pistol and some ammunition.

The conspirators met on Friday, 2 October, and again on Sunday to make the final plans. Farag fulfilled his promise: he supplied the weapons. Khaled had made detailed preparations. He had obtained three passes giving his accomplices permission to enter the camp which served as the parade staging ground. Three regular members of his gun crew were out of the way. One had become ill, another had been given leave, and a third had been assigned special duty elsewhere. The rest of his unit had been told that three soldiers would replace the absentees. He hinted that they would be from a branch of the intelligence and would be checking on security in the parade. Sunday afternoon they all assembled at the parade staging ground.

On Monday, the day before the parade, orders were given that all arms were to be concentrated in storage tents and that all firing pins should be removed from weapons and given to each unit commander. Khaled directed two of the "intelligence men" to be in charge of security, one to guard the tent and the other to collect firing pins.

Early Tuesday morning, 6 October, the day of the parade, Khaled took four machine guns from a storage tent and loaded them. Since the driver of the truck was not aware of the plan, he had to be handled carefully. When Khaled wanted to hide the four grenades under the seat of the cab, he sent his driver to buy a sandwich. When he returned, the weapons had been hidden.

Khaled's truck was on the right side of the column, closest to the reviewing stand. After the order for the start of the parade was given, and just as they came abreast of the presidential box, Khaled drew his pistol and ordered his driver to stop. The frightened man stopped so abruptly that the vehicle skidded out of line toward the reviewing stand. At that moment, Khaled leaped out and hurled a grenade. Sergeant Abbas stood up in the truck and began firing at the president. His first shot hit Sadat in the neck, wounding him fatally. Khaled rushed forward and shot repeatedly into the body of the president. By the time all the firing had ceased and three of the four conspirators had been seized, Sadat and seven others were dead and twenty-eight wounded.

The Takeover of Assiut

Assiut, the third largest city in the nation, lies about 250 miles south of Cairo. It is known as the "Coptic city" because of its large Christian population. In fact, early in this century, missionaries from the West erected their headquarters in Assiut because they found it compatible with their missionary activities. It is no surprise, therefore, that the flexing of muscles by *al-Jihad* was most obvious in Assiut.

They intended to attack and occupy the city police headquarters, as well as the government offices and its main police stations, making use of their weapons. A later section examines the historical event which took place in Assiut on the eighth of October, 1981, and how the southern part of the movement advanced the plans, even when their northern brethren failed.

During the hearing of the incidents in Assiut, numerous witnesses were brought forward by the government to implicate the accused in the killing of 82 policemen, four of whom were high ranking police officers. The killings all took place between 6:00 A.M. and noon on the eighth of October.

Immediately after the attack on the presidential reviewing stand on the sixth of October, the government moved quickly to silence the media, including radio, T.V., telephone, and telegraph. Therefore, the leaders of the upper Egypt branch were uninformed about the progress toward the success of their plans. The Assiut branch, in the absence of information from their fellow revolutionaries in Cairo, assumed that everything was operating according to plan and that they were perhaps in the process of taking over the radio and T.V. building in Cairo.[170]

Based on this assumption, they moved to fulfill their duties, namely, to assume the power of police and political leadership in general. This created a shoot-out with the police in which they indiscriminately attacked and occupied government buildings, including police stations, until fresh police troops came and regained control. Some of the accused escaped, but most of them were arrested.

Government-Orchestrated Response

Since then, the twofold response of the government has been to try to quell such movements, which have been rampant since the late sixties and the early seventies. Self-styled religious leaders like Farag are escalating in number and attracting scores of followers. They vary in their teaching from simple *Sufi* preachers to those who claim divinity, for example, al-Samawi and al-Faramawi, who each has his own followers. Mainly, the government has attempted to turn public opinion against these movements and their ideologies which are often described as "extremist."

First, the government has engaged these groups in open debate and discouraged them from operating underground. During 1983, it was a weekly event to watch a debate between the *ulama* and disaffected members of some of these groups on the one hand, and self-styled Islamic leaders on the other. All this is done in an effort to discredit them, expose errors in their teaching and, at the same time, direct the attention of Egypt toward progress and education.

The debates are not limited to the university halls but are televised nation-wide and conducted within the prisons. Members of the different groups who are imprisoned thus have an opportunity to discuss their views with the leaders of Islam. These, too, are well covered by government newspapers.

---

[170] Personal interview.

For example, in a confrontation between the *ulama* and al-Faramawi,[171] the extreme teaching of Faramawi's school was accentuated by asking one of his former members to tell of how he forbade them to visit doctors when they were very ill because doctors are "infidels." One follower would not take his son to a doctor and left him to die.

In a debate, al-Samawi, whose teaching resembled that of *al-Jihad* and *al-Takfir wa al-Hijrah*,[172] refused to respond at all, even when he was challenged to present his views so that people could have a chance to argue or refute his teaching. He spoke in general terms and refused to be specific.

When two of the most prominent members of the Islamic Research Council met with former members of *al-Takfir wa al-Hijrah*,[173] the media were careful to express the "accurate teaching" that "Islam is the religion of mercy, and to say a person is an infidel and must be fought is a big crime in the sight of God, since God does not ask men to know what is in the heart of others." As in every such case, the paper concludes with the repentance of the group member who declares that he has discovered the falsehood of his ways and has returned to the true Islam (the government's Islam).

Another important issue that was constantly raised by members of the *Jihad* group pertains to the *shari'a*. In the weekly discussions, the members of *al-Jihad* often asked the *ulama* when the government would apply the *shari'a*,[174] and the *ulama* always replied that the adoption of the *shari'a* would only occur when the necessary atmosphere was produced.[175] The *ulama* explained that, for example, as long as hunger exists, people steal food in order to survive. To cut off the hand of such a person is inconsistent with Islamic justice. Thus, there can be no *shari'a* until the right atmosphere (*al-manakh*) exists, and young people should busy themselves in preparing the right atmosphere in order that the *shari'a* might come without delay.[176]

Second, the other part of the government response is the repudiation of such religious thinking through the allotment of space in government-run media (newspapers, radio, T.V., etc.) to the *ulama* who are in agreement with the government's point of view. In their writings and interviews, these *ulamas* explain that the right Islam is more concerned with the individual life and the struggle with sin and leaves the government to govern. The most prominent feature of these writings and teachings is the representation of Islam as "the religion of peace and any talk of the spilling of blood, etc., is not really true Islam."

---

[171] *Al-Ahram*, 11 February 1983, p. 15.

[172] *Al-Ahram*, 8 April 1983, p. 13.

[173] *Al-Ahram*, 12 November 1982, p. 13.

[174] *Al-Liwaa', al-Islami*, 25 March 1982, pp. 4-6.

[175] *Al-Ahram*, 21 January 1983, p. 15.

[176] *Al-Ahram*, 5 November 1982, p. 13.

In weekly articles in *al-Ahram*, one of the highest Islamic authorities, Dr. Abd al-Mounaim al-Nimr, explained that *ijtihad* is an ongoing process.[177] The following will summarize these articles:

* *Ijtihad* is extending one's effort physically and intellectually in order to progress and develop, just as the farmer, the laborer, the doctor, and the engineer work diligently to progress. Since people differ in their resources, the results of their *ijtihad* will also differ.

* *Ijtihad* is a part of human nature that Islam hallowed. Since *ijtihad* is associated with knowledge and Islam is the religion of knowledge, it is natural that the two are closely related.

* In Islamic jurisprudence, *ijtihad* has become the expenditure of energy to generate rules and laws for which there is no clear revelation.

* *Ijtihad* advanced during the first 300 years of Islam when Islamic lawmakers (*rejaal al-fiqh*), who never conformed to the whims of the *caliphs*, expressed their own distinct views and offered their own original interpretations of Qur'anic laws (Malik, Abu Hanifa, al-Shafi'i, and Hanbal comprised the main schools). They held to the dictates of their conscience and their knowledge of both the Qur'an and the social conditions in which they lived.

* When they became great, the groups of adherents began to segment, and the different followers aligned themselves with various leaders; then, they ridiculed each other's views and called each other demeaning names. Many times people lost their confidence in the *ulamas*; consequently *ijtihad* stopped.

* *Ijtihad* halted without a government decree a thousand years ago; likewise, it should resume without a government decree today.

* The Muslim today most desperately needs *ijtihad* because the culture is changing. The modern development of technology requires that we address Islamic jurisprudence to the correlative conditions.

* Invention, progress, creativity, and innovation seem to be acceptable in all areas except that of Islamic jurisprudence.

* The problem is that legislators are always satisfied with the status quo.

The irony here is that most of the *ulama* have served as rubber stamps to government policy by finding religious rationalizations for government decisions. Therefore, it is the hope of many that the writing of Dr. Nimr is not just rhetoric and can eliminate the image that the *ulamas* have become a reviewing board rather than an instrument of innovation.[178] The whole cultural struggle within Islam revolves around the *ulamas'* reaction to Western civilization: some attack the West bitterly, while others praise the West, declaring that the secret of its success lies in Islam.

---

[177] *Al-Ahram*, 31 December 1982, 7, 14, 21, 28 January 1983, articles by Dr. al-Najar.
[178] A comment by an intellectual in a personal interview.

While the next section will deal with such details, it is important to mention here that as long as Islam is entangled with politics and denies a separation between the two, the following question will continue to preoccupy its intelligensia: "How can we exercise our power over society?" They noticeably fail to ask a more important question, "How can we make society better?" The betterment of society, incidentally, does not necessarily have to be based on a Western model.[179]

A Muslim society, such as that in Egypt, would do well to pour its energy into developing a progressive, technical Islamic society, learning from its past religious heritage, as well as western development, without blindly following either. One might question why Islam does not create alternative social institutions that would develop their economy, instead of emulating Western civilization because it supposedly originates in Islam.[180]

While al-Jihad and similar millenarian movements are not representative of the main doctrine of Islam, they are at least opening the minds of the people to the possibility of change, unlike the Islamic religious leaders who are constantly blessing the status quo.[181] Offering alternatives, in time, opens the door to progress, even though the alternatives (such as the ideology of al-Jihad) may not be desirable. Interacting with new ideas gives society the opportunity to explore new systems rather than adapt old, rigid ones.

---

[179] Interview with Rich Wills, an Australian Islamicist working in Egypt.
[180] Al-Ahram, 1 April 1983, p. 12, article by Sami Khashaba.
[181] Personal interview with an Egyptian intellectual.

SECTION THREE

COMPARATIVE ANALYSIS

INTRODUCTION

The study of the *al-Jihad* movement presupposes that though social movements have different aims and doctrines, they may exhibit common organizational structures and tactics.

This section will examine *al-Jihad* from a social science perspective, that is different in scope from previous studies of other Islamic social movements.

Previous studies, whether they were of the Iranian revolution or the Muslim Brotherhood, were treated either from a historic or popular and journalistic perspective. In both cases, they lacked an understanding of the dynamism of social change in general and an understanding of people in particular, especially people whose motivation arises from a contrary world view such as that held by Islamic militant groups.

Conversely, political scientists have concentrated on the study of ideas or "theories" which, as components of a philosophical system, require ongoing evolutions and logical consistency. The meaning of these ideas is not applied to the concerns of the people en masse. Recently, however, somewhat more attention has been given to this subject than before.[182]

While it its true that this study is concerned with intrinsic ethical values, it cannot ignore altogether the sociopolitical effectiveness of *al-Jihad*, simply because the "Islamic religious" nature of this movement renders its sociopolitical effectiveness inseparable from its ethical values.

In addition, since Islamic religious movements have received little attention in the writings of most social anthropologists, the usual definitions cannot be adequately applied to this research. Consequently, a new definition that is more relevant to the subject at hand needs to be stated.

For the purpose of this study, an Islamic social movement can be described as:

> An attempt by the dogmatic and doctrinally purist element in society to bring about in the existing social order a radical change that is both integrative and reactive.

This definition *by no means* would fit all types of Islamic social movements. It is a definition that is primarily relevant to *al-Jihad*. Secondarily, it serves as a proto-type definition for a number of Islamic social movements such as

---

[182] For example, see James P. Piscatori, *Islam in the Political Process*, (Cambridge: Cambridge University Press, 1983); John J. Donahue & John L. Eposito, *Islam in Transition—Muslim Perspectives*, (New York, Oxford: Oxford University Press, 1982); H. A. R. Gibb, *Modern Trends in Islam*, (Chicago, Ill: The University of Chicago Press, 1947); Alexander S. Cudsi and Ali E. Hillal Dessouki, eds., *Islam and Power*, (Baltimore and London: The Johns Hopkins University Press, 1981).

the Wahhabi movement in Arabia. In Chapter 18 we shall see that other progressive ideas within Islam are under debate today.

Indeed, only the purists in Islam would agree with the above definition. By purists I mean those Islamic constituents who insist that the *Shari'a* must be implemented literally. This act in itself would create radical changes in existing Muslim societies such as Egypt. The Iranian revolution is a good example of what can result when the *Shari'a* is implemented literally.

Islamic social movements such as *al-Jihad* seek to effect changes in society by attempting to conform social institutions to what they believe to be the will of the Supernatural, i.e., the will of Allah and the *Shari'a*. This normally happens under certain circumstances, namely, in reaction to what is perceived as foreign influence and domination. In this case, they believe that their society is purportedly an Islamic society which, in reality, dances to a Western Christian tune by incorporating Western technology, Western lifestyles, and Western culture as a whole. Their reaction has not produced a comprehensive alternative to the "foreign" one, but rather offers the vague utopian notion that applying "the law of God" will remedy everything.

This section will specifically examine aspects of social movements that are relevant to our study. These will be under the following headings: (1) The general conditions that give rise to social movements, particularly *al-Jihad*; (2) the nature of social movements, i.e., the classifications of social movements and the relative position of *al-Jihad*; (3) the structure and stages of development of social movements, with special consideration given to why *al-Jihad* failed and the role of the carrier agent.

CHAPTER FIFTEEN

THE GENERAL CONDITIONS THAT GIVE RISE TO
SOCIAL MOVEMENTS AND "AL-JIHAD" IN PARTICULAR

Generally speaking, social movements appear in the midst of cultural confusion, social heterogeneity, individual discontent, and the proliferation of
mass communication.[183] These characteristics normally follow what Anthony
F. C. Wallace called "the steady state."[184]

The cultural confusion or cultural stress occurs when inconsistency and
instability become the primary marks of society. "The polls could not
possibly survive in a country where people by and large agree with each
other."[185]

Confusion and a lack of synthesis creates a cultural vacuum in which people
resort to the most bizarre mechanisms for coping with stress. It is no surprise
therefore that *al-Jihad* took advantage of the opportunity to provide an
answer and deliver a "promise" to the bewildered population.

The death of Nasser (1970) and the succession of Sadat, as well as the
dislocation of social and economic order created a dizzy uncertainty in the
culture. Sadat denounced socialism and even Nasser himself, who was looked
upon by a large segment of the population as "the great hero." Moreover,
the Soviet Union, which was the country's "great ally" under Nasser, was out
and the United States of America, which was the "great enemy of the people," and its European allies were in.

Then, further contributing to the confusion, the Camp David Accords
followed Sadat's visit to Israel. Israel, the "enemy of Islam" and the "dagger
in the side of the Arab body," overnight became "our friend" with whom a
treaty of peace was signed. In the words of one fundamentalist Muslim
shaykh and a former member of Parliament, Shaykh Salah Abu Ismaiel, during his testimony in court in regard to the theological accuracy of the book
The Missing Religious Precept,

> The former president (Sadat) covered truth with falsehood and suppressed the
> truth and used the Qur'anic text which said, "If they seek peace, then you must
> respond," and he was the one who sought peace, not they. He knew that God

---

[183] C. Wendell King, *Social Movement in the United States*, (New York: Random House, 1967)
p. 13.

[184] Anthony F. C. Wallace, "Revitalization Movements," *American Anthropology*, vol 58
(April 1956).

[185] Hadley Cantril, *The Psychology of Social Movements*, (New York: John Wiley & Sons,
Inc., 1967), p. 10.

said, "Do not call to peace when you have the upper hand and God is with you and He will not forsake you and your works." He tried to get close to them by ways and means that are contrary to Islam, for example, building a Jewish temple in Sinai and declaring that Jesus was crucified in Jerusalem, despite the fact that his religion says, "They did not crucify him; they did not kill him." He was a man who danced to everyone's tune.[186]

Obviously, such reversals have an enormous impact upon culture, specifically through the uncertainty and confusion they induce.

Economy

The economic open-door policy obviously benefited a few business entrepreneurs, but very little accrued to the bulk of the population, especially those rural urban migrants who sought a better life with dreams of education and job opportunities. Most students who came from the villages into the city to attend university either had parents who were public servants or parents who had modest incomes. With the price of accommodations escalating, many became homeless or were crammed four or five students to a room in some of the poorest suburbs of Cairo, Alexandria, and Assiut. When they came to the city and saw the stores bulging with imported goods and gadgets, most of which were well beyond their means, a sense of jealousy was nurtured. This caused some introspection about self and identity which, in turn, led to alienation with the political system and its values. A Muslim zealot who had attended Cairo University expressed it this way,

> Under Nasser, we were all poor and at the same time lacked our moral values because we did not have the law of God, but experimented with socialism. But now we see some very, very rich and most of us have become very, very poor and we still have no moral values ... We would rather be all poor if the religious values are going to be missing anyhow.[187]

These words profoundly reflect the nature of thinking exercised by the members of the Islamic groups.

In the urban environment, economic disputes are pronounced, affecting the daily lives of the vast population, crushing those with inadequate financial resources with frustations. In the cities, very few have adequate housing. Public transportation, when it works, is for the most part overcrowded to the point that just as many people hang outside the bus as sit inside. People pressed together in the buses watch large American cars pass, often driven by one person. The lines outside the government co-ops that sell American chickens and eggs at reasonable prices (well beyond the means of the average person) extend thirty deep.[188]

---

[186] *Al-Nour*, 15 May 1983, p. 3.
[187] Personal interview 1981.
[188] See John Waterbury, *Egypt—The Burdens of the Past, Options for the Future*, (Bloomington and London: Indiana University Press, 1978), p. 45ff.

In the midst of this confusion, Islam appears tranquil, its values seem to provide a comprehensive set of norms.[189] It promises salvation from the mire of disequilibrium in society.[190]

Understandably, people turned to religion for clear direction when faced with the personal ambivalence and hostility, or duplicity of government actions or inactions. As Bellah indicated "... In traditional Muslim society the only political community that could transcend the local ties to village, quarters, or tribe was the Islamic *ummah*. Nationalist leaders could appeal not to 'citizens,' a meaningless concept, but only to 'believers.' " It was only after the death of Sadat that the trials of a few of his friends, and even his own brother were allowed to proceed. Most of them became rich illegally through exploitation of his social position and tax evasion. (In six years, his brother moved from being a modest driver to accumulating over twenty-three million dollars.) Such opportunism coupled with Sadat's policies intensified the cultural confusion.

It was noted earlier that government orders forbade interference with the religious groups in Assiut, indicating to them that the government was not adverse to the increase in their activities. At the same time, President Sadat declared in his speeches, "No religion in politics and no politics in religion." This statement is clearly alien to Islam.[191] Thus, in the minds of many, Sadat's commitment to Islam was dubious. He was the *state*, not a religious doctrine or philosophy, in this case, Islam.

Sadat's own behavior in the domestic political arena belied his repeated declarations that Egypt was an Islamic country and that he was a Muslim president. The most striking example of this, as we have seen, was his willingness to sign the Camp David agreement. A high-ranking police officer, now retired, spoke of the ambiguous signals that they constantly received from the government: first, leave the Islamic groups alone; next, crack down on the Islamic groups; so that "we, the police, were confused."[192] Thus, religion seemed to hold the promise of justice, equality, and a better world, especially after the government promised yet failed to deliver all of this.

Social heterogeneity

Although not integral to the development of all social movements, cultural heterogeneity was a decisive factor in the growth of Egyptian social

---

[189] Cudsi & Dessouki, eds., *Islam & Power*, p. 107.

[190] Bronislaw Malinowski, *The Dynamics of Cultural Change*, (New Haven and London: Yale University Press, 1965), p. 48.

[191] Robert R. Evans, ed., *Social Movements: A Reader and Source Book*, (Chicago, Illinois: Rand McNally College Publishing Company, 1973) pp. 54-72.

[192] Personal interview.

movements. The very presence of several million Christians, the pervasive influence of their church and, above all, the social equality with Muslims
guaranteed to them by the constitution were together a source of continuous
irritation to the purists.

The application of the Islamic *shari'a*, would automatically render Christians and all non-Muslims the protected of the state, and would exert subtle
yet obvious pressure upon them to convert to Islam in larger numbers than
currently estimated (about 700 per month), especially if they were to expect
the advantages of free rather than protected citizens. This particular law could
easily become open to abuse by whomever is in power—a thought that sends
shivers to the bones of the Copts.

In response, the jittery Coptic Christian community began to raise voices
of opposition to the application of the *shari'a*. Former Egyptians who have
settled in many of the western countries, such as the United States, Canada,
and Australia, applied pressure on the governments of their adopted countries
to counsel the Egyptian government against this move. Thus, Islamic groups
view the Copts as an obstacle to the introduction of what they perceive to be
"the perfect law of God."

This matter revived the historical tension between the Muslims and the
Christians. The attacks upon Christians took many lives, and the violence
between the two communities threatened to create another Lebanon. In addition, one of the *ulama*, Shaykh Sharawi, attacked Christianity publically on
a weekly telecast. When a priest, Rev. Basili, produced and distributed tapes
which presented a Christian response to the diatribe, he was jailed on 5
September 1981, in order to please the Muslim extremists. This decision
roused the wrath of Copts both inside and outside of Egypt.[193]

The government tried to cover up many of these skirmishes and killings by
calling a conciliatory referendum, which did not satisfy either group.

The religious conflict provoked a power struggle in which there was an
effort to activate religious principles. In this inevitable collision there could be
no compromise because Islamic fundamentalism denies the separation between either religion and state or religion and the power to rule by Islamic
religious codes.

Moreover, there was a basic heterogeneity between *al-Jihad* as a social
movement and the government itself, which members of the movement
described as "anti-Islamic" (*kafirah*) and, therefore, to be fought. "The true
Muslim was to rebel against it and endeavor to replace it with a truly Islamic
government"; this remains the stated aim of the movement. Thus, the movement was fighting on two fronts: the Copts and the government.

---

[193] *The Copts*, Vol 19, No. 1 & 2, (February 1982), p. 6.

Individual stress

Individual stress also contributed to social unrest, that is, anxiety about the future, present frustrations, and tension because of unsatisfactory decisions.[194] When a group of frustrated, anxious, or dissatisfied individuals congregate and work collectively, a social movement is born.[195] In this case, the Islamic associations or groups provided a venue through which individuals could display their status. Thus, they were not just one of forty-seven million people who, on completing their university studies, found themselves unemployed, or employed by the government and paid about 20 percent of what a graduate of Cairo's American University earned working with foreign companies.

A middle-school graduate earned 20 pounds per month (roughly US $ 25). A university graduate earned about 40 pounds (roughly $ 50) per month. The rent for a small, very modest one-bedroom apartment usually cost more than this. Meat was consumed exclusively by the upper class; the middle class usually ate it about once or twice a month because of the cost.

These strained economic circumstances created discontentment, dissatisfaction, and disenchantment leading the individuals to be responsive to new ideas and suggestions. The force of al-Jihad hinged on the receptivity of the populace to an answer, a plan of action for change of what was and what should be. It was shown earlier that the recruiters look for individuals who appear to be particularly religious and who, in the minds of al-Jihad members, are obviously suffering from stress and seeking from religion a panacea to help them cope with societal pressures. Understandably, the majority of the members of al-Jihad were university students from the villages who came to the city where they faced enormous difficulties in coping with and adjusting to city life, inflation, the huge gaps in living standards, and who thus staunchly supported any idea that would bolster their hopes in a better Islamic world. The answer, therefore, was jihad. "This is how we, who are at the bottom of the ladder, will be able to rule ... but if we die in jihad, then paradise is waiting for us. Who would not choose paradise over this miserable life?"[196]

Mass communication and mobility

In terms of both the size of the audience and the speed of transmission, the impact of press, radio and television, has served to intensify the state of con-

---

[194] Herbert Blumer, *Elementary Collective Behavior*, Alfred McClung Lee, ed., (New York: Barnes and Noble, 1951), p. 171ff.
[195] Cantril, *The Psychology of Social Movements*, p. 49.
[196] Personal interview.

fusion and upheaval, and thus has aided the reactionary shift in value and belief systems.

Egyptians congregate every evening around the television: some gather in their houses, but most of them assemble in cafes and other public places because they cannot afford a television set. They avidly watch, among other things, English and French advertisements for perfumes and luxury items that the vast majority of Egyptians can only dream about. The sexually suggestive advertisements impinge on the longings of young people (especially in the middle class) who are unable to marry because of the poor economic conditions. This has compounded the confusion of the individual in his search for identity and satisfaction within his own culture. The mass media bombard individuals with ideas, standards and information which otherwise would reach him in smaller proportions or not at all.

It is no surprise, therefore, that the members of a movement like *al-Jihad*, especially the young people, rejected non-Islamic ideas which they believed were propagated by the Christian West, the Zionists, and the Communists in an apparent attempt to destroy Islam. They perceived their role to be to reject this conspiracy of ideas and work toward eliminating it altogether so that they could turn their society into a pure Islamic society.

Nonetheless, members of *al-Jihad* did not hesitate to use all forms of modern media to achieve their ends. It was through the media of radio and television that the group in Assiut was able to receive the signal to implement their side of the plan. Also, they planned to call the people into the streets for demonstrations by using public address systems. It was through mass media that members of the group were able to maintain contact with their overseas supporters, in addition to the mobility of some members in search of funding and support overseas. Thus the media have played and continue to play a dual role by advancing utilitarian purposes and by creating discontent. They have been utilized in the growth of the social movement as well as in the creation of dissatisfaction within a given culture, especially the Egyptian culture.

CHAPTER SIXTEEN

THE NATURE AND VARIETY OF SOCIAL MOVEMENTS

While the characteristic instruments of social movements are political, neither the aims of the social movement nor the actual results of the process of the social movement are exclusively political.[197] Unlike social institutions, the sole purpose of social movements is *change*—change from the existing norms of society to alternative ones, not merely the replacement of the administrative personnel or the system of government, but rather "a sweeping fundamental change in political organization, social structure, economic property ... thus indicating a major break in the continuity of development."[198]

Despite the desire to bring about radical change on the part of most social movements, some movements contract in the face of a serious threat and conform to the status quo, thus ceasing to be a social movement. Instead, it becomes one of the many agencies that functions to promote some degree of society's stability.[199] This is clearly shown in what happened to the Muslim Brotherhood movement and the Y.M.M.A. (Young Muslim Men's Association) in Egypt.

When members of *al-Jihad* saw that the influence of the Muslim Brotherhood, once a forceful and catalytic giant, had declined, they took it upon themselves to promote comprehensive and radical change. They would have altered the whole existing social order had they succeeded.

Change for *al-Jihad* was not merely a superficial or perfunctory change. For example, they advocated the public whipping of any Muslim who broke the fast of Ramadan, normally a moral and religious matter which is left to individual descretion. They wanted to introduce legislation that would render the testimony of non-Muslims invalid in the courts of law. Society at large, however, denounced such a step as unjust and intolerable.

No matter how unrealistic one may consider these sought changes they are very real to the members of the movement. Clifford Geertz explains that,

> "... the conviction that the values one holds are grounded in the inherent structure of reality, that between the way one ought to live and the way things really are there is an unbreakable inner connection."[200]

---

[197] Heinz Lubasz, "What is Revolution?" *Why Revolution?*, Paynton & Blackey, ed. (Cambridge, Massechusetts: Schenkman Publishing Company, 1971), p. 256.

[198] Sigmund Neumann, *The International Civil War*, World Politics #1, 1948-1949, p. 333.

[199] King, *Social Movements in the United States*.

[200] Clifford Geertz, *Islam Observed*, (New Hagen: Yale University Press, 1968), p. 97.

This inner connection would have manifested itself on the international arena. Indeed, the founder of the movement reasoned that God had shown the Prophet Muhammad the earth and had told him that he would own what he saw. He argued further that since the appropriation had not yet happened, the non-Islamic world should be viewed as potential converts. Logic of this nature would have obviously interfered in foreign policies."[201]

In more concrete terms, the founder of the movement asserted that the eastern part of the Roman Empire had already been taken over by Islam, and, in the future, the western part of the Roman Empire (meaning western Europe and the West in general) would be taken over by Islam.[202] The author continued in a positive and confident manner to explain that "this prophecy (taking over Europe for Islam) will take effect in you (his followers) as God wills it, but He can take it away when He wills it too."[203]

Al-Jihad aimed at financial banks as their primary target. The movement planned two alternatives: close the banks permanently and confiscate the money or immediately conform banking policies to Islamic laws that prohibit the accrual of interest. A devout Muslim bank manager who works for a government bank referred to the Islamic banks as "a bunch of *nasabeen* (con men). They earn their money the same way our bank earns its money. All they are doing is changing the name from 'interest' to 'shareholding' or from 'banking' to 'helping develop the country.' These are not changes." A member of the Islamic group, however, when faced with the above statement, gave a response that sharply diverged from official doctrine: "Who said that Islam is a static religion that refuses to adapt to changes?"

On the whole, the rise of social movements indicates that a new social world is being conceived, new hope is being expressed, and faith is being renewed in the idea that humanity, through its own efforts, can make this world better.[204] In this sense, the efforts of *al-Jihad* to enforce the will of God will make the world not only a better world but also a "perfect" world.

Another characteristic of social movements is *collective organization*. Some sort of division of labor exists in most social movements, and its level of sophistication plays a decisive role in either the success or the failure of the movement. We noted above that *al-Jihad* to some extent contained a recognized hierarchy or system of rights and responsibilities with which participants had to cooperate.

A collective organization is more solid and durable than a passing fad or collective behavior that is based upon modulations in style. The interaction between the various members of the group solidifies the movement. Even

---

[201] Farag, *The Missing Religious Precept*, see Appendix I.
[202] Ibid., see Appendix I.
[203] Ibid., see Appendix I.
[204] Wilson, p. 4.

though the government secret police tried to isolate and undermine them, they greeted each other very warmly when they met in court and showed remarkable resilience under government pressure in jail. This front of solidarity serves to encourage those members who are still at large, those who have been released, the rank and file, and the lower echelons on the hierarchical scale.

Correlative to the collective organization is the element of *charismatic leadership*. Max Weber defines "charisma" as "a creative quality of an individual personality by virtue of which he is set apart from ordinary men and treated as endowed with spiritual, super-human, or at least, specifically exceptional qualities."[205]

Weber also indicates that it is not sufficient that the charismatic leader alone recognizes these qualities in himself; others must acknowledge these qualities, too. This recognition by the followers seems to give the leader a hold over them. Therefore, social movements based upon charismatic legitimization tend exclusively to depend upon the initiative and reflect the personal nature of the charismatic leader. Pure charisma has an inherent antinomian and anti-institutional disposition.[206]

Without exploring the predisposition of the charismatic leader (which belongs to another study), it is of utmost importance to reemphasize that *al-Jihad* cannot fit the norms of Weber's definition of charismatic leadership and its visible manifestation in a given movement. To illustrate, the five accused of the assassination of Sadat, who represented the highest order in the movement, are as follows:
— Muhammad Abd al-Salam Farag, Electrical Engineer, Founder, Age 27.
— Hussein Abbas, Army Sergeant, Age 28.
— Ata Rayil, Electrical Engineer, Army Reservist, Age 26.
— Abd al-Hamid, Air Force Lieutenant, Age 28.
— Khaled al-Istamboully, First Lieutenant, Army, Age 25.

The consistent element is that they were all under the age of 30. In the Egyptian culture as a whole, youth is associated with immaturity; therefore, to gain acceptance, especially among older age groups, they brought an outsider, as it were, and grafted him into the leadership. They named a polished older man with a doctorate in Islamic studies *al-Amir al-Aam*, but Dr. Abd al-Rahman was, nonetheless, a figurehead and not the real leader. The founder, Farag, was the leader who gave the movement its impetus. In a sense, the neck moved the head rather than vice versa which would be an unnatural situation, given the theory of charismatic leadership that is accepted among most social scientists.

---

[205] Weber, *Charisma and Institutional Building*, p. 48.
[206] Ibid., p. XXV.

After examining this matter of charismatic leadership as it related to *al-Jihad*, it is apparent that the fact that its founder and leader was not visible and recognized was (a) due to its culturally normative nature, and (b) may have played an important role in the failure of the movement. To illustrate, the apparent lack of a leader capable of popular appeal attenuated the support and admiration of the masses of people. The aims of the movement and the hopes of the masses were not allowed to converge in a tangible reality ... in one leader. This stands in contrast to the Iranian revolution, throughout which the popularity and the charismatic leadership of Ayatollah Khomeini was evident, even while he was abroad. The visibility of this charismatic leader eventually brought a resounding success.

Membership

Social movements consist of a plurality of people, each fulfilling a task. The size of the membership of the movement can determine its success or failure. Large membership does not necessarily mean success, for in the case of a small group, it is much easier to maintain intimacy, closeness and secrecy.

Founders of movements find themselves in the paradoxical position of wanting to increase the membership on the one hand and retain the intimate consensus on the other.[207] To resolve this paradox, the charismatic leader is constantly having to convince his followers that he has something they do not have in an effort to engender a cohesive dependency upon him. He also must be aware of those followers who endeavor to usurp his power position as leader.

The astute leader, in order to exercise social control within the movement, stresses the importance of the disciplined minority, both as a form for the total movement and as a "hard core" which educates, mobilizes and directs the masses of the larger movement when additional members are brought in.[208]

Generally speaking, accurate numbers in Egypt are hard to determine, especially when trying to assess an underground movement like *al-Jihad*. Thus, one cannot claim strict accuracy for the following figures. It is estimated that between one hundred and one hundred-twenty members comprised each Islamic group, and between fifty to eighty groups were affiliated with *al-Jihad*. Numerous others were available in time of need, but the hard-core group consisted of no more than five to ten thousand members.

The number of sympathizers would reach, without a doubt, into the hundreds of thousands, perhaps even millions. If one were to categorize the typical sympathizer as a lower middle-class university student or a recent

---

[207] Cameron, p. 13ff.
[208] Farag, *The Missing Religious Precept*, see Appendix I.

graduate of an elite college (engineering, medicine, agriculture, etc.), who probably originates from a village or small town but currently resides in Cairo, Alexandria, or Assiut, who is moreover a high achiever, dynamic, and one of the most intelligent of Egypt's young people, then the figure of hundreds of thousands is justifiable. These types would have comprised the body of the movement in addition to, of course, former members of the Muslim Brotherhood, who would have supported the movement initially but not on a long-term basis.

It is evident from the court proceedings, though, that the real decision makers were the members of *al-Majlis al-Shouri al-Aam*, under the leadership of the founder and the author of the book which is deemed the constitution of the movement.

The oath of secrecy was one of their most solemn and highly regarded initiation ceremonies, and an important factor in the group's cohesion. The hallowed concept of secrecy found its precedent in the wars that the Prophet Muhammad led. He tried to insure that an increase in size would not cause laxity in commitment.

Goals and Objectives

The goals and objectives of social movements vary depending upon the portion of social life that they want to change. Some movements are concerned with a very narrow segment of the culture, while others attack major parts of the culture. Still others are "totalitarian" in their attempt to control the entire structure of the existing social institutions and thereby alter the whole culture.

The stated purpose of *al-Jihad* is simply "the rule of God should replace the present infidel system," even if it is to be realized by destroying its opponents. In other words, to them the end justifies the means, and if the end or the goal is in direct obedience to the supernatural, there is all the more reason to ignore the ethical and moral issues which are involved in achieving their goal.

Of interest is a statement that, in line with *al-Jihad's* stress on moral and social change, Islamic social movements may find a kindred spirit with American fundamentalist movements such as the Moral Majority. George Marsden, for instance, pointed out that fundamentalists insist "... God is punishing America for her depravity ... God's blessings and curses ... are contingent on national righteousness or sinfulness."[209]

Just as other social movements distinguish their goals and objectives from all others in order to justify their formation, the founder of *al-Jihad*, as outlined in the previous chapter, recounted the objectives of all past movements

---

[209] Mary Douglas and Steven M. Tipton, ed., *Religion and America*. (Boston: Beacon Press, 1982), p. 161.

in order to emphasize the weakness of their goals and the methods that they use to achieve their goals. He concluded that his goal is unique, and his methods of effecting it are not only the most efficient but also adhere most closely to the religious tradition of the Prophet of Islam.

Whereas some social movements attach importance to one segment of the culture, i.e., economic, religious, political, and so on, most, if not all, Islamic movements are primarily concerned with the total culture. In discussing this matter with former and current members of Islamic groups in Egypt, it is evident that much time in their meetings, *nadwah*, was devoted to the purpose of the movement, In fact, the intense and exclusive concentration upon its goal generated hostility, not only in non-members, but also the police. For example, they harrassed people in the streets whom they thought were not in conformity with Islamic dogma [see Chapter 14]. The active members simply categorized as "infidels" and "hypocrites" anyone who did not understand and sympathize with their goal. Conversely, the outsiders call the members of this social movement "fanatics" (*mota'assibeen*), "extremists" (*motatarrifeen*), and "misguided."

The goals and objectives of any social movement cannot be properly assessed unless the particular nature of the movement is understood and generalizations are dissipated. Thus, we need to classify social movements in order to delineate the purpose of *al-Jihad*. There are a great number of classifications of social movements.[210] The classical distinctions between religious and secular movements, between reformative and revolutionary, etc. are helpful in that they help to identify the kind of movement with which we are dealing. However, they may not be perfectly adequate to describe *al-Jihad* movement, simply because Islamic social movements are not as systematic as those in other cultures. For example, one cannot apply the distinction between religious and secular movements since in Islam such a distinction essentially does not, or at least should not, exist.

All typologies represent some distortion of reality simply because of their conscious selection process. The function of typologies should more or less serve as a primitive model, ordering and selecting data while, at the same time, suggesting questions about them.[211]

Aberle has four basic classifications of social movements which can serve here as a summary of all other classifications.

---

[210] For example, Aberle, *The Peyote Religion Among the Navaho*, (Chicago: Festinger, 1966); *When the Prophecy Fails*, (University of Minnesota Press, 1956); Geerd, *The Interpretation of Cultures*, (New York: Bacis Books, 1973); V. W. Turner, *Schism and Continuity in an African Society*, (Manchester University Press, 1957); Peter Worsley, *The Trumpet Shall Sound*, (London: MacGibbon & Kee, 1957); William Bruce Cameron, *Modern Social Movements*, (New York: Random House, 1967); John Wilson, *Introduction to Social Movements*, (New York: Basic Books, 1973).

[211] Wilson, p. 15.

1. *Transformative movements* These are movements which aim at a total change in supra-individual systems. Here we can include millenarian movements, revolutionary movements, etc. There are ample examples of these, the Russian Revolution, the French Revolution, etc.
2. *Reformative movements* These are movements which aim at a political change in supra-individual systems. The child labor law movement and the Protestant Reformation are good examples of this type of movement.
3. *Redemptive movements* These types of movements aim at a total change in the individuals. Numerous sectarian movements which aim at not only conversion, but also a total change in lifestyle and separation from society such as the Mennonite movement and the Peyote cult would fit this classification.
4. *Alternative movements* These are movements whose aim is partial change in the individuals, i.e., birth-control movements, anti-abortian movements, etc.

These classifications are theoretical and will vary a great deal on the empirical level, especially in our study of *al-Jihad* which, to some extent, fits the definition of the *transformative movements*. The main reason for this description is the revolutionary nature of *al-Jihad*, which rejects the existing social structure as not only inadequate but inherently evil. Social and political institutions, as well as the leadership of these institutions, are infidels (*kafir*); and the movement wishes to supplant them with a system that they deem not just desirable but "perfect." Even if many in the society do not see its perfection, they will appreciate this utopia when they experience it.

The drive for total change caused the media to denounce *al-Jihad* as "radical," "extremist," "misguided," "terrorists," etc. With a revolutionary movement such as *al-Jihad*, the term "radical" is more pertinent to the intensity of the movement than the direction of its action.

Millenarian is a concept that can be applied to this transformative movement with some qualifications. It is true, Farag, the founder of the movement, talks about the *Mahdi*, the Messiah, who shall come to fill the earth with justice and happiness, yet he is somewhat vague on this notion.[212] Since Islam, unlike Christianity, is "this worldly" oriented, it would be difficult to speak specifically regarding the millenium (i.e., the rule of God on earth).[213]

The vagueness as to whether the founder saw himself to be the *Mahdi* or merely the forerunner for the *Mahdi* is not of major significance in *al-Jihad*. Actually, the prime motivation of the movement did not reside in the figure of the *Mahdi*. More importantly, the movement believed that God's rule is not a future contingency, but rather a Qur'anic precept to be realized now; unfor-

---

[212] Farag, *The Missing Religious Precept*, see Appendix I.
[213] Sears, 1924; Fistinger et al;. 1956, Schwartz, 1970.

tunately, corrupt men are delaying its application because they want to be the rulers in the place of God. The application of God-given laws will establish the perfect *ummah*.[214]

Duration

One of the features of social movements that distinguishes them from other manifestations of discontent such as riots and strikes is that they are recurrent phenomena. Social movements seldom die: they are modified, and though each time they are visibly manifested in a different format, the foundation of the social movement persists through the change.

Riots, which often constitute one single action, can at times be a visible manifestation of well-organized social movements. As we have seen, the strategies of *al-Jihad* included deliberately creating and controlling mass panic, as well as attacking police and other citizens in order to test its hold over society.

The following questions need to be asked here: How long has the movement been in existence? Is it a phase of a continuous history of social movements or did it just happen in response to a peculiar sociological setting? What is the apparent life expectancy of a given movement?

Answering these questions in the light of the data about *al-Jihad*, we see that *al-Jihad* was formed in 1980 and apparently dissolved toward the end of 1981. These dates are really parenthetical and, like most dates, tend to oversimplify the evolvement of the social movement. Since the foundation in 1928 of the Muslim Brotherhood movement (in reaction to the British occupation and to combat Western influence upon Islamic society), there has been an unbroken line of successive social movements, varying in their visible manifestation or methodology, but not in their overriding ideology.

While the founding of the Muslim Brotherhood was a response to peculiar socio-political conditions, namely the British occupation and the feeling that the state of Islam was "in danger," the spirit of this movement is ongoing and alive even today. Furthermore, to say that *al-Jihad* died in late 1981 is again to oversimplify the matter. While the government and the state would like to think that the movement died with the arrests of its core leadership, the alert social anthropologist is sensitive to the movement's pulsebeat.

As one searches for an answer to the question of whether or not the movement is dead, one finds that the opposite is true, i.e., the movement is far from dead. For example, some of the released members are completely unrepentant and many of them are reorganizing (mid-1983). The court appointed to prosecute *al-Jihad* members, in their proceedings, highlighted on

---

[214] Farag, *The Missing Religious Precept*, see Appendix I.

a daily basis the fact that large numbers of the accused membership were still at large. In every court's opening hearing, the government prosecutor indicated that all accused were present except for the sick and those "at large." Some of those who are "at large" were involved at the highest level of leadership and were very close to the founder of the movement. Knowledgeable sources have observed close contact between those who are at large and those who are currently imprisoned, even though the founder and four others were executed.

While it is comparatively easy to examine the birth of the movement, it is extremely difficult to detect the movement's demise, especially since it may have survived in a different fashion.

The next question that arises is whether the movement must succeed in order to be considered a movement, and what in the structure of the movement helps it to succeed. This will be dealt with in the next chapter.

CHAPTER SEVENTEEN

THE DEVELOPMENTAL STRUCTURE OF SOCIAL MOVEMENTS

Although social movements differ in their cultural manifestations, they all share certain common traits. These traits consist of genotypical structures independent of local cultural differences; these generalities are observed in widely differing cultures.[215] Furthermore, social movements are linked with past movements through shared ideology.[216]

In spite of their similarities with other social movements, Islamic social movements are unique in many ways, as this study has shown.

There are a number of theories regarding the developmental structure of social movements. For example, the process of social movements is often related to social dramas and applied to individual relationships as well as the society at large. Thus, Victor Turner sees four phases in any social change.[217] These phases can be summarized as follows: first, the *breach* of regular norm-governed social relations; next, the phase of mounting *crisis* which cannot be ignored; then, the phase of *redressive action* in order to deal with the crisis; and, finally, the phase in which there is a *reintegration* of the disturbed social group or the *social recognition and legitimization* of the irreparable division of society.

Rex Hooper suggests a division similar to that of Victor Turner's.[218] *First*, any social order or society may be viewed as a sort of moving equilibrium of culturally held values and socially acquired attitudes. *Second*, however, disorder occurs (for whatever reason) and creates fear and dissatisfaction which, in turn, further disturbs social order; and the process of social disorganization sets in. When this happens, attitudes and values begin to diverge which means, *third*, that social change has taken place. If and when social disorganization eventuates in the recognition of attitudes and/or values which result in a significant social change, then, *fourth*, change on the institutional level occurs. In short, the change of attitudes in individuals is normally followed by change in institutions. Hence, revolutionary change is the kind of social change which occurs when the basic institutional values of a social order are rejected and new values accepted.

---

[215] A. F. Wallace, *American Anthropologist*. Vol 58, (April 1956), p. 268.

[216] H. G, Barnett, *Innovation: The Basics of Cultural Change*, (Mc Graw Hill, 1953), p. 181.

[217] See Victor Turner, *Dramas, Fields, and Metaphors*, (Cornwall University Press, 1978), p. 38ff. See also King, *Social Movements in the U.S.*, p. 39ff, Wilbert Moore, *Social Change*, p. 69ff.

[218] Rex Hooper, *Social Movements*, Robert Evans, ed., (Chicago: Rand McNally, 1973), p. 55ff.

E. J. Hobsbawm, in his book entitled *Primitive Rebels*, categorizes the typical millenarian movement in Europe as having three characteristics. First, a profound and total rejection of the present, evil world and a passionate longing for another one. Second, a fairly standard "ideology." Here Hobsbawm stresses that most classical millenarian movements in Europe occur in countries that are affected by Judeo-Christian propaganda and that the concept of millenarianism is alien to Hinduism and Buddhism. It is worth noting that he ignores Islam altogether. In any case, the third characteristic, according to Hobsbawm's schema, is that millenarian movements have a fundamental vagueness about actual ways in which the new society will be brought about, probably because of the expectation of the divine revelation when the time comes.

For the purposes of this study, however, A. F. Wallace's renaming social movements as "revitalization" movements and his breakdown of the process of change is more adequate, simply because he takes culture as a whole into account.[219]

Wallace provides five overlapping stages of what he calls "revitalization movements." These five stages can be summarized as follows:

1. A steady state which is a period of moving equilibrium. Although some changes occur during this stage, these changes are relatively slow.
2. A period of individual stress when the sociocultural system is "pushed" progressively out of equilibrium by various changes such as climatic and biotic changes or epidemic diseases, wars and conquests, social subordination or acculturation. Under such conditions, an increasingly large number of individuals are placed under what is to them intolerable stress by the existing system and the failure of the system to meet their needs. With this perception in mind, widespread dissatisfaction sets in.
3. A period of cultural distortion in which some members of the society attempt, in a fragmentary manner and ineffectually, to restore personal equilibrium. Small changes at that time will not be able to reduce the impact of the forces that have pushed the society out of its equilibrium and, in fact, are likely to lead to continuous decline in the organization.
4. A period of revitalization. Once severe cultural distortion has occurred, it is difficult for the society to return to a steady state without the institution of a revitalization process. Revitalization, however, depends on the following foundations:
(1) Formulation of a code, i.e. an alternative to the existing social system. Normally at this point there is a contrast between the old system and the new one, often highlighting the new as being much better.

---

[219] A. F. Wallace, *Religion—An Anthropological View*, (New York: Random House, 1966), p. 30ff.

(2) Communication. With an evangelistic zeal, the formulation of the code needs to be preached in the endeavor of making converts. In other words, being able to sell the ideology—in most cases, showing how salvation can come, or will come, at the hands of the group.

(3) Organization. As the movement increases in number, the organization falls into two categories—a set of disciples and a set of mass followers; the disciples end up as the leaders and the mass followers continue to devote part of their time and money for the continuation of the movement.

(4) Adaptation. Because of the revolutionary nature of the organization, it threatens the status quo, but it also tries to take advantage of the status quo. Since the code is never complete, inadequacies in the code are discovered. The response of the code formulators and disciples is to rework the code and, if necessary, to defend the movement by political and diplomatic maneuver and eventually by force. Ultimately, the movement becomes hostile to nonparticipating fellow members of the group who will be defined as traitors, and outsiders become enemies.

(5) Culturation transformation. If the movement is able to capture both the seat of power and a large number of adherents, the transference of culture almost always is effected. The revitalization, if successful, will be attended by a drastic decline of the old culture and the disappearance of cultural distortions. For such a revitalization to be accomplished, however, the movement must be able to obtain internal social conformity without destructive coercion and must have a successful economic system.

(6) Routinization. When the preceding functions are satisfactorily completed, the reasons for the movement's existence as an innovative force disappear, and the role of the movement changes from innovation to maintenance. If the movement is a religious movement in orientation, it becomes a cult or a church that reworks the code and maintains it through rituals. If the movement is primarily political, its organization will become a bureaucracy and routinized into stable bodies, administrative, police, military, and so on, whose function is to make decisions and to maintain moral order.[220]

With the routinization of the movement, a new steady state may be said to exist. A steady state does not imply a static condition in the cultural process; changes, small though they may be, occur nonetheless. Many of these changes are extensions of the fundamental change which the movement originated. In particular, changes in the value structure of the culture may lay the basis for ongoing changes in other areas. An example of this that Wallace gives is the economic and technological consequences that followed the dissemination of the Protestant ethic after the Protestant reformation. Thus, in addition to the

---

[220] Max Weber, pp. 54 & 55.

change the revitalization movement accomplished during its active phase, it may control the direction of the subsequent equilibrium process by shifting the values that define the cultural focus.

Al-Jihad, at this point of its history, has gone through the earlier stages of the process and, according to government officials, has died, or according to some of the former members and former supporters, has only temporarily subsided.

Most segments in Egyptian society accept that after the 1973 war with Israel (in which Egypt believed itself to have defeated Israel for the first time in their long history of enmity) the Egyptian economy began to deteriorate badly. The economic policy following the 1973 war changed from socialism to the "open door" policy of President Sadat. This "open door" policy produced a skyrocketing rate of no less than 80 percent inflation, a scarcity of food and accommodations, and a dislocation of the middle class which made up the bulk of Egypt's urban population. In other words, the society experienced what Wallace would call a severe yet still tolerable stress that destabilized the society's equilibrium. The severity of the shock was fully felt when the government tried to raise food prices in January 1977. The people responded with a nationwide, violent protest which surpassed all others in magnitude. However, instead of facing the dilemma and admitting the reality of the situation, Sadat began to blame the Soviet Union for instigating the violence.

What Sadat failed to realize is that his economic "open door" policy had pushed the society into an intolerable economic condition, and it had no alternative but to collectively express its frustration and anger by demonstrating in the streets. This opposition was not organized or under any kind of leadership, but was a spontaneous action directed against the government and the rich. Thus, in the perception of the mob, overturning and burning buses and cars was stating, "We are unable to find food while you people drive big cars."

In one sense, this kind of frustration resembled to a great degree Karl Marx' description of the proletariat parties whose aim is "the formation of the proletariat into a class, the overthrow of the bourgeoisie supremacy, conquest of political power by the proletariat."[221] Observers believed that many of the muslim groups were attacking churches not only to show disdain for the high visibility of Christians in a "muslim" land, but also to attract the government's attention. This was their unorganized way of expressing their dissatisfaction with the direction that the government was pursuing, both in its inability to deal with the horrendous economic problems and in its foreign policy, which seemed to be drifting away from "the true Islamic path."

---

[221] *The Marx-Engels Reader*, Robert Tucker, ed., (New York and London: W. W. Norton & Company, 1978) p. 484.

In the latter part of 1977, the year in which Sadat traveled to Jerusalem, extreme Islamic ideologies began to appear and by 1980 *al-Jihad* was born. By that time, the stress upon individuals, particularly those in the large cities, noticeably intensified. Both peaceful demonstrations and subtle, yet incisive, verbal attacks on the government in some of the Muslim fundamentalist magazines and newspapers increased.[222]

Cries for introducing the *shari'a* were heard from religious as well as political spheres of influence. These cries represented the Egyptian Islamic cultural mores, and attempted to deal with the problems created by the "open door" economic policy which jolted and disoriented individuals, especially when they saw a sudden influx of Western luxury goods accompanied by sexually alluring advertisements. In one sense, while the population reluctantly embraced Nasser's rule, his blatant socialist policies, and his alliance with the Soviet Union, at least they felt that there had been equality. Under Sadat, five percent of the population became extremely rich and increasingly adopted Western lifestyles, while the rest merely had a subsistence or below subsistence existence. Under these conditions, religion was seen as a boat of salvation in the midst of crashing waves.

Anxiety over the changing behavior pattern and the fear of the unknown created a state of confusion in the minds of some educated, middle class individuals, who began to behave in a bizarre manner in order to cope with the tension between their religious heritage and foreign acculturation. Two examples will suffice here. One is the case of the man who refused to sit at the table to have his meals, protesting that the Prophet Muhammad did not eat off a table. Another pulled the tiles off the floor, claiming that the Prophet did not have tiles on his floor.

During this time, Abd al- Salam Farag preached with messianic zeal that the answer could be found in "the missing religious precept." The way to combat all this cultural distortion is to establish *jihad* as the duty of every Muslim to be carried out against infidels. The West with its "evil and wicked culture invading our Islamic society" constitutes, in part, "the infidels," but it is not the primary concern. The "evil infidels" inhabit the very homeland of Islam; they are the rulers who allow the acculturation process to take place and even emulate Western lifestyles with the result of destroying the Islamic way of life and bringing about upheaval in the culture. Therefore, Farag argued Muslims must fulfill their mission and protect their culture. The only way they can insure this is by applying the *shari'a*.

Like all revolutionary movements, *al-Jihad* was not satisfied by simply calling upon the government to implement the *shari'a* or demanding that the government bring about the desired change; they saw that nothing short of

---

[222] See, for example, *Al-Da'wah* and *Al-Intizaam* between 1977 and 1979.

taking over the seat of power would bring about and enforce the "law of God."

If one is to transplant the heart of Marxist theory in *al-Jihad*, if only in methodology, then the words of Marx become relevant in this context:

> Someday, the worker must seize political power in order to build up the new organization of labor. He must overthrow the old politics which sustained the old institutions ... it is force to which we must someday appeal in order to erect the rule of labor.[223]

To be sure, *al-Jihad* was not founded as a Marxist movement in doctrine. However, as one spends hours listening to members bitterly attacking the "rich" and the "corrupt," it is impossible to ignore that the spirit of Marxism in its revolutionary fervor is very much evident in the heart and the soul of the movement.

By 1980, *al-Jihad* became well organized as a movement with a hierarchical structure. This advanced level of organization was no more evident than during the time when the Egyptian masses poured into the streets demonstrating their disdain, while the rest of the world stood in admiration of Sadat's courage to receive the homeless Shah of Iran into Egypt. One eyewitness, in describing the well-organized demonstration, chanted the following words, "Ya phar'oun al-asr moush awzeen al-shah fi masr." ("Oh Pharaoh of this age, we do not want the Shah in Egypt.") This became the slogan of thousands of students who demonstrated. The eyewitness explained that the main street of Assiut, the stronghold of *al-Jihad*, was completely covered with religious students shouting this and other slogans. As the police moved in, the fearful students fled so quickly that the ground was covered with the sandals they left as they ran. This event was one of the most powerful expressions of the masses' obvious affinity with the Khomeini Islamic revolution and their rejection of Sadat as an infidel. By calling him "pharaoh," the ancient Egyptian dictator who knew not Allah, they showed their utter disdain for him.

In any case, *al-Jihad* was progressing according to most norms of social movements' developmental structure when the original plan was to be effected in a nationwide revolution in 1983.

External events affected the planned process of this movement. In September of 1981, President Sadat ordered a series of arrests, which totaled more than fifteen hundred, in the hope that this would quell the tension between the Christians and the Muslims which eventuated in massive bloodshed. Both the nature of the arrests and the reaction to it on the part of *al-Jihad* contributed equally to the abortion of the movement.

When the secret police were ordered to arrest "extremists of both sides," Christians and Muslims, the arrests of members of all opposition parties,

---

[223] Tucker, p. 523.

journalists, and many innocent citizens soon ensued. This aggravated the severe tension in the society and confirmed to the members of *al-Jihad* that the government would deliberately and ruthlessly try to crush them.

Among those arrested were members of *al-Jihad*. Some were close relatives of the highest level of leadership in the movement. At that point, panic spread in the camps of the movement, which tried to accelerate the plans for taking over power and move the date forward from 1983 to October 1981. At the same time, they were caught unprepared and misread the mood of the masses.

Although the masses were frustrated and readily sought change, the arrests of September 1981 terrorized many former activists. The fear of failure that permeated the history of the Muslim Brotherhood haunted them and pushed them back into the corner of passivism. These activists as well as the potential activists were deluged with thoughts such as, "They won't get me" or "I don't want to go to jail again" or "I had my fair share of suffering at the hands of the secret police." In other words, they were not prepared to take the risk of supporting an "unknown quantity" (a group of young men with high ideals). Thus, the "carrier agent" ingredient was missing in this social movement, whose total strength resided in a few thousand enthusiastic young men who thought they could easily bring the masses into the streets just as had happened in Teheran, Iran, in 1978 and 1979. *Al-Jihad*, however, failed to recognize their own limitation in that while they initially received tacit support from the pillars of the Muslim Brotherhood, the alliance evaporated when the situation became critical and *al-Jihad* found themselves solely responsible.

The plan was worked out between Abd al-Salam Farag and members of *al-Majlis al-Shouri al-Aam*, then brought to Dr. Abdul Rahman, the figurehead leader, to receive his blessing. Hence, on the morning of the sixth of October, when society at large was transfixed to its television sets watching the ostentatious military parade celebrating the 1973 "victory," President Sadat and the entire leadership (political as well as military) were to be killed in a one-minute attack upon their reviewing stand. However, only Sadat and a few others were the victims and the remainder of the leadership and the elite of the society survived. *Al-Jihad* planned that as soon as the killing took place, they would move into the media headquarters, declare the revolution and call the masses out to support and bless the new government.

That was not to be, and the movement came to an end—at least formally. Over one thousand arrests were made in the weeks following the assassination. Some of these people were subsequently released, but more than 350 were in jail at the time of the writing of this study (mid-1983). The state prosecutor has asked the court that 48 of the accused be executed for their terrorist attacks, primarily upon the police headquarters in the city of Assiut and the killing of 84 policemen on the eighth of October 1981.*

---

* See afterword.

How would the movement have implemented its ideology had it succeeded? What parts of the existing social order would have been destroyed or adopted and how quickly? These and many other questions must be left solely to speculation.

More importantly, however, the question is asked, "Given all our knowledge of Egyptian society, can this kind of movement succeed in the future?" The answer to this question shall be dealt with more fully in the following concluding chapter.

CHAPTER EIGHTEEN

FROM THE PRESENT TO THE FUTURE

On the 31st anniversary of the July '52 revolution, President Hosni Mubarak declared that "the continuation on the revolutionary road does not mean repetition or stasis, but it means that we positively put aside the past and freely look to the future with optimism and hope."[224]

In this historic speech in July 1983, Mubarak set the tone of the policies out of which he intends to carve the future of Egypt, whose facets will include democracy, Western-style progress, both social and political, and a secular, as opposed to religious, government because Egypt cannot "turn back the clock ... or return to barbarianism ... but rather must go on to strengthen and support the scientific and technological revolution."[225]

Mubarak's statements were far more blunt than this. He requested the masses to change a great many of their embedded cultural habits and cultural mores. "Since we have chosen the road of democracy, we must think and breathe democracy ... work hard and forget our reactionary past," said Mubarak.

Has Mubarak called upon traditional Islamic society to become Westernized in its outlook upon democracy, nationalism, secularism, and technology? One can hardly answer this question in any way other than in the affirmative, given the speech and its context.

Mubarak and the present Egyptian government as a whole have now clearly come out on the side of modernism.

The historic background illustrated that ever since Shaykh Muhammad Abduh's profound influence upon the thinking of Egyptians, there has been a split down the middle of society—a split between modernists and orthodox Muslims. The modernists accept and follow Western social and technological progress with minimum amount of modification and were represented by Lotfi and Taha Hussein and others. The others, who have interpreted Abduh along conservative, orthodox Islamic lines and put themselves on the side of strict Islamic dogma, were represented by such people as Reshid and Heikal.

These two main segments in society remain the dominant schools of thought in modern Egypt. Even now, the *ulama* are no longer speaking with one voice, but they, too, are divided on their interpretation of the Islamic *shari'a* and its relation to the social and economic life of society.[226]

---

[224] *Al-Ahram*, 22 July, pp. 1, 3, & 5.
[225] Ibid.
[226] *Al-Nour*, 15 June 1983.

Where does Islamic society as a whole and Egyptian society as its microcosm go from here? The answer to this question will encompass both direct experience and a great deal of speculation.

The same two main streams of Islamic thought that existed earlier in this century continue to exist today, albeit, in a different manner. Now there are numerous splinter groups from both interpretations of Islamic teaching, which are like railroad lines—parallel in their conviction of Islamic truth, yet never meeting on the application of this truth to social life.

The group which we may call "modernists" interprets Islam more on contemporary Western (even Christian) terms than Islamic, thus failing to satisfy the masses. In other words, they see Islam as the true religion, but it is a personal relationship with God and no human being should dictate to another human being what he should and should not do in the area of religious observance. Therefore, to attempt to apply Islamic law and enforce it would be a disservice to Islam. For this interpretation, they have textual and traditional support.

On the other hand, the "orthodox" Muslims who are calling for the application of the *shari'a* without delay and without change, see Islam as the truth, the only truth. Islam is not merely a religion like other religions, but the fulfillment of all other monotheistic religions. Furthermore, Islam is not just a relationship with God, but it is also "this worldly," i.e., "*Dien wa Doniah*." There was no separation of church and state under the rule of the Prophet, and there should be no separation today.

There are left and right wing proponents (as westerners understand those terms) in both streams of thought, although Marxists are to be found only under the umbrella of the modernists. But there is no lack of supply of socialists among the orthodox Muslims. To both groups, however, Islam is a potent social force providing the main social cohesion for the majority of their members. On the whole, Islam is the legitimizing force for both segments of the society, a source of cultural identity and a distinguishing factor from the non-Muslim world.

The debate between the two groups has been raging since the middle seventies. Nageeb Mahfuz, one of Egypt's foremost thinkers, explained that "the application of the *shari'a* would make society a living contradiction"; he lists all the social and economic problems of society that are in existence today, and questions why innocent people are punished. "How difficult the problem, but how easy the punishment," Mahfuz concludes.[227]

On the other hand, the former rector of al-Azhar University, the stern and uncompromising theologian Dr. Abd al-Haleem Mahmud, insists that "to say that we must reform the individual first then apply the *shari'a* is an obvious

---

[227] *Al-Ahram*, 17 May 1977.

deception because the law itself is the most powerful means for reforming the individual. This is putting things upside down and reversing the desires of the believers ..."[228]

Islamic Nationalism in Historical Perspective

The argument of the "orthodox" Muslims is crisp and clear: the ideal Islamic state was supposedly established by the Prophet and *al-Kholapha al-Rashidun* (the four immediate successors to the Prophet). There has been sharp division within Islam ever since that time on whether or not the Prophet founded a "state" or a "community of believers within the state." The question that has preoccupied the minds of the thinkers within the Muslim world is whether the sacred laws are sufficient in themselves for ruling the community or if a necessary ingredient in an Islamic nation is the presence of an enforcer of the sacred laws. But the crux of the problem here can be summarized in Bellah's words that, "... The main criticism of contemporary Muslim thought and its impact on society is that it fails to distinguish adequately between the realms of reason and faith, and that explicitly or implicitly it binds and restrains the use of reason in the solution of social problems."

The ideas operating today in the Muslim world are forces generated from within the Muslim community, even though the main thrust of the ideas is foreign—in the case of the orthodox, the modernist, or even the revivalist segments alike. It is self-evident that many of the modernists have been so influenced by Western thinkers that sometimes their thinking seems to be an extension of Western thought, as was illustrated earlier in the historical analysis section.

There are some who argue that modernization in the last 150 years has politicized Islam.[229] Since the *shari'a* has nothing to say about complex economic issues, secular rulers gradually took over functions in society that previously had been performed by traditional religious leaders and used religion for political purposes. In fact, this has created new urban masses that now express their economic and political grievances in Islamic terms. Their demands are modern, but the formulation remains traditionally Islamic.[230]

Without arguing the merits or flaws of the above theory, it is important to point out here that historically, Muslims attached to the Caliphate the function of enforcing and interpreting the *shari'a*. When the political systems in the Muslim world diverged from this theoretical ideal, the Muslims' first loyalty was to the Islamic institutions; negative feelings and rejection were expressed toward the secular leader, in tandem with the rise of Messianic

---

[228] *Al-Ahram*, 7 May 1976.
[229] See, for example, *Islamic Resurgence*, pp. 174ff.
[230] Ibid.

idealism in Islamic society. This may or may not be attributed to modernism, but it must be attributed to any thought or ideal that is perceived as non-Islamic. The best example of this was the rejection of the Ottoman rulers by the Wahhabis in the Arabian peninsula.

Modernization, however, does not account entirely for this, and it is important to note that revolutionary notions of Islam, especially in our epistemological study of that religion, show a lack of appreciation for concepts such as turning the other cheek, and peaceful or passive resistance. Islam was born on the battlefield and stayed there throughout its history. More often than not, revolutions and ruthless dictators have used Islam to conquer and achieve personal gain; yet, in the essence of Islam, one cannot escape the militance and seeking after power.

Well before Nicholas Copernicus developed his concept of *De Revolutionibus Orbium Celestium* (On the Revolutions of the Heavenly Bodies),[231] prior to the sixteenth and seventeenth century European development of the concepts of revolutionary change and, of course, long before Karl Marx's discovery that "revolutions are the locomotive of history," Muhammad of Arabia invoked revolutionary change in the social and religious structure of Arabia. True, the French Revolution, the Marxist theory, etc., have inspired many Muslim revolutionaries in the past fifty years, yet Islamic revolution has an inherently religious tone that would baffle most Western political scientists.

Probably this study will stimulate discussion and further research in the revolutionary nature of Islam. If class conflicts are the means of resolving the question of the power of the bourgeoisie, then Muhammad's revolution in 611 was the first of this kind. For as was shown earlier, Muhammad's own clan of Hashim was the poorer side of the Qurayshite tribe. The clan that enjoyed wealth and power were the Umayyads; thus Muhammad's revolution was just as much economic and social as it was religious.[232] Trade introduced Arabia to foreigners and foreign culture; this change in turn caused social dislocation and the rise of a new class of traders, which are the two main ingredients necessary for revolution.[233]

The reaction of the first Islamic revolution toward the non-Muslims was understandable. For Muslims in Arabia who used to distinguish between "them" and "us" continued to distinguish, not on the basis of tribal or clan loyalty, but on the basis of religious loyalty. Accordingly, the Muslim world view is segmented into the "House of Islam" (*Dar al-Islam*) and the "House of War" (*Dar al-Harb*). The very outsiders who brought about the two ingre-

---

[231] *Why Revolution*, Paynton & Blackey, ed., pp. 16ff.
[232] M. A. Shaban, *Islamic History*, (Cambridge University Press, 1971), p. 9.
[233] Theda Skocpol, *State and Social Revolution*, (Cambridge University Press, 1979), p. 14.

dients for the first Islamic revolution are to be treated as enemies less they spoil the purity of the new found community. It is no surprise, therefore, that in most subsequent Islamic revolutions, the demarcation line between "us" and "them" becomes entrenched and more highly stressed.

The modern Western technological invasion of the Egyptian society has had a tremendous impact upon the society, and, indeed, intensified the pressure and necessitated the desire for change. However, in the typical Islamic environment, crisis culminates in the emergence of supposedly "new," but in most cases old, sociopolitical arrangements, i.e., the return to the "first century Islam" with all this entails of utopian ideology.

Where does utopia lead?

If utopia is "predominantly that of an idea which is in principle unrealizable,"[234] then the idea of a strictly Islamic state in which Islamic sacred laws would exist and function in modern times is indeed utopian at its best. For Mannheim explains that in the light of the Hegelian and Droysen theory "all movement in the history would go on in this way: Thought, which is the ideal counterpart of things as they really exist, develops itself as things ought to be ..." Moreover, "thoughts constitute the criticism of that which is and yet is not as it should be ... Out of the already given conditions, new thoughts arise and out of the thoughts, new conditions—this is the work of man."[235]

Ever since the first Islamic century, Muslim activists throughout all ages have sought to recreate this magical moment of history in their own time. *Al-Jihad* is no exception in this regard. Yet how much of this movement was motivated by implementing the truth in the sacred laws as they saw it, and how much of it was the rejection of the depressing status quo of the socio-economic conditions in the society is difficult to detect. One suspects that the answer perhaps lies somewhere in between.

The revolutionaries in *al-Jihad* were not Islamic theologians, they were laymen through and through. The members have consistently illustrated that Islam has no division between theologians and lay people as in Christianity. Yet, the existing system of their hierarchy would dispute their claim. Even the clothes that the theologians wear distinguish them from the laymen. In any case, the members of *al-Jihad* are referred to by the young Communists in Egypt as the "proletariat." "They are like us ... except that they hide behind Islam because they know that this is a 'quick fix' ... they can turn on the emotions of the people much easier if they find justification in Islam to bring

---

[234] Karl Mannheim, *Ideology and Utopia*, pp. 49ff.
[235] Ibid., pp. 179-80.

about change ... we take the hard road. Communism is a swear word here in Egypt. Who wants to be unpopular?"[236]

Regardless of the motivation, the message of the revolutionaries is clear· "We reject society as it stands and we want to change it to what we think it ought to be." In many ways this is akin to revolutionary messianism in medieval and reformation Europe. At that period of history, Europe suffered from social dislocation and economic uncertainty which created a desperate feeling of the need for redemption. Moreover, there was the feeling of cultural and religious imperialism by Rome and many conditions in England, Germany, France and elsewhere necessitated the search for cultural and religious independence.

At that point, it was the religious leadership that led Europe out of its slumber by seeking the very things that are sought today by Islamic revolutionaries, i.e., the return to their first century and a rejection of pomp and ceremony and the displaying of religious opulence.

It is important to note the other part of this analogy, namely, as we saw in the European reformation, that seeking after their own religious roots and heritage did not necessarily mean the return to those original conditions. Thus, Islamic revolutions will not necessarily mean the return to "the Islamic *ummah*."

However, these revolutionary movements opened the door to truly Islamic progress which is, of course, highly desirable, Open debate and discussion regarding the *shari'a* and its function and relevance to modern society have been helpful by allowing room to vent ones frustrations and strive for economic and social progress.

We saw two examples of this debate about the *shari'a* in this chapter. Al-Ashmawi, who currently holds the high post of a consultor at the Cairo High Court of Appeal, in his book *Usul al-Shari'a* (Principles of the Shari'a)[237] makes a distinction between Islamic faith and religious thought. He argues that the *shari'a* is not a specific body of rules and regulations governing the conduct of the Muslims, but rather these were revealed in response to specific circumstances and needs. Thus the Qur'anic surahs revealed to Muhammad in Mecca deal exclusively with matters of faith, sin and salvation. They did not relate to the community of the faithful. The revelations in Medina, however, (later revelations) dealt with personal conduct and social relationship among the faithful. The *shari'a* therefore, Ashmawi argues, is a guide, a dynamic ethic.

As far as the Islamic *ummah* (state) is concerned, Ashmawi argues that there is not a single passage in the Qur'an about such a state and form of

---

[236] A member of a young communist group in Alexandria University.
[237] *Principles of the Shari'a*, (Cairo, 1979).

COMPARATIVE ANALYSIS

government. Until the death of the Prophet, there was no state in Islam; only a community led by the Prophet. The Qur'an always addressed itself to the faithful, not the citizens. In fact, citizenship is an alien concept to Islam. In conclusion, Ashmawi asserts that religion has to do with man and his social environment and not with states and empires.

Just as the subsequent generations of the European Protestant reformers discovered, upon examining the New Testament documents academically and technically, that the early church was not as perfect as reformers first thought, al-Ashmawi also reminds his utopia-seeking fellow Muslims that the idealistic past had its own human problems, such as the Umayyad dynasty. Moreover, the *shari'a* never specified a form of government.

But like Taha Hussein before him, he became the object of the wrath of the Islamic groups, specifically the Muslim Brotherhood.[238] It remains to be seen whether al-Ashmawi's school will flourish or die a premature death. For this kind of courageous Islamic thinking can be choked not only by the revolutionary Islamic groups but also many of the *ulama* who are trying to protect their own turf. But if one is to conclude, as indeed Tipton did, that the importance of religious movements "lies chiefly in the ideas they carry,"[239] then one holds a great deal of hope for the Ashmawi school, especially after the apparent failure of the Iranian revolution and its drive to apply the *shari'a* literally.

One vital historical note is that the utopian Islamic revolutionary movements have suffered the usual fate of their kind. From the earliest centuries of Islam, political control was in fact executed by secular governments. Today, most utopian movements continue to receive this same fate because the secular powers are in control even in the Islamic heartland such as Arabia.

Utopia-seeking Islamic revolutionaries have found themselves with two alternatives in dealing with such governments. One is to submit on the principle that tyranny is preferable to anarchy; the other is to assert by violence the supremacy of the sacred law.[240] In the past, most Muslim activists have chosen the first, with the understanding that the secular government would not interfere with the Islamic socioreligious institutions. Lately, however, whether it be the Muslim Brotherhood in Syria or *al-Jihad* in Egypt, the extremists who seized the Holy Mosque in Arabia, or the *Amal* Shi'ite group in Lebanon, it seems that Muslim activists are moving more and more toward the second alternative.

As the next generation observes the failure of the application of the *shari'a* in Pakistan, Iran, Sudan and other places and the struggle of Arabia to hold

---

[238] *Al-Da'wah*, October 1979.

[239] Steven M. Tipton, *Getting Saved From the Sixties*, (Berkeley, Los Angeles, London: University of California Press, 1982), p. 280ff.

[240] Gibb, *Modern Trends in Islam*, p. 117.

off the flood of Western technology and foreign ideas in order to shelter its citizens and force them to keep to the rigid and outmoded desert lifestyle, they will begin to reexamine the dogmatic approach of the revolutionaries. At that moment, the whole Muslim world would be ready for an alternative mode for progress that is different from its Western counterpart. The emergence of a developmental progress that is compatible with Islamic ethic will become wholly acceptable.

Today the West may boast of its development, but that development seems to have bankrupted the very moral values upon which it was founded. An Islamic development which would combine both moral values and willingness to develop and progress is what most Muslims would welcome. Some, however, question whether the Islamic ethic, which is basically desert-nomadic in its nature, can achieve this. The alternative is, of course, to adapt and modify the Western codes of development into their cultural milieu, following the example of countries like Japan, Korea, Singapore, and others. Struggling with ideas has its price, but ultimately it is the "truth," when it is known, that shall make men free.

APPENDIX I

THE MISSING RELIGIOUS PRECEPT

IN THE NAME OF GOD THE MERCIFUL

"Is not the time ripe for the hearts of those who believe to submit to Allah's reminder and to the truth which is revealed, that they become not as those who received the Scripture of old but the term was prolonged for them and so their hearts were hardened, and many of them are evil-livers." (LVII:16)

Abd Allah Ibn al-Mubarak of whom Salih al-Marie told us through Ibn Abbas who said, "God has slowed the hearts of the believers and rebuked them on the 13th day of the coming down of the Qur'an and said, 'Is not the time ripe ... (text)'"

Introduction

All praise is to God. We praise Him, seek His help, and ask for forgiveness and guidance. We flee to Him from our sins and our wrong doings. He whom God guides will not go wrong, but he whom He leads astray will have no guide. I testify that there is no God but God alone and He has no partners (*Shariek*) and I testify that Muhammad was His slave and messenger. I believe that the saying in God's book is the best guide, the guidance of Muhammad. The most evil thing of all is to modernize these sayings. All modernizing is a fad and all fads are misleading. To be misled is to experience the fire of hell.

Jihad (struggle) in God's way, despite its extreme importance and the danger that its neglect bears upon the future of this religion, has been neglected and ignored by modern *Ulama* (men of learning). They have neglected it even though they know that it is the only way to return to and raise anew the glory of Islam. Every Muslim has gone his own way in his thoughts and philosophies. They have left the God-given way of *Jihad* which is the only source of honor for those who worship God.

There is no doubt that the ruthless traitors of this earth have only been eliminated by the power of the sword. Thus says the Prophet, "You gave me the sword to my hands until God alone is worshiped without partner. He let my success be under the shadow of my arrow, and He let all the defeated and the little ones be those who disputed my command and those who wanted to imitate a group of people. He is one of them. (A saying by Imam Ahmed quoting Ibn Amr and Ibn Rajab). In commenting on the saying of the Prophet regarding the sword, Imam Ahmed stated that God sent him with the sword proclaiming the unity of God. After he attempted explanation and argumentation and reconciliation, the people still did not believe, thus the use of the sword became necessary.

Hadiah in Mecca said that when the Messenger of God addressed the ruthless leaders of Mecca he said, "Listen to me, O people of Quraysh, or else by Him who has the breath of Muhammad in His hand I will come to you with slaughter." They took his word and there was no man among them who did not feel as if this were a bird falling on his head. Even the strongest said to one another, "Run, O Aba al-Kasim. By God, I was ignorant of what the Prophet meant when he said, 'I come to you with slaughter.'" When he was in Mecca, he showed the straight way in which there is no argument and no armistice with the leaders of infidelity and the leaders of corruption.

Islam is Coming

The establishment of the Islamic nation and the return to the caliphate is exactly what the Messenger of God preached. This is different from considering *jihad* to be merely one thing among many other things of God. *Jihad* is the duty of all Muslims and they should spare no efforts to execute this duty.

A) The Prophet said, "God showed me the earth so that I saw the east and the west and if I obey I will own what He showed me." (This was told by Abu Dawod and Ibn Majah and al-Tirmizi) This has not happened yet since there are countries which Muslims have not yet taken over. But this will happen when God wills it (*in shaa Allah*).

B) The Apostle said, "This matter shall be as clear as the difference between day and night. There will be no house in the cities or in the villages or among the Bedouins which this religion will not enter, either victoriously or by defeating those who object. God gives victory to those who accept Islam; defeat and humiliation will be the lot of the objecting infidels." (This was told by Ahmed and al-Tabrani who Hathmi called men of learning.)

C) In the book (*Al-Hadith Al-Sahih*) Ibn Qabeel said, "We were at the place of Abd Allah Ibn Amr Ibn al-As and he asked, 'Which of the two cities (Constantinople or Rome) is to be conquered first?' Abd Allah asked for an open box from which he took a book and he said, 'When we were with the Apostle of God there was a conversation going on and he was asked that very same question. The Apostle of God said, "The city of Heraclius, Constantinople, is to be conquered first."'" This was told by Ahmed and the Darami. (Rome is the capital of Italy today).

The conquest of the first city took place under the leadership of Muhammad al-Fateh al-Uthmani more than 800 years after the prediction by the Prophet. The conquest of the second city, God willing, will become a reality in the future. You will see the reality of his prediction though you may have to wait for it.

D) The prophecy will take effect in you when God wills it. He also takes it away when He wills. The same thing is true of the caliphate. It becomes yours if you wish, but when God takes it and renders it compulsory, it is what He wants it to be, and He can take it away altogether if He wishes. Also, the caliphate, like the prophecy, works in people by the Sunnah (tradition of the Prophet) and Islam meeting opposition on the earth, for which the dwellers of Heaven accept, but, O dwellers of the earth, be careful because Heaven can stop its blessings and the earth will not grow fruit. (Unknown author, but told by al-Hafiz al-Iraqi from the way of Ahmed who said this is true.) Corrupt rulers are finished and the king who forces his rule by coups rules our people against their wishes. The discussion regarding the good news of the return of Islam, which will occur in the present age after the Islamic awakening, prophesies a great future in the area of economics and agriculture.

Answer to Those Who Have Lost Hope

Some of those who have lost hope have responded to this good news by quoting the Prophet's saying through Ans, "Be patient. Until you meet your Lord, no time will come which will be better than the time before." I heard this from God's Prophet (peace be upon him). Al-Nazmezi said this is true. Thus they say, "No need to waste your efforts and time and dreams."

But remember the saying of the Prophet when he said, "My *Ummah* is a blessed Umma. You do not know which is better, its beginning or its end." This was told by Ibn Askor quoting Umr Ibn Athlan pointing to al-Sout who speaks well of him. Moreover, there is no contradiction between the two sayings since the speech of the Prophet was directed toward the companion generation until they meet their Lord; hence, the saying is not a general saying but a "specific general" case. The evidence to this is the saying of the *Mahdi* (Messiah) who will appear at the end of time and fill the earth with justice and blessings after it was filled with injustice and darkness.

God told some believers, "God praises those who believe and perform good deeds. They will multiply in the earth as He multiplied those before them. He will establish this religion which pleases Him and He will exchange their fear to worshiping Him in safety and they will not associate with Him another thing. God does not go back on His promise." May we ask Him, Who is so highly exalted, to make us one of those.

The Establishment of an Islamic State

This duty is denied by some Muslims and ignored by others despite the fact that the duty of establishing an Islamic state is so clear in the book of God, blessed and exalted is He. Thus God said, "Rule them by what God has revealed." And He also said, "If it is not ruled by what God revealed, these are infidels." And He also said (highly exalted may He be) in Surat al-Nour regarding the duty of Islamic rule, "*Sunnah* we brought down and imposed upon you." Thus, the imposition of the rule of God upon this earth is the duty of all Muslims. Consequently, the establishment of an Islamic state is the duty of all Muslims. If our duty cannot be fulfilled except by fighting, then it is our duty to fight.

All Muslims have agreed that the institution of the caliphate is a duty. The establishment of the caliphate presupposes the presence of a seed, the Islamic state. He who dies without giving his allegiance to the caliph dies in *jahiliyah* (pre-Islamic); thus, it is the duty of all Muslims to strive for the return of the caliphate so that he may not be under the condemnation of God's saying.

The Abode in Which We Live

We must ask ourselves, "Do we live in an Islamic state?" The mark of an Islamic state is Islamic rule. Abu Hanifa explained that the abode of Islam became the abode of infidels if three conditions are found:
1) Its laws are the laws of infidels
2) The safety of Muslims is in question
3) The proximity between Muslims and the abode of infidels becomes a source of danger and Muslims are unsafe

Also Imam Muhammad and Imam Abu Yusef, friends of Abu Hanifa, said that those who live in a society follow the rules of those who control it. So if the rules that control society are Islamic, it is the "abode of Islam," but if the rules that control society are not Islamic, it is *Dar al-Kafr* (abode of infidels). Shaykh al-Islam Ibn Taymiyya in the book of rulers, section 4 of the book of *Jihad* was asked about a town called Mar Dien which was ruled by Islamic rulers then taken over by people who ruled it by the rules of infidels, "is it *Dar al-Harb* (abode of war) or *Dar al-Islam* (abode of Islam)?" He answered, "It is neither *Dar al-Islam* nor *Dar al-Harb*. It is a third division in which the Muslim is treated as he deserves and the outsider is treated as he deserves." Truly we don't find contradiction between these sayings because Abu Hanifa and his friends didn't say its people were infidels because "peace to him who deserves peace and war to him who deserves war." The nation of Egypt is ruled by the laws of infidels despite the fact that the majority of its people are Muslims.

The Ruler Changes What God Has Revealed

The rules that control Muslims today are rules of infidels yet Muslims follow them. God says in Surat al-Ma'idah, "... whoso judgeth not by that which Allah hath revealed: such are disbelievers." (V:44) After the end of the caliphate in 1924 and the uprooting of Islamic laws from the land, the infidels substituted their own laws. This situation has become like the situation of the Tatars as is proven in Ibn Katheer's interpretation of the following text. Ibn Katheer said that anyone who deviates from the law of God denies God Himself because God's law is inclusive. He forbids evil and implements justice. Men who express other opinions and thoughts and did not support the shari'a of God are like the people of jahiliyah (pre-Islamic times), they rule in ignorance and in lies. They made up their opinions and thoughts on different matters. Indeed, this is the way the Tatars ruled their kingdom. Their king, Genghis Khan, gave the al-Yasiq which is an amalgam of rules taken from different law codes including Judaism, Christianity, the Islamic millet and others. Many of his rules were only mere whims which became law. Now they prefer this over and above the book of God and the tradition of His Apostle.

He who does this is an infidel and he must be fought until he returns to the rule of God and His Apostle. No one but him should rule — no more and no less. (Ibn Katheer, 2nd section, p. 67)

Today's rulers have increased the ways of infidelity. They have digressed from the Islamic faith to the point that there is no relation between what they say they are, and the way they rule.

Shaykh al-Islam Ibn Taymiyya in the book of al-Fatawi al-Kubra the section on Jihad p. 288, Chapter 4. All Muslims agree that following any religion other than Islam or any shari'a other than that of Muhammad is deemed kafir (infidel). Also, anyone who believes in some of the book, but not all of it is also kafir, as God said. Those who do not believe in God and His Apostle, those who make a division between God and His Apostle saying, "We believe in one, but not the other," and those who choose for themselves another way, those are infidels and punishment is prepared for all kafirs.

The rules of Islam today regarding "Ridda" (going out of) Islam

The rulers of this age are far from Islam. They grew up under imperialist rule, be it that of the Crusades, Communism or Zionism. They are Muslims in name only even though prayer and fasting are part of their daily life. The Sunnah has declared that the punishment of the murtadd (the backslider) is greater than the punishment of the kafir. For many reasons the murtadd is to be killed. His punishment differs from the punishment of the kafir in the matter of death in all the schools of Islamic laws like Hanifer, Malik and Ahmed. Thus, the belief of the people that the murtadd be killed is the teaching of Malik, Shafie and Ahmed. The murtadd is ineligible for inheritance, forbidden sexual intercourse; also, no one should eat from his sacrifice. Again this distinguishes him from the one who is already kafir and any other such rulers.

If the *ridda* of the *murtadd* is greater than the lack of faith of the infidel, it follows that the *ridda* from the *shari'a* is greater than the infidel. (Ibn Taymiyya, p. 293)

Sunnah decided that the *murtadd* punishment is greater than the punishment of *kafir* in many aspects: The *murtadd* is to be killed; he does not pay the jizya; he is not to enter into any covenant (*zimeh*) like the *kafir* (*trans*: This is repeated three times on the same page.)

Ibn Taymiyya also says on p. 281: Any group that does not abide by the Islamic *Shari'a*, even if disputed, must be killed by agreement of the Muslim members if there are two witnesses for this. If they do not pray five times a day, they will be beaten until they pray. If they do not give alms, fast in *Ramadan* and visit Mecca, they must be beaten until they do these things. They must be punished if they do not forbid debauchery, adultery, gambling, the drinking of wine or any of the actions associated with the backslider, (for example, failure to rule on matters of blood, money and honor and also failure to rule by the book of *Sunnah*); also if they fail to prevent evil and encourage good, fail to demand *jizya* from the infidels on peril of the sword, encourage rulings that are contrary to the book of the *Sunnah*, follow the *Salaf* by showing disbelief in the name of God and His texts or calling God's laws lies or doubting His power or doubting the rules of the people of God during the age of the caliphates (mainly the first four). After the attack upon the first Muslims, whether they were of the *Muhajereen* (immigrants) or *al-Ansar* (supporters), in all these matter God said, "Fight them until there is no sedition and all religion is God's alone." (VIII:39) God said, "Those who believe, follow God. Throw away what remains from *riba* (usury), if you believe. If you do not, wait for the war by God and His Apostle." These texts came to the people of al-Taa'if when they entered into Islam and held fast to prayers and fasting, but did not refrain from usury. As far as God was concerned, they were fighting Him and His Apostle until they gave up usury. Usury is the last evil which God forbade. If they were fighting God and His Apostle by not forbidding usury, how much worse it is to rebel against so many other important Islamic laws. Thus, they must be fought until all believe in Allah's religion.

The Muslim *Ulama* agreed that if a group of people transgressed some of the Islamic duties which are obvious and consistent, they must be fought. If they say the *Shahadetain* (two testimonies) but do not pray or give alms or fast in the month of Ramadan or visit the house of God (pilgrimage) or do not submit to the rule of the Book and the *Sunnah* or do not forbid debauchery, drinking of wine, illegal sex, stealing money without right, the practice of usury or gambling or do not wage *jihad* against the infidels or refuse to collect the *jizya* from the people of the book and neglect other Islamic laws, they are to be fought on these issues until they submit completely to the religion of Allah.

Comparison between the Tatar and the present rulers

1) It is obvious from the saying of Ibn Katheer in his interpretation of God's saying, "Do they want the rule of *jahilih*? What is better than God's rule for any people who are making rules." (p. 6 in his book). He does not distinguish between those who have departed from God's rule and the Tatars. The Tatars rules by al-Yasiq, a combination of Jewish laws, Christian laws, the Islamic *millet* and other codes, selected according to their whim. Without a doubt *al-Yasiq* is better than the rules established by the West which have no relation to Islam whatsoever.

2) In a question directed to Shaykh al-Islam ibn Taymiyya from a Muslim zealot, the questioner described this condition to the Imam saying, "Is it still important for us to fight those Tatars who come to the Levant time after time, who have testified with the *Shahada* and who are no longer infidels? Is it forcing Muslims to fight against their own army? And what about the members of their army who are men of learning in religious matters?"

What can be said about those who pretend to be Muslims and fight against Muslims? "Both of them are wicked, thus one should not fight with either of them." This is similar to the situation we have today. We shall explain later on, if God wills. (Fatawi al-Kubra, pp. 280-281, case 516.)

3) Ibn Taymiyya, in describing the Tatars, said, "They do not have safety in their nation. They were the most evil of all creation. A wicked hypocrite does not adopt Islam internally without showing it on the outside, but the Tatars are evil and makers of evil such as *al-Rafidah*, *al-Jahmiah* and *al-Itihariah*. These are the worst kind of people and most wicked. Despite their ability to go to Mecca from their countries, they did not go, although some of them prayed and fasted and gave alms." Isn't this what is happening today?

4) While they were fighting for their King Genghis Khan, they allowed anyone who followed their rules to become a Muslim, even if he was an infidel. Those who broke their rules became an enemy even if he was the best of Muslims. They did not fight for Islam and did not implement the *jizya*, but they made Muslims equal with Jews and Christians, even making them leaders in their ranks. (Al-Fatawi, p. 286)

Don't these pages reflect the characteristics of the rulers of today and those who surround them and blindly glorify them more than they glorify their maker?

5) On page 287 Shaykh al-Islam adds that insiders who surrounded Genghis Khan and praised him became, in their eyes, true Muslims. They considered themselves Muslims although they were fighting Muslims and taking their money and obeying every rule put down by their infidel King, al-Mushrik, (one who associates other things with God) who resembles Pharaoh or Nimrod. This was the greatest corruption on earth.

6) Ibn Taymiyya adds that he who entered into the *jahiliyah* (pre-Islamic) obedience and *Sunnat al-Kafr* (infidel laws) was their friend. But he who disobeyed and disagreed with them was their enemy even if he was one of the prophets of God. (p. 288)

7) Shaykh al-Islam speaks also regarding the time of the Tatars and says: "Their contemptible leader, who was called al-Rashid (the guided one), rules over these people and prefers the worst Muslims to the best of the people of the faith. Those who were qualified for power were those who were closer to corruption and uncleanness and disbelief in God and His Apostle. Infidels and Jewish hypocrites and atheists who pretended to accept the *shari'u* became high in his administration. Their minister, a deceptive, atheistic hypocrite, dared to say, "The Prophet accepted the religion of the Jews and the Christians. He did not deny them their rights and he did not call them to leave their religion and convert to Islam." As proof, this ignorant, devious man used the text that said, "Say, O infidels, I do not worship whom you worship and you do not worship whom I worship. I will not worship whom you worship and you will not worship whom I worship. You have your religion and I have mine." He declared that this text is not *mansukh* (canceled). (pp. 288-289, al-Fatawi al-Kubra.) Isn't this kind of Tatar like what we have today in the attempts at religious brotherhood and the ecumenical movements? Our present situation is worse than under the Tatars.

The Fatawi of Ibn Taymiyya is helpful today. Thus it is good for us to take some of the Fatawi by Ibn Taymiyya and apply them today. We talked before about the town of Mar Dien which the Tatars ruled by their laws. Ibn Taymiyya said of Mar Dien, "It is advised that if Muslims can use him and he can benefit them, then he should not leave, but stay and work as an inside man as it were. However, going forth in the *jihad* which God and His Apostle have made is better than volunteering in worship, prayer, pilgrimage, and fasting. God knows best.

Rules regarding their money

(Case 514) Question: If the Tatars entered the Levant and embezzled the money of Christians and Muslims and then the Muslims took the money back from the Tatars, it is right or wrong to take the money?

Answer: Everything that is taken from the Tatars is right to take and should be used.

On fighting the rulers

(Page 298, case 217) Ibn Taymiyya said, "Fighting the Tatars who came to the Levant is the duty of all Muslims because God said in the Qur'an, 'And fight them until persecution is no more, and religion is all for Allah.

(VIII:39)'" Religion is obedience. If part of the religion is God's and another part is not God's, fighting is a duty until all religion is God's. That is why God said: "You who believe, fear God, and end what is left of usury. If you believe but do not obey you are at war with God and His Apostle."

This text was revealed to Ahl al-Taa'if when they were newly converted to Islam. They prayed and fasted, but they refused to give up usury. Thus they were described as fighting God and His Apostle. If fighting them was necessary, how much more important it is to fight those who omit so many elements of the *shari'a* like the Tatars. All Muslim *ulama* have agreed that any group of people wo refuse to perform any of the obvious Islamic duties must be fought. If they recite the *shahada* but do not pray or fast or give alms or go on the pilgrimage or refuse to obey the rule of the book and the *Sunnah* or fail to forbid debauchery or the drinking of wine or having sex with other than their wives or taking advantage of people or their money without having a right to it or forbidding gambling or usury or failure to fight the infidels or failure to collect the *jizya* from the people of the book and so many other Islamic laws, then they must be fought until all religion is God's.

It is said that when Umar consulted Abu Bakr regarding those who refuse to pay the *zakat*, Abu Bakr said, "How could I not fight those who are omitting the duties which are set down by God and His Apostle. By God, if they refuse me as much as a camel's halter which they gave to the Apostle, I will fight them for refusing to give it to me."

Umar said, "It was not until that time that I saw how God had blessed Abu Bakr for fighting and then I knew it was the truth." It has been said in the *Saheeh* tradition, speaking to the Muslims concerning the *khawarja*, that "they pray like you, read the Qur'an like you and fast like you, but their reading does not go past their throats. Given half a chance they would desert Islam as fast as an arrow from a bow. Whenever you see them, fight them, for it is better to fight them now than on the day of the resurrection."

The *Salaf* and the *ulama* agree on fighting the *khawarja*. The first one to fight them was Ali Ibn Abi Taleb. Muslims continued to fight them in the time of the *Umayyad* and the *Abbasad Caliphates*. Rebellion against Islamic law is greater than refusing to pay the *zakat* and the *khawarja* (backsliding) of the Ahl al-Taa'if who refused to turn away from usury. Those who doubt the importance of fighting them are the most ignorant of all men regarding the religion of Islam. "When fighting proves necessary, we must do it even if we do not like it."

Is it wrong to fight them?

Ibn Taymiyya said on page 283 in the section on *Jihad*, "Some may think that these Tatars are just rebellious Muslims and that we should rule they are like those who refuse the *zakat*, like the *khawarja*, but we shall show the error of this thinking if God wills." Ibn Taymiyya said on page 296, "As the Prophet said in the traditions concerning martyrs: He who is killed while fighting for God without his money is a martyr; he who is killed while fighting for God without his blood is a martyr; he who is killed without his wife is a martyr.

How much more killing those corrupt backslidden people is neccesary. The killing of those attackers is fixed in the *Sunnah* and *Ijmaa*. Those attackers are attacking Muslims and their money and their women. This is the worst kind of oppression and yet they say that the Imam is communicating with them. They fight God and His Apostle; they are filling the earth with corruption. They are *khawarja* from Islam and yet they claim that to be better Muslims in knowledge and practice.

The rule of those who paid them homage against Muslims

Ibn Taymiyya said in page 291 (section on Jihad), "Everyone who runs to military leaders is ruled by their rules. Among them are backsliders from the laws of Islam. If the *Salaf* described as backsliders those who refuse to give alms, despite the fact that they fast and pray and do not fight Muslim groups, how much worse are these enemies of God and His Apostle who kill Muslims. Ibn Taymiyya also said on page 293, "By this we know that a Muslim who backslides is more wicked than the Turks who were infidels. When a Muslim backslides from some of the Islamic laws, he is in worse condition than those who did not enter into Islamic laws, whether he is a *Sufi*, a scholar, a merchant, a writer or any other of those wicked Turks who did not enter into Islamic *Shari'a* and insisted on infidelity. That is why Islam is more hurt by those than by a new convert who is led to Islam and its law and the obedience of God and His Apostle. Such converts are much greater than those who are halfhearted about obedience of Islamic laws and become hypocrites, putting on an appearance that they are religious and believe.

The rule regarding those who go out to fight in their ranks

Ibn Taymiyya, page 292 said, "A good Muslim should not willingly join those rulers who are Muslims in name only, those who are hypocrites, corrupt, and wicked. If he is forced to go out with them to fight, he must be true to his convictions. We must fight all soldiers without distinguishing between those who have been coerced to join the others. This should be a warning to those forcing them to go. Ibn Taymiyya warns those who force Muslims to join the ranks (pages 295, section on *Jihad*), "He who is forced to fight in a rebellion does not have to fight. He may destroy his weapon and patiently await an unjust death. A person who is forced to fight against Muslims on the side of dissenters from Islamic laws (like those who refuse to pay alms, backsliders, and others like them) should refuse to fight even if it means being killed by Muslims.''

Opinions and whims

But there are opinions in the Islamic world that omit the importance of *jihad* in the establishment of God's laws. Let us examine the accuracy of whims and opinions.

Charitable associations

There are some who say we should establish associations supported by the government which encourage people to pray and give *zakat* (alms) and do good works in general. Prayer and *zakat* and good works are things of God and we must not minimize the importance of them.

But if we ask ourselves, ''Will all these good works establish an Islamic nation?'', the answer has to be unequivocably, ''No!'' Moreover, the associations would belong to the present government and would be registered in its records and follow its rules, therefore they would be tainted by the current order.

Obedience, discipline and increase in worship

There are those who say we ought to get busy obeying God by encouraging the discipline of Muslims. They say we must be more active in worship since all the miserable conditions in which we live are the result of our sin; we are reaping what we have sown. In support of their argument, they normally quote the wisdom saying of Malik Ibn Denar when he said that God said, ''I am God, the King of Kings; the hearts of Kings are in my hand. Kings who obey me, I bless and kings who disobey me I curse. So do not worry yourselves about the kings, but repent and I will make them kind to you.''

Anyone who thinks that this wisdom has cancelled the duty of *jihad* is causing himself to perish and causing others who obey him to perish. Anyone who truly seeks the highest form of obedience and wants to reach the height of worship must begin the *jihad* in the way of God and must not ignore the other pillars of Islam, The Apostle of God described *jihad* as the highest glory of Islam and says, ''He who does not fight is dead as if he were in the pre-Islamic time (Jahiliyah).'' Thus the *Mujahid* in the way of God, Abd Allah Ibn al-Mubarak, said, ''Oh, servant of the two sacred places, if you were perceptive, you would have realized that you are playing with the emotions of Muslims who wet their cheeks with tears, and their tears later turned into blood.''

Others say that involvement in politics hardens the heart and diverts the person's attention from the things of God. Those who say that ignore the saying of the Prophet who said, "*Jihad* is preferable to living under the rule of a weak ruler." The truth must be said: Anyone who proclaims these opinions either does not understand Islam or he is a coward and does not want to stand firm in God's rule.

The establishment of an Islamic party

There are some who say we must establish an Islamic political party as one of the present parties. Truly this will increase the charitable associations, but this will be associated with politics. The purpose of *jihad* is to destroy the infidel government. Working through a political party will have the opposite result; it will help to build infidel nations. The party would be part of legislative committees which delegate without God.

On achieving high positions

There are some who say that Muslims must try to achieve high positions so that these positions will be filled by Muslim doctors, Muslim engineers. In this way, they claim, the present system will collapse without effort and a Muslim ruler will be put in place. When one hears these things for the first time, one thinks it to be mere imagination or a joke, however, there are many in the Islamic world who go along with this despite the fact that it has no support in the book and the *Sunnah*. Thus, this kind of thinking continues without facts to support it. No matter how many Muslim doctors and engineers we have, they are helping to strengthen the current system in our nation. In any case, no Muslim can reach a ministerial (cabinet) position unless he is loyal to the system. He would have to compromise his faith in order to reach such a position.

The "call" only

Some of them say that the way to establish an Islamic nation is only through the "call" and the establishment of a wide base of popular support. This does not establish the nation despite the fact that some have made this point the basis for their refusal of *jihad*. The truth is that those who can establish the nation are the believing minority, those who walk in the way of God and the tradition of the Prophet. The proof is in what God said, "Few are those who worship me with thankfulness." God also said, "There are many on the earth who will mislead you from the way of God." This is God's way (Sunnah) on His earth. Where will you find this majority? Remember that God said, "There are so many people if you take out the believers."

Islam does not care about large numbers. God said, "How many times a small group of people defeats large groups of people by the will of God." And

God said, "The day will come when you become proud of your number and you will need not anything else done and the earth will become small for you." The Prophet said, "God will serve your enemies and strengthen you." Then he said, "How few of us are apostles of God, but God's riches make up for our smallness."

How can this "call" succeed when all the media is under the control of infidels and corrupt people who are fighting the religion of God. The true endeavor is to liberate the media from their hands. As soon as victory comes we will see the answer of God for He said, "When the victory of God comes, you will see people enter the religion of God in large numbers."

Hence, our Lord answers those who say that the people have to be Muslim before they are receptive to the application of Islamic law. Anyone who believes or unconsciously thinks that Islam is incomplete or incapable of being self-sufficient is wrong because this good and wholesome religion is relevant and can be applied at any time and in any place and is capable of handling anyone: Muslims, infidels, the corrupt and the good, the knowledgeable and the ignorant. If people are happy to live under the rules of the infidels, how much happier they will be when they find themselves under the just rule of Islam.

Let me not be misunderstood. I do not mean that we should refrain from calling people into Islam. The basis of my argument is that we must take Islam as a whole. What I said above is in response to those who make their case to be the formation of wider support in the country in the place of *jihad*, thus stopping *jihad* altogether.

Flight

There are also those who say that the way to establish an Islamic nation is by fleeing to another country and establishing it there; then returning later as conquerors. To save their effort, they should first establish an Islamic nation in their own country and then go out of it conquering others. Is such a flight to another country legal or not? To answer this question, we should study the variety of flights in the *Sunnah*. In one of the interpretations, it is clear that flight to God and His Apostle is permissable; but flight to wordly possessions or a wife is not. Ibn Hajar said that flight, leaving one thing for another, in the *Shari'a*, is fleeing from what God has forbidden. In Islam, this happens in two ways:

First, fleeing from fear to safety as in the flight to Ethiopia and the beginning flight from Mecca to Medina.

Second, fleeing from the abode of infidelity to the abode of faith. This happened after the Prophet had established himself in Medina and Muslims went there to be with him. It is amazing that some say that they should go up to the mountain like Moses, then come down and meet Pharaoh — and God will destroy Pharaoh and his armies just as He did in Moses' case. All these fantasies only help to exclude the only right and legal method for establishing an Islamic nation! God said, "Warfare is ordained for you, though it is hateful unto you; but it may happen that ye hate a thing which is good for you, and it may happen that ye love a thing which is bad for you." (II:216) Again God said, "Fight them until sedition is no more, and religion is all for Allah." (VIII:39)

The diversion of knowledge seeking

There are those who say that the way forward now is by seeking knowledge. They ask, "How can we struggle without knowledge?" Seeking knowledge is a duty, but we do not hear anyone say we must neglect a legal command or a duty of Islam in order to pursue knowledge, especially if the duty is a serious one.

How can we learn the smallest and the most popular of all religious duties and call people to it and yet leave out the one that is made great by the Apostle of God? Why has *jihad* and the punishment for neglecting it slipped by those who have all knowledge and understand its depth and its width? Those who do not know what *jihad* is need to know that *jihad* is fighting. Because God said, "*jihad* is appointed to you." It is known that a man declared the two *shahadas* at the hand of the Apostle of God, then went into war and fought until he died. This was before he had a good knowledge of worship, but the Apostle of God declared that his small work had a much greater reward. He who learns of the duty of prayer, must pray. He who learns the duty of fasting, must fast. Also, he who learns the duty of *jihad*, must fight. Anyone who claims to be ignorant of *jihad* must know that the rules of Islam are easy to those who have good intentions. Thus, he must have good intentions in fighting in the way of God and after that the rules of *jihad* can be studied easily and in a short time. He who wants to get more knowledge over and above that of *jihad* can, for knowledge is available to everybody and it is not exclusive. There is no sole right upon knowledge, but to delay *jihad* for the sake of seeking knowledge is a false excuse. There have been men struggling since the time of the Prophet until recently and they were not *Ulama* (men of knowledge). God, through their struggle, opened and conquered many territories. They did not neglect *jihad* by using the excuse of seeking knowledge or the knowledge of *Hadith* (tradition) or the *Fiqh*' jurisprudence. At their hands God gave victory to Islam, victory that the *Ulama* of al-Azhar itself could not achieve when Napoleon and his soldiers entered into Al Azhar with horses and shoes. What good was all their knowledge in the presence of this humiliating experience?

So knowledge is not a sharp-edged sword which cuts off the heads of the infidels, but it is a sharp-edged sword that God mentioned when He said,

"Fight them. God will torment them at your hands and He will shame them and make you victorious and will heal the bruises of the believing ones." We are not belittling knowledge or men of knowledge (ulama). We believe in it, yet we do not use it as an excuse to forsake duties imposed by God.

The Islamic *Ummah* differs from other nations in their method of fighting. This is explained by God. In previous nations God brought down His torture upon infidels and enemies of His religion through nature's own rule — earthquakes, floods, and strong winds. This differs from Muhammad's *Ummah* for God spoke to them saying, "Fight them. God will torment them at your hands and He will shame them and make you victorious and will heal the bruises of believing ones." In other words, it is the duty of the Muslims first of all to carry out God's command by fighting. After this God will interfere by using the laws of nature. In this way, victory will be achieved at the hands of the believers of God.

Rebelling against the ruler

In the *Sahih* (tradition) Nawawi tells of an incident from the life of Ibn Abi Amia saying, "We entered into the presence of Ibn al-Samit while he was sick and we said to him, 'Tell us one of the sayings of the Prophet which would benefit people for God's sake which you heard from the Prophet of God.' And he said, 'The Prophet of God called us and we gave him our allegiance. After we gave him our allegiance, he told us, "If you have proof of infidelity, we must fight it."'" And the Nawawi quoted al-Qadi Aiad in explaining this saying. The *ulamas* agree that the office of the *Imamate* is not to be given to an infidel. If he becomes an infidel, he should be removed. He should also be removed if he forsakes the call to prayer or follows fads which stray from the true faith. Some say the *Imamate* should be given to such a person if he at least claims to be Muslim. The al-Qadi said, "If he becomes an infidel during his rule and changes the rule or follows a fad, he should be released from his duties as ruler and no one should obey him. It is then the duty of Muslims to turn against him and throw him out and install in his stead a just *Imam*, if they can do that." (Sahieh, Muslim—section *Jihad*. This section is also an answer to those who say fighting is impossible unless it is under the leadership of the caliph or *Amir*.) Ibn Taymiyya said that any group of people who broke one of the *Shari'a* of Islam, especially the clear-cut ones, must be fought. A'immat al-Muslimeen agreed with this statement—even if those groups declared the two *Shahadas*. (Section *Jihad*, page 281.)

The near enemy and the far ones

There is a saying that the battlefield of *jihad* today is the liberation of the Holy Land. The truth is that liberating the Holy Land is an important duty for all Muslims, but the Apostle of God described the believer as an intelligent being, i.e., one who knows what is beneficial and what is changeable and makes a decision. This needs explanation:

First, fighting an enemy who is nearby takes precedence over fighting an enemy who is far away.

Second, when a Muslim's blood is shed in order to achieve this victory, the question is: Is this victory beneficial to an Islamic state or is it beneficial to the present infidel order? In this case, a victory would strengthen the nation which is outside the laws of God. These rulers take advantage of the nationalist feelings of Muslims to achieve their purposes which are non-Islamic (even if its appearance is Islamic), so fighting must only be done under Islamic leadership.

Thirdly, the reason for the presence of imperialism in Islamic nations is precisely these rulers. So if we want to end imperialism, we must begin with these rulers. To fight the imperialist is a waste of time. We must begin with our Islamic country by establishing the rule of God in our nation and highly exalting the word of God. Thus, the first battlefield for *jihad* is the uprooting of these infidel leaders and replacing them with an Islamic system from which we can build.

An answer to those who say that jihad is for defense only

In this we respond to those who say that Islam was not spread by the sword and that *jihad* in Islam is for defense only. This is a faulty view which is frequently repeated by some prominent leaders in the Islamic world. The answer to this was given by the Apostle of God when asked, "Which *jihad* is in the way of God?" He said, "He who fights to make God's word to be the highest, he is fighting in the way of God." So fighting in Islam is to lift up high the word of God in the earth whether it is in defense or in attack. Islam expanded and spread by the sword and in the face of these leaders of infidelity who hid it from humankind and afterward they did not force anybody. It is the duty of all Muslims to raise their swords in the face of leaders who hide the truth and show evil, or otherwise the truth will not reach the hearts of people. Read with me the message of the Apostle of God to Heraclius which was told by Ibn Abbas in the Sahieh al-Bukhari: "In the name of God the Merciful, the Compassionate, from Muhammad the servant of God and His Apostle, to Heraclius the Great of Rome. Peace upon the followers of the right guidance. I call you with the call of Islam. Accept Islam and save yourself. God will give you a double reward. I call you. I also call the Arians. Oh people of the book, come without dispute to worship the one God without associating (sharak) with Him. We do not take Lords from among ourselves other than God and say we are Muslims." And we add the message of the Prophet to Chrosroes also. "In the name of God the Merciful, the Compassionate. From Muhammad the Apostle of God to Chrosroes the Great of Persia. Peace upon those who follow guidance and believe God and His Apostle and testify that there is no God but God alone without associates and that Muhammad is His servant and messenger. I call you in the name of God, for I am the messenger of God to all people warning all those living and telling the infidels to become Muslim in order that you may be saved. If you refuse, the sin of the *maji* rests upon you.'' (This was told by Ibn Hazier and quoted by Ibn Iskah.)

The Bayqi quoted the message of the Apostle of God to the people of Nijran this way: "In the name of the God of Abraham and Isaac and Jacob from Muhammad the prophet, the messenger of God, to the Bishop of Nijrah and the people of Nijrah, give yourselves up. For I am the praised one sent to you by the God of Abraham and Isaac and Jacob. I call you now from worship of the human to the worship of God; give Him your allegiance instead of giving your allegiance to a mere man. If you refuse this, you must pay the *jizya*. If you refuse the payment, I will have to go to war with you. Salaam.''

The Apostle of God sent similar messages to Makokas (Bishop of the Coptic church), the king of Yemen, al-Mondher Ibn Sawi the Great of Bahrain, al-Harith ibn Abi Shamr, al-Ghassani, al-Harith Ibn Abd Kalal al-Hamiri, and the King of Oman and others.

The text of "The Sword"

Most interpreters have touched on the text "The Sword" (*al-Saif*) in which God said, with the exception of the Holy month, to kill the *mushrikeen* (those who associate with God) wherever you find them. Spy on them, surround them, capture them. Al-Hafiz Ibn Kathir, in interpreting this text, quoted Al-dahhaak Ibn Mezaheim saying: "This text has cancelled all other covenants between the Prophet and all *mushrikeen*." Al-Ofi quoted Ibn Abbas saying in his text: "Since the appearance of this text none of the *mushrikeen* have any right of a covenant of protection."

Al-Hafiz Muhammad Ibn Ahmed Ibn Muhammad Ibn Jizy al-Kalbi, the author of *al-Tafsir al-Tashiel Leuloom al-Tanzeel* (*The Knowledge of the Revelation made Simple*) states, "Here we see what cancelled other texts that call for peaceful existence with infidels, forgiving them, and delaying injuring them and killing them." There is no need here to repeat all the texts that this one text has cancelled. Suffice it to say that in the Qur'an there are 114 texts in 54 Surah (chapters). They were all cancelled when God said, "Kill all those who associate with God wherever you find them. Fighting is appointed unto you."

Al-Hussein Ibn Fadel also commented on this text saying that it cancelled every text in the Qur'an that mentions other beliefs. How amazing it is to see some use these cancelled texts as proof to forsake fighting and *jihad*.

Al-Imam Abu Abd Allah Muhammad Ibn Hazim who died in the year 56 (AH) said regarding the *Naasikh wa mansukh* (which text cancelled which) in the section on forcing the *mushrikeen (those who associate with God), "The 114 texts in 48 Surahs* were all cancelled when God said, 'Fight the Mushrikeen wherever you find them.'" If God wills we shall mention this in context.

Al-Imam Muhaqqiq Abu al-Qasim Hibat Allah Ibn Salamah: "Fight the *mushrikeen* where you find them." The third text is the most important. It cancelled 114 texts of the Qur'an. Thus its end cancelled its beginning and God's saying if they repented and prayed and gave alms, leave them alone. (*Kitab al-Naasikh wa Mansukh*) (written and cancelled).

When you meet the infidels hit them in the necks

Both the Sadi and Al Dahak agree that the text of "The Sword" (*al-Saif*) is cancelled by the text that said, "When you meet the infidels hit their necks until you take hold of their noose and tighten it until they either seek redemption or are gotten rid of." This text is much harsher toward the *mushrikeen* than the text of "The Sword." I do not know of anyone who taught contrary to this other than al-Suyooty when he said in the book of agreement (*Al-Ittifaaq*), "When Muslims are a minority or weak, they should be patient and forgiving," thus cancelling the duty of fighting. The truth is that it is not cancelled, but belongs to *Mansiyaat* who forgot what God said, "... or we forgot it and what is forgotten is the command to fight until the Muslims become strong and in weakness the ruler must be patient in punishment." This weakens what others have taught. Others have said that what was revealed is similar to what is found in Surah al-Baqara when it said, "Forgive until God commands." This is not *Mansukh* (cancelled), but postponed. Despite al-Suyooty's difference with other interpretations, there is no doubt that the others are more accurate. Moreover, he is mistaken when he says that texts promoting peaceful co-existence and forgiveness are not cancelled and replaced by the two duties of *jihad* and the command to do good and refrain from evil; he is mistaken when he eliminates *jihad* as a duty. The Apostle of God says, "*Jihad* continues till the last day." Abd al-Wahab Khalef in his book, *The Origin of Jurisprudence*, page 227, explaining the meaning of "continues to the last day," states that it means that *jihad* will continue as long as this world remains. So to delay *jihad*, by using the excuse of the "forgotten" is not only stopping the attack (*ghazw*) but it also stops the intention of *ghazw*. The danger of this is seen in the saying of the Prophet, "He who does not attack (*yaghzw*) or he whose soul does not incline him to attack them, is dead as if he were in paganism (*jahiliyah*)."

What can be agreed upon here is that for Muslims to fight, they must have power—and this power will not come if we delay *jihad*. God said, "You must be prepared (see Onjad) to go out to fight and God will discourage your enemies." So if you do not go out, then you will not have the power. So he who stopped the duty of *jihad* also stopped the source of power for *jihad*. The Prophet says, "If any of you went astray after money (*dinariis* and *dirhams*) and left the *jihad* in the way of God and sinned, God will bring down plagues from Heaven and will not rescind them until you return to your religion."

The position of Muslims in relation to fighting

Muslim armies over the years have been small in number and they have normally faced armies many times their size. Some will protest by saying that this success was given only to the Prophet and his followers. The answer to this is that God's promise of victory is true as long as the heaven and the earth endure. It is helpful to look at what happened to Zahir al-Babr who faced the King of India (Dana Snimgy) and his army. Although he only had 10,000 and the Indian army was 200,000 strong, the Muslim leader was victorious after he refrained from drinking wine. There are many examples of such victories.

There are those who claim that we do not live in a Meccan society, settled like Mecca after the wars with the local pagans. If this is their license for forsaking *jihad* in the way of God, they should also forsake prayer and fasting and eat pork. Since usury (*riba*) was forbidden in Medina, that should also be forsaken. The truth is that Meccan society was at a time of expansion of the call, as God said, "Today I fulfilled your religion for you and I completed my grace and gave you Islam as a religion." This text had cancelled all other thoughts regarding the excuse of not living in a Meccan society. For we are not beginning where the Prophet began, we are picking up where he left off. We are not in a Meccan society, or Medinan community for that matter, but the society in which we live is actually backslidden.

Today fighting is the duty of every Muslim

When God commanded fasting he said, "Fasting was appointed to you." In the matter of fighting he said, "*Jihad* is appointed to you," in other words, fighting is a duty. There are those who say fighting is a duty, thus "If I do my duty of the 'call,' I have discharged my obligations for *jihad*. If I seek education, I am fighting in the way of God."

Let us go back to the text of *Hadith*. The purpose of the text is clear. *Jihad* is confronting your enemy and spilling his blood. The question here is: When does *jihad* become an absolute duty? *Jihad* is a duty on three different occasions:

1) When two armies face each other at the war zone, it is forbidden to retreat. The Prophet said, "O you who believe, if you meet those who have become infidels, do not let them go."

2) If the infidels come to a town, the inhabitants of that town must fight them and send them in retreat.

3) When the Imam calls on the people. God said, "O you who believe, when it is said to you to go in the way of God, do not refuse and do not prefer this life over eternal life. If you refuse, your torture will be great and God will raise someone else to take your place. He will not suffer, and God is able to do everything." The Apostle said, "When you are called, go."

Now, in Islamic countries, the enemy lives in our midst. The enemy is even in control; in fact, the enemy is those rulers who took over Islamic leadership, thus fighting them is an absolute duty. Moreover, the Islamic *jihad* today needs every drop of sweat of all Muslims.

Since *jihad* is an absolute duty, it is obvious that there is no need to get permission from one's parents to go out for *jihad* as one of the *Foqahaa* (law makers) says. *Jihad* is like prayer and fasting.

Jihad is divided into degrees, not stages

It is clear that *jihad* today is the duty of every Muslim, Despite this, we find some who say that *jihad* is self-discipline and that there are stages of *jihad*. We are still in the stage of personal *jihad*, they say, and they support their argument by the stages of *Jihad* listed by Imam Ibn 'al-Qayim'
1) The *jihad* of one's self
2) The *jihad* of Satan
3) The *jihad* of infidels and hypocrites

This argument indicates either complete ignorance or terrible cowardice, because Ibn al-Qayim divided *jihad* into degrees, not stages. If they are stages, we should stop fighting Satan until we finish the stage of fighting with ourselves. The truth is that all three are equal. We do not deny that the strongest in the faith among us who fights evil in himself is the most firm, but anyone who studies the life of the Prophet will find that when he called for *jihad* everybody responded in the way of God, even new converts and those who sinned.

It is said that a man became a Muslim during the fighting and died. The Apostle said of him, "He performed little, but gained much." In the story of Abu Mahjin al-Thaqafi, an alcoholic who was involved in the war with the Persians, he and Ibn al-Qayim heard the saying, "We entered the big *jihad* from the small *jihad*," and he asked, "What is the big *jihad*, O Apostle of God?" He responded, "*Jihad* with oneself." (*Hadith* subject, *al-Manar al-Maif*). This does not mean to belittle the *jihad* by the sword or divert the attention of Muslims from fighting infidels and hypocrites.

Fear of failure

There are those who say, "We fear the establishment of an Islamic nation because after a day or two there would be a reaction that would destroy everything we have done."

The answer to this is that by establishing an Islamic nation we are carrying out the command of God. We are not asked to produce results. Those who hide behind this excuse should realize that they are discouraging Muslims from performing their legal duty which is establishing the laws of God. They have forgotten that as soon as the infidel rulers fall, everything will be in the hands of the Muslims. Also, Islamic laws are not inept or weak in bringing into submission every corruptor in the land who departs from the rule of God. Moreover, the laws of God are just and will only find welcome, even from those who do not know Islam. To clarify the position of the hypocrites in this event and in order to comfort those who fear failure, here are the sayings of Surah al-Hajr (Exile), "Hast thou not observed those who are hypocrites, how they tell their brethren who disbelieve among the People of the Scripture: If ye are driven out, we surely will go out with you, and we will never obey anyone against you, and if ye are attacked we verily will help you. And Allah beareth witness that they verily are liars." (LIX:11)

This is the promise of God, and if the hypocrites see that power is on the side of Islam, they will return humbly. So, do not be deceived by these voices, they will quickly die down. The position of these hypocrites is that of all enemies of Islam. God says, "If you lift up God, He will lift you up and will strengthen your feet."

The leadership

There are those who complain because there is no leadership to lead on the road of *jihad*. There are those who relate *jihad* with the presence of *Amir* or *Caliph*. Those who are saying these things are the ones who lost the leadership and stopped the march of *jihad*. The Apostle calls Muslims to form leadership. Abu Dawood in the book of *jihad* quotes the Prophet to say, "If three people are going on a journey, one of them should lead." From this we see that Muslim leadership is in their hands and they have to produce it. The Prophet said, "If someone in a group pleases God, then he can lead them with the blessing of God, His apostles and the Muslim group." (This was told by al-Hakiem and al-Suyooty declared its accuracy.)

Thus leadership must go to the best Muslim. It should be given to the strongest; this is a relative matter. We can conclude that the leader of Muslims can be produced by them. We should not use the lack of leadership as an excuse. We may find a man of knowledge in Islamic laws but he may be out of date in relation to modern leadership and we may find the opposite, but all this does not excuse us from finding leadership through the *Shuri* system (consultation). Anything that is incomplete can be completed. Now we have no excuse for any Muslim to forsake his duty of *jihad*. We must begin to spend every effort to organize the *jihad* to return Islam to this nation and establish the *Ummah* and uproot the oppressors who have not found anyone to convince them of the command of God.

Submission to fighting and death

Al-Bukhari tells the story of Salmah when he said, "I submitted to the Prophet, then I looked at the shadow of the tree when all the crowd had gone. The Prophet said to me, 'O son of al-Akwaa, will you not submit?' I said, 'I submit, O prophet of God ...' He asked again, so I submitted to him a second time. I said to him, 'O Aba Selmah, on what did you submit?' Then he said, 'We submitted to death.' " This was also written by Muslim. Also, when someone came to Abd Allah Ibn Zayd saying, "Ibn Hanzalah makes people submit unto death," Ibn Zayd said, "I don't submit to anyone except the Apostle of God." (*Muslim fi 'l-Ain* page 15 and *al-Habqy*.)

The above story shows the importance of submitting till death, but we can not study here the position of Abd Allah Ibn Zayd. There is a difference between submission to death and absolute submission to the Caliph only. This does not mean that the *Amir* of a group is not to be obeyed. For the Apostle of God said, "He who obeys me, obeys God and he who disobeys me, disobeys God. He who obeys the *Amir*, obeys me, and he who disobeys the *Amir*, disobeys me." (agreed upon)

Also Ibn Abbas commenting on God's saying stated, "Obey God and the Apostle and those who are above you." (This was sent down by God.)

The exhortation to fight in the way of God

Muslims must not prepare themselves to fight except in the way of God. The Apostle said, "He does not remember anyone who went out except in the way of God and believing in me and witnessing to my apostleship for he will guarantee that I will enter paradise or I will return him to his home with booty." Also the Prophet said, "He who genuinely desires martyrdom, God will give him the honor of being a martyr, even if he dies in his bed." Muslim and Bukhari quoting Abu Hurayra said, "A man came to the Apostle of God and said, 'Tell me about any work that is equal to *jihad*.' The Apostle said, 'Nothing is equal to *jihad*.' The man repeated, 'Are you able to tell me?' 'If the fighter (*mujahid*) can go out and enter his mosque and pray without ceasing and fast without breaking his fast.' And he said, 'But who can do that?' " Abu Hurayra said, "The reward of the *mujahid* (fighter) is untold." (This was told in *al-Bukhari*)

The Apostle also said, "The martyr has six rewards in God's sight. His sins will be among the first to be forgiven and he will be given a seat in Paradise. He will avoid the torment of the tomb. He will be calm during the cataclysmic event. He will wear the suit of faith. He will marry the beautiful eyed women. He will intercede on behalf of 70 of his relatives."

The punishment for forsaking jihad

Forsaking *jihad* is the reason why Muslims today are suffering humiliation and are divided and torn. They indeed prove the saying of God,

> "O ye who believe! What aileth you that when it is said unto you: Go forth in the way of Allah, ye are bowed down to the ground with heaviness. Take ye pleasure in the life of the world rather than in the Hereafter? The comfort of the life of the world is but little in comparison with that in the Hereafter. If ye go not forth He will afflict you with a painful doom, and will choose instead of you a folk other than you. Ye cannot harm Him at all. Allah is Able to do all things. Surah IX:38,39.

Ibn Kathier said commenting on this text that this is God's warning to those who stayed back when the Prophet attacked Tabouk. When he waited in the heat so that the fruit became ripe in the heat, God threatened those who forsook *jihad* saying, "Unless you go, God will punish you with pain." Bn Abbas said God punished them, indeed.

The Prophet said, "If people loved money and forsook *jihad* in the way of God, the Heavens will pour plagues on them that will not be stopped till they return to their religion. It is not right for Muslim men to be satisfied to stay behind with the women."

There are others who are afraid of going into battle reasoning that among those who will face him are Muslims as well as infidels. They ask, "How can we fight Muslims when the Apostle of God said, 'The killer and the killed will go to hell.'?" Shaykh al-Islam Ibn Taymiyya discusses this in one of the significant questions on page 517. He answered those who refused to fight the Tatars because some Muslims were forced to fight with the Tatars. He answered that anyone who doubted fighting them is ignorant of Islam since fighting is their duty. And if there were among them those who were forced against their will, then they can say what al-Abbas said when was taken prisoner at the War of Badr, "O Apostle of God, I went out against my will." The Apostle replied, "Your outward appearance is ours, but your secrets are with God." The *Ulama* agreed that fighting the armies of the infidels is correct even if they hide behind Muslim soldiers in order to stop Muslim soldiers. As for the Muslims who are fighting with the other side, do not fear their fate because the *Ulama* have said that if they get killed they will be martyrs. *Jihad* must not be forsaken even if Muslims may also die during the killing of the infidels.

In the *Sahihain* it is written that the Prophet said, "When an army attacked it was said, 'O Apostle of God, among them are some who have been forced against their will.' They will be judged according to their intention. If any among those armies who attack Muslims are fighting against them they will have much more torment. God will torment them at the hands of the Muslims even as God himself said, ... we shall wait till God touches you from above or else at our hands.' " We know that it is difficult to distinguish between those who are fighting willingly and those who are fighting against their will. If we fight them in the name of God we are excused and if any of them are killed because they couldn't refuse them, their good intention will be revealed in the day of judgment. If he is killed while fighting with the infidels, he is not greater than the Muslim soldier who fought for the establishment of the religion. But if any of them escape, then those who are killed are guilty. If they have a whole battalion who refuse to fight, is it right to follow their leader and kill the persons and their wounded? According to two famous sayings by the *Ulama*, that must not be done.

The accurate view is that these people are not guilty because they are not infidels but rather they are *Khawarj* who refuse to give alms and *Ahl al-Taa'if* who were fought because of their departure from Islamic dogma.

The method of fighting

With modernization and the development of man since the time of the Prophet the methods of fighting today are different from the time of the Prophet, what is the proper method of fighting in the modern day? And does one have to use his imagination and mind?

The art of fighting in Islam

It is said that "war is a trick." The Nawawi also said that it is agreed among the *Ulama* that deceiving the infidels in war is right and deception without contradicting covenants is impossible. It is a fact that there is no true covenant between us and them since they are fighters of God's religion. Therefore, Muslims are free to choose any means they wish to fight in their aim of fulfilling the deception. It is the means of victory with a minimum of loss.

Methods of fighting in conquering the parties (Ghazw al-Ahzab)

After the leaders of the Jews were successful in turning the infidel parties against the Prophet and his call and the situation became dangerous, the Muslims quickly formulated a plan which was so unique that most Arabs had never heard of it before, for they only knew the open fields of war. Al-Farsi said that the Muslims dug a deep trench around the city, so methods of fighting are not inspired or fixed, but Muslims have to use their minds and plan and consult.

Lying to the enemies

Lying is permissible in three areas according to the *Hadith*. Al-Tabari said that lying is permissible in war. This is prudent in your fight against God's enemies. God knows best. (Nawawi's interpretation).

Islamic strategy

From studying secret plans, Muslims created strictly Islamic plans and continuous tricks which became effective and binding upon many Muslims, for example:

1) The secret of the assassination of Kaab Ibn al-Ashraf in the third year (AH): In the *Sahieh al-Boukhari*, Gaber Ibn Abd Allah reported that the Prophet said, "He who supports Kaab Ibn al-Ashraf is hurting God and his Apostle." Then Muhammad Ibn Muslimah said, "Do you want me to kill him, O messenger of God?" The apostle said, "Yes." Then he said, "Allow me to say one thing, that is, to say words that make me appear to be one of the infidels." The Apostle gave him permission and he did speak words contrary to the faith in order to trick Kaab Ibn al-Ashraf. The message here is that it is possible for a Muslim to appear as if he is submitting to the enemy in war even if he appears to associate with God (*sharak*) and infidelity.

(*trans.* Here the author gives a long and complicated story on how Muhammad Ibn Muslinah deceived Kaab Ibn al-Ashraf and killed him.)

From this story we have many useful lessons in the art of fighting and killing. The orientalists have described the killing of Kaab Ibn al-Ashraf to be deception and trickery, but this infidel went to hunt the Muslims. The Jews came to Muhammad after the killing of Kaab Ibn al-Ashraf and said, "O Muhammad, one of our gentry was killed innocently last night," and the Prophet said, "Had he followed us as others have, he would not have been assassinated, but he was hunting us and causing us grief." (page 71 *Al-Sarim al-Masloul ala Shutaa'im al-Rasoul* by Ibn Taymiyya)

2) The secret of Abd Allah to Abu Sufyan in the fourth year (AH): The reason for this assassination was that the Prophet was told that Shaban Ibn Khaled al-Hadhli, living in Yaamor, was gathering crowds to fight the Muslims. The Prophet ordered Abd Allah Ibn Anies al-Jehani to kill him.

(*trans.* Again the author tells of how al-Jehani hid in order to kill this man in the most gruesome way.)

This kind of lying is not forbidden.

3) The story of Naim Ibn Messoud in the attacking of the parties (Ghazw al-Ahzab)

(*trans.* In this story the author explains how and where a Jew was converted to Islam and was told to keep his conversion a secret until they destroyed the Jewish tribe of Banu Quraiza).

Here is an important point: Ibn Taymiyya said that it permissible for a Muslim to infiltrate the ranks of the infidels and appear to be one of them. He can do so without it bothering his conscience if it is to the advantage of the Muslims. (page 296, Section on *Jihad*, Ibn Taymiyya)

Muslim tells the story of Ashab al-Akhdoud, the prophet in the *Sahieh*. In it we hear of the boy who killed himself for the benefit of the religion. And thus, the four major schools of Islam made it permissible for a Muslim to infiltrate the ranks of the infidels. If he sees that they have discovered him and will kill him, it is fine if it will bring benefit to the Muslims. The point of these words by Ibn Taymiyya is that infiltration of the infidels by Muslims is permissible even if his death comes before he sees the benefits for himself.

The "call" before fighting

Concerning permission to attack without notice those infidels who have received the call to Islam, Al Imam Muslim told about Ibn Adi saying: "I wrote to Nafi' to question him regarding the call before fighting and he wrote to me saying that in the beginning of Islam, the Apostle of God raided Banu al-Mustahiq while their camels were drinking water. They killed some and took others."

Explanation: Al-Nawawi said, regarding this incident, that this means it is right to raid without warning the infidels who have received the call to Islam. Concerning the legality of such action, there are three positions described by the al-Mazy al-Qadi. One said that they should be very clearly warned. This was the position of Malik and others. This is a weak position. The second is: No warning should be given at all. This position is weaker or even false. The third said a warning is permissible if they did not receive the call and is not permissible if they received the call but did not respond. This view is preferable and accurate and is supported by the following: Nafi'a Moli Ibn Umr, Hasan al-Basri, al-Thauri, al-Laith, al-Shafi'i, Ibn-Thawr, Ibn al-Mondher and al-Jomhou. Ibn al-Mondher said that this is the most intelligent, enlightened position.

There was a saying told by Ibn Abbas regarding al-Saib Ibn Jethhamah's conversation with the Apostle. He asked, "What should we do with the women and children of the infidels who are killed in these raids?" The Apostle of God said, "Since the rules of their party brought this punishment upon them, they should be permitted to live by their own rules, not Muslim laws." (Quoted from Muslim by Hanomi in the *Jihad* section.)

Ibn Amr said: "The Apostle of God was passing by and found a woman who had been killed in one of the Apostle's raids and he ordered an end to the killing of women and children." Ahmed and Abu Dawod tell of one of the Apostle's raids. They saw a woman killed in the raid and they stood looking at her and her features. The Apostle asked who killed her. They said, "Khalid." The Apostle said, "Tell him not to kill children or the weak."

These two different *Hadiths* are not contradictory to one another since each case is different.

Seeking the help of Mushrikeen

Aishah (one of the wives of the Prophet) said that once when the Apostle of God was in need a man came up to him to help him and the Apostle asked him, "Do you believe in God and his Apostle?" The man said, "No." The Apostle said, "Go back. I can't receive the help of a *mushrik*." Then he came after him again and the same conversation took place. Then it happened for the third time, but this time the man said, "Yes." So the Apostle let him help (told by Muslim).

Al-Nawawi said that there was another *Hadith* stating that the Prophet sought the help of Sufyan Ibn Umayyah before he embraced Islam. So, a group of *Ulama* took the first *Hadith* as authoritative and al-Shafi'i and others said that if the infidel has a good opinion about Muslims and you need his help, then seek his help or else force him to help.

These above two *Hadiths* give two different situations and the major schools in Islam have fallen into these two categories. For example, Malik said you can use them if they are servants of Muslims. Abu Hanifa said that they can be used only if Islam had the upper hand. Al-Shafi'i permit it only on two occasions (1) when Muslims are in the minority, and (2) when the *mushrikeen* have good intentions toward Islam. They would be given fixed wages and are not to share with the Muslims in the booty.

Cutting the infidel's trees and burning them

Al-Imam Ibn Muslim told about Nafi' who said Abd Allah Ibn Amr reported the Apostle of God burned the palm tree of Banu al-Nadeer. Then a word came from God saying, "Whether you cut down a man's livelihood or leave it in its place, God will shame the corrupt at your hand." (section 12, Muslim Shah al-Nawawi.)

Al-Nawawi said in explaining this that it is permissible to cut down the tree of infidels and burn them.

(*trans.* The author, quoting Abu Hurayra, gives a long and complicated story explaining the example of the Prophet's lack of hesitation in killing and destroying their livelihood since they were infidels.)

The order of Islamic army according to Ahmed and al-Bukhari and Abu Dawoud

According to Amr Ibn Yaser, "The Apostle of God preferred that a man should fight under the banner of his group." (told by Ahmed)

According to al-Baraa Ibn Azib, the Apostle of God said, "You shall face the enemy tomorrow. Your slogan should be ... they must not be victorious!" (told by Ahmed)

According to al-Hassan who quoted Qais Ibn Ayad who said, "The friends of the Apostle of God hated noise during the fighting." (told by Abu Dawoud)

According to Kaab Ibn Malik, "The Prophet went out on a Thursday to conquer Tabouk and he was supposed to go out on a Thursday." (agreed upon)

According to al-Nu'maan Ibn Magraan, "The Prophet would fight from the break of day to its end, when the sun sets and the wind blows and victory comes." (told by Ahmed and Abu Dawoud and supported by al-Bukhari who also said, "Wait until the wind blows and the attendance of prayer.") (Prayer for victory is a must when you face your enemies in battle.)

This is one of the Prophet's prayers for victory: "o God, who sent down the book (the Qur'an) and moves the clouds and is the defeater of the parties, defeat them and give us the victory over them." (Sahieh, Muslim)

An important matter to which we must be alert:

Sincerity in *jihad* in the way of God. Sincerity means the emptying of oneself from all foreign or ulterior motives, bringing one closer to God. It is said that if one wants to forget the creation, one must constantly direct his attention to the creator.

In the section on the devil's interference in the battle, Imam Ibn al-Jawzi said, "The devil came upon many people, so they went out to fight. Their intention was hyprocrisy and pride so that people can say that so-and-so is a conqueror. Or maybe their intention was that they want people to dub them courageous or perhaps they were seeking booty. But action is dependant on intention."

Abu Mosa said that a man came to the Prophet and said, "O apostle of God, have you seen the man who was fighting so courageously, even fighting his in-laws and fighting usury? Which conflict (with in-laws or against usury) is fighting in the way of God?" The Apostle of God answered him, "He who fights in order to make the word of God high above everything else, he fights in the way of God."

It was said by Ibn Mas'oud, "Don't you dare say so-and-so died a martyr, for the man who fights for personal gain or fights in order that he may be remembered or fights to make himself a place is not a martyr." This was supported by Abu Hurayra when he said, "There are three types of people who will be judged first in the day of the resurrection:

First—one who died will be brought forward and asked about a certain blessing. He will say, "I have a hand in this blessing and fought for it until I died." Then he will be told that he is lying because he actually fought so that people would say that he is courageous. And they said so. Then he will fall on his face and be thrown into the fire.

Second—a man of learning who had knowledge and read the Qur'an. He will be brought forward and asked to identify a blessing and he will do so. Then he will be asked, "What was your part in it?" He will answer, "I taught it and I have read the Qur'an." Then it will be said, "You are lying, for you have read the Qur'an so that you may parade your knowledge and people would say you are learned." And they said so. Then he will fall on his face and be thrown into the fire.

Third—God was good to him and gave him all kinds of material riches. He will be brought forward and asked to identify a blessing that he had. Then he will be asked, "What is your part in it?" He will say, "I spent it in all kinds of charities." Then it will be said, "You are lying because you did all these things so that you would be called a charitable and kind man." And this was said of him. Then he will fall on his face and be thrown into the fire. (This was produced by Muslim.)

Here is supportive evidence by Abu Hatem al-Razi who said, "I have heard Abd Allah Ibn Sulayman say: 'We were in a battalion with Abd Allah Ibn al-Mubarak in the Roman countries and we faced the enemy. When the two armies faced each other, one of the enemy's men came forward and challenged one of our number to face him in a sword duel and one of us went out and fought him, stabbed him and killed him. Then there was another, but this second man (of the enemy's camp) killed the man from our ranks.

'The people crowded around him and I was one of those who crowded around him. He was lying down, covering his face. I stretched him out to identify who he was; it was Abd Allah Ibn al-Mubarak. I said, "You, O Aba Amru, look and see how this sincere and faithful one, how he sought not the praise of people; see his faithfulness and praise him for covering his face."

Ibrahim Ibn Adham fought yet never took his share of the booty. The fighter who fights for booty is demon possessed. Because he may take some of the booty which is not his. He may see the goods of infidels and, if he has knowledge, he knows that he is allowed to take it, but what he may not know is that greed for booty is sin.

In the *Sahiehain*, the *Hadith* of Abu Hurayra said, "We went out with the Apostle of God to 'Khaybar' and God gave us victory. We did not have gold in our booty, only food and clothing. Then we went to the valley with the Apostle of God. He had his slave with him who took some booty for himself, then died. We said, 'Blessings be upon him the martyred, O Apostle of God.' The Prophet said, 'By Him who has Muhammad's breath in His hand, the fire of what he took will continue burning, either a share of fire or two shares of fire.'"

It is possible that the invader knows what is forbidden, but he sees the booty and is not patient enough. Or he may think fighting will absolve his action. Here we see the effect of faith and knowledge. We have mentioned before, with supporting evidence, how Hurayra Ibn al-Ashaf told of Abu Abedah al-Anbari saying: "The Muslims came down and gathered the Copts together who were with him and asked him, 'Did you take anything from them?' He said, 'I would not have brought them to you.' They knew that he was someone of importance. They asked him, 'Who are you?' He said, 'If I told you, you would praise me and you would be persuaded to help.' They followed him and then they knew that he was Amer Ibn Abd al-Qais."

There are those who should be kept from the way

There are those who love comfort and ease and despise hard work and pain. This is their motivation, like the Qur'an tells of the disputers in Surah al-Tauhah when God said of them,

> "Those who were left behind rejoiced at sitting still behind the messenger of Allah, and were averse to striving with their wealth and their lives in Allah's way. And they said: Go not forth in the heat! Say: The heat of hell is more intense of heat, if they but understood.
> (Surah IX:81)

"They have an example regarding the weakness of their consciences and the softness of their wills. Many of them try to escape from effort and run away from hard work and prefer cheap comfort to honorable work. They prefer humbling security to the danger which is dear. They fall sick behind the lines of those who march forward knowing the cost of their call. Those lines continue in the road which is full of difficulties and thorns. They will not give up because they know that fighting difficulties is part of man's nature and it is much more enjoyable than sitting down in lazy comfort." In the Qur'an it is said, "Those who chose comfort over hard work in the hour of difficulty and missed the march even once, they are not useful in fighting and should not be included in the fight. They should not have the privilege of *jihad*. If God returns you to one of these groups and they ask your permission to go out (for *jihad*) say, 'You will never go to fight on my side. You have refused to go the first time. This time then, you stay with the hopeless!'"

The call needs straightforward, solid characters willing to count the cost in the long struggle. The line which will be infiltrated by the weak and the uncertain will not last because they will let them down in the time of desperate need. They should live in the state of humiliation and weakness. They should be sent far away from the front line lest they come back. To forgive them is suicide to the entire line.

Fatawi al-Fuqahaa regarding the purification of the front line.

The *Salaf* has a great deal to say regarding this matter.

The first is by Imam al-Shafi'i in his book in which we find continuous incidents regarding the sharing (or lack of it) of profit from the conquests and a warning to anyone who tries to become famous in subsequent generations of Muslims. The description of such people should be considered a yardstick by which we measure the standards of today's leaders and punish them in the way outlined in this book.

Al-Shafi'i says, "The Apostle of God raided and those who feared the cost of fighting escaped and thus he was defeated at the war of 'Uhud.' Three hundred of them left him. Then they stood with him in the day of al-Khandaq and spoke of what God said of them, saying, 'We have promised God and his Apostle only deception.' Then the Prophet raided Banu al-Mustaliq and they saw him and spoke of what God called hypocrisy. Then he raided Tabok and a group of them wanted to kill him, but God saved him. Others stayed behind. Then God commanded the raid of Tabok and he said if they would go out (to fight) do not take them, for God hated their halfheartedness. They were crossed out and stayed behind with the retreaters."

Al-Shafi'i said God revealed to his Prophet their secret and he told them that since they do not have good intentions they will stay behind. Ever since it has become known that anyone who does not fight with the Muslims is to be forbidden fellowship for he is a harm to them.

Al-Shafi'i said, "It is not allowed for the Imam to call such people for war because of their sedition. He should bring them low and shame them. Also, they could increase in number by influencing their friends and relatives—and that is dangerous." (Al-Shafi'i 4:89)

The Fiqh continued on this teaching until Ibn Qudamah al-Moqaddes who said, "The Amir is to force people into battle and hardship—even those who say the heat of summer or the cold of winter is too much and this or that hardship is too much. He is the one who said, "The secret of the Muslims has been betrayed. They do not have food or energy, but the infidels have energy and patience. There are spies from the infidels who have been appointed to spy on the Muslims to discover news, strategy and leaders. There are Muslims who are helping those spies. They are creating enmity between Muslims and spreading corruption. True Muslims should not accomodate these spies and should shun anyone who creates enmity. As God said, 'God hates their going forward (to battle)' thus they should stay with those who are left behind. If they go out with you, they will hamper you and create division among you. They are harmful to Muslims, thus they should be stopped." (Mughni, Ibn Qudamah 8:301)

The conceit of Faqieh forbids his leadership

In the Fiqh of Umar Ibn Abd al-Aziz we find permission to put away a leader who loves appearance and is conceited. This is for his own protection and especially to protect the reputation of the call.

It is said that when Rashid V became Caliph he sent to Abu Abd al-Mazgi whom he trusted. There were elders from Awza'i and Malik and others of the Caliphate's aides. Umar said to him, "This is the way to Palestine and you are from there and you are qualified for it." (presumably the governorship) He said to him, "O Amir al-Moumeneen (Caliph), if you saw Abu Ubaid, consult him." And the Caliph said, "True, he is more deserving, but he is arrogant." (Tahdhieb al-Tahdhieb 11:158)

To the leaders of islamic groups this day: kill every leader who looks for fame, wealth, power and social station like Umar Said to Abu Ubaid.

They understand who would only know leadership thus. You have lost your way in reaching your goal, so you passed by the house of those who advocate the call and humility and sacrifice and strategy. This is the road to leadership and such persons deserve leadership.

APPENDIX II

Postscript

Since this book went into print, a most dramatic and unexpected turn of events has taken place in regard to the pending court case that are discussed in the book.

The Egyptian government-controlled newspapers recently announced that the government case against the organization named "Al-Jihad" has been dropped without any explanation. But it was not until the opposition newspapers began to raise questions that the president of the country made mention of his matter in an interview with the "Magala" magazine (interestingly enough in Germany) which was then reported in detail in the three government newspapers on Friday the 2nd of November 1984.

When the interviewer asked President Mubarak a question regarding why the government dropped its case against this group, the president asserted that the government has never interfered in the case in any shape or form. This was a matter of the court's decision without the interference of the government. He added that this was a matter of the judge's conscience.

The question that is on the mind of the man on the street still remained unanswered: how and why the court dropped a case that was open and shut— against an organization that, according to the prosecutor's record, plotted to overthrow the government?

Al Ahram newspaper dated Saturday the 3rd of November, quoted the report by Judge Abed Al Ghafar Mohamed, Chief Justice of Egypt's Supreme Court, giving the reasons for the court's judgment.

This report, said the newspaper, is contained in a 677-page ruling on the trial. The newspaper gave only a portion of this report, in which the court accused the nation's security forces of having tortured more than half of the 281 moslem fundamentalist who belonged to "Al-Jihad."

Al Ahram said the report called for a prompt inquiry to identify individuals responsible for torture. "Contrary to the Middle Ages," said the report "torture to extract confessions is unacceptable in modern times."

On September 30, 1984, the court gave many defendants sentences that were considered lenient—and acquitted more than half of those accused of murder, attempted murder, and attempting to overthrow the government of Egypt.

While the state prosecutors had demanded the death penalty for nearly all of the accused, the court sentenced 16 defendants to life imprisonment with hard labor, 89 to terms of between 3 and 15 years with hard labor, and 2 to 2-year terms. The court acquitted 174. Initially, 302 people were accused in the case, but 2 died before the trial began and 19 were never apprehended.

Al Ahram reported that the court was lenient partly because of the torture, "It is established beyond doubt that security authorities subjected the majority of the defendants to physical abuse, causing serious injuries, some of which required treatment in hospitals," the newspaper quoted the court document as stating.

The court report also accused the sucurity police of incompetence in failing to detect the existence of the extremist group, known as "Al Jihad when it was established in 1980.

The ruling is significant in at least two ways:

First:

It is the first time that the judiciary, or any branch of government for that matter, has publicly accused the most powerful segment of the government apparatus (the state security) of abuse. This apparatus was organized and empowered by the state under the nasser regime, and continues to serve the government well.

Second:

While the official reason for throwing the case out of court is "torture," the most common speculation is that the Islamic extremist group is so powerful and widespread that both the government and the court do not want to jeopardize their safety and what appears to be the government efforts to establish a genuine democracy.

The most important development in all this, however—and indeed the most telling—is the demonstration by the released prisoners outside the prison immediately after their release. According to an eyewitness account, the demonstration was filled with enthusiasm and slogans such as "Islamic revolution is comming..." This no doubt opens a new chapter, which will occupy a future volume.

GLOSSARY

Ahl al-dhimmah: a follower of a religion tolerated by Islam, i.e., Christianity and Judaism.

Amir: literally prince, in this usage a leader in religious terms.

Al-Amir al-Aam: the head leader.

Caliph: a successor of the Prophet.

Copts: the Christian minority in Egypt.

al-Da'wah: the call

Dar al-Harb: House of War

Dar al-Islam: House of Islam

Fajir: dawn

Fatwa pl. Fatawi: legal casuistry.

Fedan: about an acre.

Felaheen: peasants

Fiqh: in the first instance, jurisprudence, but may be regarded as the entire set of rules derived from the shari'a.

Ghazye: conqueror

Grand Mufti: highest religious authority in a nation.

Hadith: normally translated as "tradition," but in actuality a report of some activity or saying of the Prophet.

Hajj: pilgrimage

Hashemites: one of the two clans of the tribe of Quraysh (Muhammad's own tribe and clan).

Hizb: a party, normally a political party.

Ijmaa: the consensus of the community as the basis for a legal pronouncement.

Ijtihad: individual, (as opposed to divine) interpretation of legal precept.

Imams: among Sunnis, the leader of the congregation in prayer, and by extension of the Muslim community. Among Shi'ia, the spiritual successors of Muhammad and the proper leaders of the umma.

al-Iqta'iyeen: feudals

Jahiliyah: pre-Islamic era in Arabia, current usage refers to any society that is not strictly observing Islamic laws.

Jamaa'a Islamiya: term designating religious community organization.

Jizya: taxes imposed by the Muslim ruler upon the Dhimmis (Jews and Christians) who live in Muslim lands.

Kaaba: Muslim's holy shrine.

Kafir: literally, "the one who covers up the truth," but generally the word for unbeliever.

Kharijism: "those who go out" refers to those who went out of Islam after the death of Muhammad.

Mahdi: Messiah or the expected one.

Al-Majlis al-Shouri al-Aam: general consultative council.

Majlis al-Shoura: consultative council.

Majlis al-ulama: council of men of religious learning.

Millet: a religious community or confessional group that became part of Ottoman governance.

Monophysites: those who believe in the one nature of Christ.

Monothelites: those who believed that Christ possessed one divine will.

Omayyad: the first Muslim Dynasty, centered in Damascus, that ruled the Muslim empire from 661 to 750 AD.

Osmanlis: Arabic term for the Ottomans.

Qur'an: the word of Allah, as received by the Prophet and embodied in the holy book of Islam.

Quraysh: the main tribe of Arabia during the time of the Prophet to which Muhammad belonged.

Salafiya: history of interpretation of Islamic Dogma.

Salat: liturgical form of prayer, recited five times per day.

Shari'a: the law or entire corpus of rules guiding Muslim life.

Shaykh al-Azhar: Rector of Al Azhar University in Cairo.

Shaykh al-Tariqa: a sect leader.

Shahada: literally witness, or testifying that there is no God but Allah and Muhammad is his Prophet.

Shi'a: a sect within Islam who declare that Ali and his descendants are the true successors of the Prophet.

Shura: literally, "the consultation," deriving from the Qur'anic commendation to believers to consult together; in modern parlance, a legislative assembly.

Sowm: fasting.

Sufism: a mystical sect within Islam.

Sunnah: the custom of the Prophet, incorporated into the Hadith.

Sunni: majority division within Islam of those who accept the entire first generation of Muslim leaders as legitimate, in contrast with Shi'ia who accept only Ali and his descendents.

al-Takfir wa al-Hijrah: literally infidelity and flight, the followers of that movement believed that since present society is an infidel society they must flee from it until it collapses then return and build a new Islamic society.

Uhud: a name of one of the battles between Muslims and the pagans of Arabia under the leadership of the Prophet.

Ulama: scholars or learned individuals, especially in the legal or religious sciences.

Ummah: the community of believers who confess Islam.

Wafd: literally means delegate, a name of the major political party that dominated Egyptian politics during the thirties and forties.

Wahhabiyya: reform movement begun by Ibn Abd al-Wahhab in the Najd in Arabia, which gained the support of the Saud family and eventually became the central ideology in the area. Generally held strict views drawn from conservative Ibn Taymiyyah who rejected much of Sufi Islam and became strongly intolerant of any form not built on the Qur'an. Preached a new form of purification of Islam. Collectively known as wahhabism.

Waqf: an endowment for religious purposes, or for the collective good, such as hospitals, libraries, etc.

Za'im: a political leader.

Zakat: a yearly "tax" paid by Muslims as a contribution to community welfare or as a charitable gift.

Zawiyas: literary corners, street corners where Muslims sometimes gather for prayer.

Zoroastrians: the original inhabitants of Persia before Islam.

BIBLIOGRAPHY

Aberle, David F. *The Peyote Religion Among the Navaho.* Chicago: Festinger, 1966.

Ahmed, Jamal Mohammed. *The Intellectual Origins of Egyptian Nationalism.* London, New York, Toronto: Oxford University Press, 1960.

Ajami, Fouad. *The Arab Predicament: Arab Political Thought and Practice Since 1967.* New York City: Cambridge University Press, 1981.

Akhtar, Karm B. and Ahmad, H. Sakr. *Islamic Fundamentalism.* Cedar Rapids, Iowa: Igram Press Co., 1982.

Allon, Yigal. "Israel and The Palestinians", *The Jerusalem Quarterly.* No. 6, Winter 1978.

Al-Mu'ti, Abd al-Basit Abd. "The Future of Democracy in Egypt." *The Jerusalem Quarterly,* no. 6, Winter 1978.

———. "Class Structure in the Egyptian Village." *The Jerusalem Quarterly.* No. 10, Winter 1979.

Al-Sayyid-Marsot, Afaf Lutfi. *Egypt's Liberal Experiment: 1922-1936.* Berkeley, Los Angeles, London: University of California Press, 1977.

Amin, Samir. *The Arab Nation.* London: Billing & Sons Ltd., 1978.

Antonius, George. *The Arab Awakening.* New York, New York: Paragon Books, 1979.

Atiya, Aziz S. *Crusade, Commerce and Culture.* Bloomington: Indiana University Press, 1962.

———. *The Crusades in the Later Middle Ages.* London: Methuea and Company, 1983.

Atiyeh, George. *The Contemporary Middle East, 1948-1973: A Selective and Annotated Bibliography.* Boston: G. K. Hall, 1975.

Ayubi, Nazih N. M. "The Political Revival of Islam: The Case of Egypt." *International Journal Middle East Studies.* (vol. 12), 1980.

Badawi, Gamal. *al-Fetna al-Ta'ifiyya fi Misr.* Cairo: al-Markez al-Arabi lil-Sahafa.

Baer, Gabriel. *Studies in the Social History of Modern Egypt.* Chicago: University of Chicago Press, 1969.

———. *A History of Landownership in Modern Egypt.* London: Oxford University Press, 1962.

al-Bahnasawi, Salim Ali, *al-Hukm wa Qadiyat Takfir al-Muslim.* Cairo: Dar al-Ansar, May 1977.

al-Banna, Hasan. *Five Tracts of Hasan al-Banna 1906-1949.* Charles Wendell, Trans. Berkeley: University of California Press, 1978.

Barnett, H. G. *Innovation: The Basis of Cultural Change.* New York: McGraw Hill, 1953.

al-Bashry, Tamg. *al-Muslimoon wa 'l-Aqbaat.* (Muslims and Copts) Cairo: al-Hay'ah al-Misriyya al-Aama lil-Kitaab, 1980.

Bee, Robert L. *Patterns and Processes.* New York: The Free Press, 1974.

Be'eri, Eliezer. "Arab Officers and Politics." *The Jerusalem Quarterly.* No. 6, Winter 1978.

Bellah, Robert N. *Beyond Belief.* New York, Hagerstown, San Francisco, London: Harper & Row, 1976.

Bennigsen, Alexandre A. and Wimbush, S. Enders. *Muslim National Communism in the Soviet Union.* Chicago and London: The University of Chicago Press, 1979.

Berque, Jacques. *Egypt: Imperialism and Revolution.* London: Faber and Faber, 1972.

Binder, Leonard. *In a Moment of Enthusiasm* Chicago: University of Chicago Press, 1978.

———. *Ideological Revolution in the Middle East.* New York: Willey Publications, 1974.

———. *The Study of the Middle East.* New York, London, Sydney, Toronto: John Wiley & Sons, 1976.

Blumer, Herbert. *Elementary Collective Behavior.* Alfred McClung Lee, ed. New York: Barnes and Noble, 1951.

Bohnstedt, John W. *The Infidel Scourge of God: The Turkish Menace as Seen by German Pamphleteers of the Reformation Era.* Transactions of the American Philosophical Society, New Series, Vol 58, pt. 9, 1968.

Boisard, Marcel A. "On The Probable Influence of Islam on Western Public and International Law." *International Journal Middle East Studies.* (Vol. 11), 1980.

Brecher, Michael. *The Foreign Policy System of Israel.* New Haven: Yale University Press, 1972.

Brockelmann, Carl. *History of the Islamic Peoples.* New York: Capricorn Books Edition, 1960.

Bush, Rev. George, A. M. *The Life of Mohammad*. New York: Harper & Brothers, 1842.

Butcher, E. L. *The Story of the Church of Egypt*. London: Smith, Elder and Company, 1897.

Butler, Alfred J. *The Arab Conquest of Egypt—and The Last Thirty Years of the Roman Dominion*. Oxford: The Clarendon Press, 1902.

Cameron, William Bruce. *Modern Social Movements*. New York: Random House, 1967.

Camp David Document: A Framework for Peace in the Middle East Agreed at Camp David (September 17, 1978) *The Jerusalem Quarterly*. No. 10, Winter 1979.

Cantril, Hadley. *The Psychology of Social Movements*. New York: John Wiley & Sons, Inc., 1967.

Cash, W. Wilson. *The Expansion of Islam*. Scotland: Turnbull and Spears, 1928.

Charnay, Jean-Paul. *Islamic Culture and Socio-Economic Change*. Leiden: E. J. Brill, 1981.

Clements, Frank. *The Emergence of Arab Nationalism, from the Nineteenth Century to 1921*. Leiden: Brill, 1976.

Coser, Lewis. *The Functions of Social Conflict*. New York: The Free Press, 1956.

Crone, Patricia and Cook, Michael. *Hagarism*. Cambridge: Cambridge University Press, 1977.

Cudsi, Alexander S. and Ali E. Hillal Dessouki, ed., *Islam and Power*. Baltimore and London: The Johns Hopkins University Press, 1981.

Cutler, Allan. "The First Crusade and the Idea of 'Conversion.'" *The Muslim World*. LVIII, 1968.

Dahrendorf, Ralf. "On The Origin of Social Inequality." *Philosophy, Politics, and Society*. Basil Blackwell, 1962.

Daniel, N. A. *Islam, Europe and Empire*. Edinburgh: University Press, 1966.

——. *Islam and the West*. Edinburgh: The University Press, 1962?

Davies, James Chowning. *When Men Revolt and Why*. New York: The Free Press; London: Collier-Macmillan Limited 1971.

Deeb, Marius. *Party Politics in Egypt: The Wafd and Its Rivals 1919-39*. London: Ithaica Press for Middle East, 1978.

Dekmejian, R. Hrair. *Egypt Under Nasir*. Albany: State University of New York Press, 1971.

Dennett, D. C. *Conversion and the Poll Tax in Early Islam*. Cambridge: Harvard University Press, 1950.

Dessouki, Ali E. Hillal, ed. *Islamic Resurgence in the Arab World*. New York: Praeger Publishers, 1982.

Dinstein, Yoram. "Peace Negotiations Fatigue." *The Jerusalem Quarterly*. No. 10, Winter 1979.

Dishon, Daniel. "Sadat's Arab Adversaries." *The Jerusalem Quarterly*. No. 6, Winter 1978.

Donaldson, Dwight M. *The Shi'ite Religion*. London: Luzac & Company, (Luzac's Oriental Religions Series, vol. VI), 1933.

Donohue, John J. and John L. Esposito. *Islam in Transition - Muslim Perspectives*. New York, Oxford: Oxford University Press, 1982.

Douglas, Mary and Tipton, Steven M., ed. *Religion and America*. Boston: Beacon Press, 1982.

Durkheim, Emile. *On Morality and Society*. Chicago and London: The University of Chicago Press, 1973.

Enayat, Hamid. *Modern Islamic Political Thought*. London and Basingstoke: The MacMillan Press, Ltd., 1982.

Evans, Robert R., ed. *Social Movements: A Reader and Source Book*. Chicago, Illinois: Rand McNally College Publishing Company, 1973.

Farag, Muhammad Abd al-Salam. *The Missing Religious Precept*. (Unpublished document in Arabic—translated from the original by Michael Youssef).

Fickelman, Dale. *The Middle East: An Anthropological Approach*. 1981.

Fischer, Michael M. J. *Iran - From Religious Dispute To Revolution*. Cambridge, Massachusetts and London, England: Harvard University Press, 1980.

Fischer-Galati, Stephen A. *Ottoman Imperialism and German Protestantism, 1521-1555*. Cambridge: Harvard University Press, 1959.

Foster, George M. *Traditional Societies and Technological Change*. New York, Evanston, San Francisco, London: Harper & Row Publishers, 1973.

Freedman, Robert O. *Soviet Policy Toward the Middle East*. New York: Praeger, 1970.

Friedmann, Yohanan. "Islam is Superior ..." *The Jerusalem Quarterly*, no. 10, 1979.

Frowde, Henry. *The Arab Conquest of Egypt*. London, Edinburgh, New York: Henry Frowde, M. A. (Publisher To The University of Oxford), 1902.

Frye, Richard N. *Islam and the West*. The Netherlands: Mouton and Co., The Hague, 1956.

Galal, Amin. *The Modernization of Poverty: A Study in the Political Economy of Growth in Nine Arab Countries, 1945-1970*. 1974.

Gaudefray-Demonbyes, Maurice. *Muslim Institutions*. New York: Barnes and Noble, 1968.

Geerd, *The Interpretation of Cultures*. New York: Basic Books, 1973.

Geertz, Clifford, *Islam Observed*. New Haven: Yale University Press, 1968.

Gibb, H. A. R. *Modern Trends in Islam*. Chicago, Illinois: The University of Chicago Press, 1947.

——. *Mohammedanism*. London, Oxford, New York: Oxford University Press, 1962.

Gibbs, David; Mueller, Samuel A.; Wood, James R. "Doctrinal Orthodoxy, Salience, and the Consequential Dimension." *Journal for the Scientific Study of Religion*, Research Report 109, 1971.

Gilbar, Gad G. "Egypt's Economy: The Challenge of Peace." *The Jerusalem Quarterly*. No. 10, Winter 1979.

Gilligan, Carol. *Do The Social Sciences Have an Adequate Theory of Moral Development?* Harvard University, March, 1980.

Gilsenan, Michael. *Recognizing Islam*. New York: Pantheon Books, 1982.

Glubb, Sir John. *Soldiers of Fortune* (The Story of the Mamlukes). New York: Stein and Day Publishers, 1973.

Golan, Galia. "Soviet Policy in the Middle East." *The Jerusalem Quarterly*. No. 10, Winter 1979.

Goldschmidt. *A Concise History of the Middle East*. Colorado: Westview Press, Inc., 1979.

Gottheil, R. J. H. "Dhimmis and Moslems in Egypt." *Old Testament and Semitic Studies*. 2 vol. Chicago: The University Press, 1903.

——. "A Fetwa on the Appointment of Dhimmis to Office." *Zeitschrift fur Assyriologie*, XXVI, 1911.

Gran, Peter. *Islamic Roots of Capitalism - Egypt 1760-1840*. Austin, Texas: University of Texas Press, 1979.

Haim, Syvia, ed. *Arab Nationalism: An Anthology*. Berkeley: University of California Press, 1974.

Halpern, Manfred. *The Politics of Social Change in the Middle East and North Africa*. Princeton: Princeton University Press, 1963.

Hana, Milad. *Naam Akbat Laken Masriou*. Cairo: Madboly Library, 1980.

Harkabi, Y. *Palestinians and Israel*. Brunswick, New Yersey: Transaction Books, 1974.

Harris, Christina Phelps. *Nationalism and Revolution in Egypt: The Role of the Muslim Brotherhood*. Stanford: Mouton & Co., 1964.

Harris, Marvin. *Cannibals and Kings—The Origins of Cultures*. New York: Random House, 1977.

Hasluck, F. W. *Christianity and Islam Under the Sultans*. 2 vols. Oxford: Clarendon Press, 1929.

Haykel, M. A. *Tarajim Misriyyah wa-Gharbiyyah*. (Egyptian and Western Biographies), Cairo, 1929.

Heberle, Rudolf. *Social Movements*. New York: Appleton-Century-Crofts, 1951.

Heikal, Mohamed. *Autumn of Fury: The Assassination of Sadat*. New York: Random House,

Heyworth-Dunne, J. *Introduction to the History of Education in Modern Egypt*. Totowa, New Jersey: Biblio Distribution Centre, 1968.

——. *Religious and Political Trends in Modern Egypt*. Washington, D.C.: McGregor & Werner, Inc., 1950.

Hobbes, Thomas. *Leviathan*. New York, London: Collier Books, 1962.

Hobsbawm, E. J. *Primitive Rebels*. New York: W. W. Norton & Company, Inc., 1959.

Hodgeson, Marshall G. S. *The Venture of Islam*. Chicago: University of Chicago, 1974.

Hoffer, Eric. *The True Believer: Thoughts on the Nature of Mass Movements*. New York: Harper, 1951.

——. *The Ordeal of Change*. New York: Harper and Row, 1963.

——. *Reflection on the Human Condition*. New York: Harper and Row, 1973.

Holt, P. M. *Egypt and the Fertile Crescent 1516-1922*. Ithaca and London: Cornell University Press, 1966.

Hooper, Rex. *Social Movements*. Robert Evans, ed. Chicago: Rand McNally, 1973.

Hourani, Albert. *Arabic Thought in the Liberal Age 1798-1939*. London, New York, Toronto: Oxford University Press, 1962.

Hunter, Robert. *Revolution: Why? How? When?* New York and London: Harper and Brothers Publishers, 1940.

Husaini, Ishak Musa. *The Moslem Brethren*. Beirut, Lebanon: Khayat's College Book Cooperative, 1956.

Hussein, Taha. *mustaqbil al-Thaqaafa fi Misr*. (The Future of Culture in Egypt), Cairo: Dar al-Ma'aarif, 1938.

Ibrahim, Saad Eddin. "Anatomy of Egypt's Militant Islamic Groups: Methodological Note and Preliminary Findings." *International Journal Middle East Studies*. Vol. 12, 1980.

———. *The New Arab Social Order*. Colorado: Westview Press, 1982.

Issawi, Charles. *Egypt at Mid-Century—An Economic Survey*. London, New York, Toronto: Oxford University Press, 1954.

———. *Egypt in Revolution*. London: Oxford University Press, 1963.

———. *The Arab World's Legacy*. Princeton, New Jersey: The Darwin Press, Inc., 1981.

Jafri, S. Husain M. *Origins and Early Development of Shi'a Islam*. Longman, London, and New York: Longman Group Ltd., 1979.

Jansen, G. H. *Militant Islam*. London and Sydney: Pan Books, 1979.

Jurji, Edward J. "The Conciliatory Tone on Ibn-Arabi." *The Muslim World*. XXVIII, 1938.

Kalidy, Mustafa and Farrukh, Omar. *Missionaries and Imperialism*. (In Arabic) Beirut, 1964.

Kampf, Herbert A. "Soviet Policy in The Middle East: Does it Make Sense for Moscow?." *The Jerusalem Quarterly*. No. 6, Winter 1978.

Kazemi, Farhad. "The Shi'i Clergy and The State In Iran: From The Safavids To The Phalavis", *Journal of the American Institute for the Study of Middle Eastern Civilization*. Vol. 1, No. 2, Summer 1980.

Kazemi, Farhad. "Iranian Revolution in Perspective." *Iranian Studies*. Journal of the Society for Iranian Studies, (vol. XIII, Nos. 1-4), Massachusetts: Bosworth Printing Company, 1980.

Keddie, Nikki R. *Roots of Revolution—An Interpretive History of Modern Iran*. New Haven and London: Yale University Press, 1981.

———. "Iran: Change in Islam: Islam and Change." *International Journal Middle East Studies*. Vol. 11, 1980.

———. *Sayyid Jamal al-Din "al-Afghani": A Political Biography*. 1972.

Kelley, Jonathan and Herbert S. Kleim. *Revolution and the Rebirth of Inequality: A Theory Applied to the National Revolution in Bolivia*. Berkeley, Los Angeles, London: University of California Press, 1981.

Khomeini, Ayatollah Ruhollah. *Islamic Government*. Arlington, Virginia: Joint Publications Research Service, 1979.

Khouri, Fred J. *The Arab-Israeli Dilemma*. Syracuse: Syracuse University Press, 1976.

King, C. Wendell. *Social Movements in the United States*. New York: Random House, 1967.

Kohlberg, Lawrence. "Development of Moral Character and Moral Ideology." *Review of Child Development Research*. Illinois: University of Chicago.

Kotb, Sayed. *Social Justice in Islam*. New York: Octagon Books, 1980.

Kritzeck, Jamen. *Peter the Venerable and Islam*. Princeton: University Press, 1964.

Kuhn, Thomas S. *The Structure of Scientific Revolutions*. Chicago: The University of Chicago Press, 1962.

Kuper, Adam. *Anthropologists and Anthropology*. New York: Pica Press, 1973.

Lanternari, Vittorio. *The Religions of the Oppressed*. New York: Mentor Books, 1965.

Laroui. "Marxism and the Third World Intellectual." *The Crisis of the Arab Intellectual*. Berkeley: University of California Press, 1976.

Lewis, Bernard. *The Emergence of Modern Turkey*. London, Oxford, New York: Oxford University Press, 1961.

Locke, John. *The Second Treatise of Goverment*. Indianapolis: Bobbs-Merrill Educational Publishing, 1952.

Lubasz, Heinz. "What is Revolution?" *Why Revolution?* Paynton & Blackey, ed. Cambridge, Massachusetts: Schenkman Publishing Company, 1971.

Mabro, Robert. *The Egyptian Economy, 1952-1972*. Oxford: Clarendon Press, 1974.

Madkour, Ibrahim. "Islam et Evolution." *International Journal Middle East Studies*. Vol. 11, 1980.

Magnarella, Paul J. *Tradition and Change in a Turkish Town*. New York, London, Sydney, Toronto: Jihn Wiley and Sons, 1974.

al-Malefijt, Annemarie De wa. *Images of Man*. New York: Alfred A. Knopf, 1977.

Abdel-Malek, Anouar. *Egypt: Military Society*. New York: Random House, 1968.

Malinowski, Bronislaw. *The Dynamics of Cultural Change*. New Haven and London: Yale University Press, 1965.

Mangold, Peter. *Superpower Intervention in the Middle East*. London: Croom Helm, 1978.

Mannheim, Karl. *Ideology and Utopia*. London and Henley: Routledge & Kegan Paul, 1936.

Mansfield, Peter, ed. *The Middle East: A Political and Economic Survey*. London: Oxford University Press, 1973.

———. *The Arabs*. New York: Penguin Books, 1976.

———. *Nasser's Egypt*. Baltimore: Penguin Books, 1969.

Marx, Karl. "A Note on Classes." *Capital: A Critique of Political Economy*, Moscow: Foreign Languages Publishing House, Vol. III.

Marx, Karl. "Karl Marx's Theory of Social Classes." *Class, Status and Power*.

Mayfield, James, *Rural Politics in Nasser's Egypt: A Quest for Legitimacy*. Boston: University Press, 1971.

Menashri, David. "Strange Bedfellows: The Khomeini Coalition." *The Jerusalem Quarterly*. No. 10, Winter 1979.

Mikhain, Kyriakos. *Copts and Moslems*. London: Kennikat Press, 1911.

Mitchell, Richard P. *The Society of the Muslim Brothers*. London: Oxford University Press, 1969.

Moore, Wilbert. *Social Change*. Englewood Cliffs, New Jersey: Prentice-Hall, Inc., 1963.

Mortimer, Edward. *Faith and Power: The Politics of Islam*. New York: Vintage Books, 1982.

Muir, Sir William. *The Caliphate: Its Rise, Decline, and Fall*. London: Smith, Elder & Co., September 1891.

———. *The Life of Mohammed*. Edinburgh: John Grant, 1923.

Murphy, Thomas Patrick. *The Holy War*. Columbus, Ohio: Ohio State University Press, 1974.

Nasr, Seyyed Hossein. *Ideals and Realities of Islam*. London: George Allen and Unwin Ltd. (Ruskin House), 1964.

Nasser, Gamel Abdel. *The Philosophy of the Revolution*. Cairo: Dar al-Ma'aarif, 1959.

Neumann, Sigmund. *The International Civil War*. World Politics #1, 1948-1949.

Paynton and Blackey, ed. *Why Revolution*. Cambridge: Schenkman, 1971.

Peretz, Don. *The Middle East Today*. New York, Chicago, San Francisco, Dallas, Montreal, Toronto, London, Sydney: Holt, Rinehart and Winston, 1978.

Perlmann, M. "Notes on Anti-Christian Propaganda in the Mamluk Empire." *Bulletin of the School of Oriental Studies*. X, 1940-42.

Pickthall, Muhammad M. *The Glorious Qur'an*. New York: The Muslim World League, 1977.

Piscatori, James P. *Islam in the Political Process*. Cambridge: Cambridge University Press, 1983.

Potter, Ralph B. "Justice and Beyond in Moral Education." Regional Conference on Moral Development of Youth, Spring Hill Center, Wayzata, Minnesota, June 1, 1977.

Qasim, Abduh. *Ahl al-Dhimmah fi 'l-Usoor al-Wusta* (Dhimmi in the Middle Ages) Cairo: Dar al Ma'aarif, 1979.

Qasim, Amin. *Tahreer al-Mar'ah*. (The Liberation of Women) Cairo: Dar al-Ma'aarif, 1980.

Quandt, William R. *Decade of Decision: American Policy toward the Arab-Israeli Conflict, 1967-76*. Berkeley: University Press, 1977.

al-Rafi'i, Abd al-Rahman. *Tarikh al-Haraka al-Qawmiyya fi Misr*. (The History of the Nationalist Movement in Egypt), Cairo, 1929.

Rahman, Fazlur. *Islam & Modernity*. Chicago & London: The University of Chicago Press, 1982.

Ramadan, Dr. Abd al-Azeem. *Ikhwan al-Muslimeen wal-tanzeem al-Sirri*. Cairo: Roz al-Yousuf Printing, 1982.

el-Raziq, Abd. *al-Islam wa Usool al-Hukm.* Cairo, 1925.

Rejwan, Missim. *Nasserist Ideology, Its Exponents and Critics.* New York: Willey Publishers, 1974.

Reck, Andrew J. "The Metaphysics of Equality." *The New Scholasticism.* Vol. XXXIV, July, 1960.

Rodinson, Maxime. *Islam and Capitalism.* Austin: University of Texas Press, 1978.

——. *Marxism and the Muslim World.* London.

Rubin, Barry. *The Arab States and the Palestine Conflict.* Syracuse, New York: Syracuse University Press, 1981.

Rubinstein, Alvin. *Red Star on the Nile: The Soviet-Egyptian Relationship since the June War.* Princeton, New Jersey: Princeton University Press, 1977.

Runciman, Steven. *A History of the Crusades.* 3 vols. Cambridge: University Press, 1941-54.

Sabuh, Michael. *Abu Bakr al-Sideeq.* Cairo: Dar al-Thaqafa al-Aamah, 1973.

al-Sadat, Anwar. *In Search of Identity.* New York: Harper and Row, 1978.

Shalins, Marshall. *Culture and Practical Reason.* Chicago and London: The University of Chicago Press, 1976.

Said, Edward. *The Questions of Palestine.* New York: Times Books, 1979.

Salem, Elie. "The Elizabethan Image of Islam." Studia Islamica, XXII, 1965.

Sauvaget, Jean. *Introduction of the History of the Muslim East: A Bibliographical Guide.* 1965.

Saunders, J. J. *A History of Medieval Islam.* London, Henley and Boston: Routledge and Kegan Paul, 1965.

al-Sayyid, Muhammad Lutfi. *Ta'ammulaat fi 'l-Falsafa wa 'l-Adab wa 'l-Siyaasah wa 'l-Iqtimaa'.* (Reflection on Philosophy, Literature, Politics and Society), Articles from al-Jaridah 1912-1914 printed in a book, Cairo, 1946.

Schacht, Joseph and C. E. Bosworth, ed. *The Legacy of Islam,* London W.I.: Oxford University Press, 1974.

Schmandt, Raymond H. *The Crusades—Origin of an Ecumenical Problem.* (The Smith History Lecture 1967) Houston: University of Saint Thomas, 1967.

Schwoebel, Robert. *The Shadow of the Crescent: The Renaissance Image of the Turk.* New York: St. Martin's Press, 1967

Shaban, M. A. *Islamic History A.D. 600-750 (A.H. 132).* Cambridge: Cambridge University Press, 1971.

Shari'ati, Ali. *On the Sociology of Islam.* Berkeley: Mizan Press, 1979.

Sivan, Emmanuel. "How Fares Islam?" *The Jerusalem Quarterly.* No. 10, Winter 1979.

Skocpol, Theda. *State and Social Revolution.* Cambridge University Press, 1979.

Smith, Adam. *The Theory of Moral Sentiments.* Indianapolis: Liberty Classics, 1969.

Smith, Wilfred Cantwell. *Islam and Modern History.* Princeton University Press, 1957.

——. *On Understanding Islam.* Netherlands: Mouton Publishers, 1981.

Southern, R. W. *Western Views of Islam in the Middle Ages.* Cambridge: Harvard University Press, 1962.

Stoddard, Philip H., David C. Cuthell, Margaret W. Sullivan (ed). *Change and the Muslim World,* Syracuse, New York: Syracuse University Press, 1981.

Safran, Nadav. *Egypt in Search of Political Community.* Cambridge, Massachusetts; London, England: Harvard University Press, 1961.

Sykes, Christopher. *Crossroads to Israel 1917-1948.* Bloomington, London: Indiana University Press, 1973.

Szyliowicz, Joseph S. *Education and Modernization in the Middle East.* Ithaca, New York: Cornell University Press, 1973.

Tabari, Ali. *Kitab al-Din wa-al-Dawlah.* ("The Book of Religion and Empire"). Lahore: Ra Publishing Company, 1970.

Tachau, Frank, ed. *Political Elites and Political Development in the Middle East.* Cambridge, Massachusetts: Schenkman, 1975.

Tabataba'i, Allamah Sayyid Muhammad Husayn. *Shi'ite Islam.* Persian Studies Series No. 5, Albany: State University of New York Press, 1975.

Tignor, R. L. *Modernization and British Colonial Rule in Egypt, 1882-1914.* Princeton, New Jersey: Princeton University, 1966.

Tipton, Steven M. *Getting Saved From the Sixties*. Berkeley, Los Angeles, London: University of California Press, 1982.

Toch, Hans. *The Social Psychology of Social Movements*. Indianapolis, New York, Kansas City: The Bobbs-Merrill Company, Inc., 1965.

Tocqueville, Alexis de. *Democracy in America*. New York: Doubleday and Company, Inc., 1969.

Tritton, A. S. *The Caliphs and Their Non-Muslim Subjects*.

Troeltsch, Ernst. *The Social Teaching of The Christian Churches*. London: George Allen & Unwin Ltd. and New York: The Macmillan Company, Vol. one, 1931.

Tucker, Robert, ed. *The Marx—Engels Reader*. New York and London: W. W. Norton & Company, 1978.

Turner, Bryan S. *Weber and Islam*. London and Boston: Routledge & Kegan Paul, 1974.

Turner, Ralph H. "The Real Self: From Institution to Impulse." meeting of American Sociological Association, Denver, August 1971, University of California, Los Angeles, Vol. 81, no. 5.

Turner, V. W. *Schism and Continuity in an African Society*. Manchester University Press, 1957.

——. *Dramas, Fields, and Metaphors*. Cornwall University Press, 1978.

——. *The Forest of Symbols*. Ithaca and London: Cornell University Press, 1967.

Vatikiotis, P. J. *Revolution in the Middle East*. Totowa, New Jersey: Rowman and Littlefield, 1972.

——. *The History of Egypt from Muhammad to Sadat*. 1980.

——. *The Modern History of Egypt*. New York, Washington: Frederick A. Praeger, 1969.

——. *Nasser and His Generation*. New York and London: St. Martin's Press, 1978.

Waken, Edward. *A Lonely Minority*. New York: W. M. Morrow and Co., 1963.

Walzer, Michael. *The Revolution of the Saints*. Princeton, N.J., June 8, 1965.

Wallace, Anthony F.C. *Religion: An Anthropological View*. New York: Random House, 1966.

——."Revitalization Movements." *American Anthropology*. Vol. 58, April 1956.

Warriner, Doreen. *Land and Poverty in the Middle East*. London: Royal Institute of International Affairs, 1948.

Wasserstein, Bernard. *The British in Palestine: The Mandatory Government and the Arab-Jewish Conflict*. London, England: Rivial Historical Society, 1978.

Waterbury, John. *Egypt—Burdens of the Past, Options for the Future*. Bloomington and London: Indiana University Press, 1978.

——.*The Hydropolitics of the Nile Valley*. New York: Syracuse University Press, 1980.

Watt, William Montgomery. *Islam and the Integration of Society*. London: Routledge & Kegan Paul, 1961.

——. *Islamic Philosophy and Theology*. Edinburgh: Edinburgh University Press, 1962.

——. *Muhammad Prophet and Statesman*. London, Oxford, New York: Oxford University Press, 1961.

——. *Truth in The Religions*. Edinburgh: Edinburgh University Press, 1963.

Weber, Max. *On Charisma and Institution Building*. Chicago and London: The University of Chicago Press, 1968.

——. "The Development of Caste" from "Karl Marx's Theory of Social Classes." *Class, Status and Power*. New York: Free Press, 1953.

——. *The Protestant Ethic and the Spirit of Capitalism*. London: George Allen & Unwin Ltd., 1930.

——. *The Sociology of Religion*. Boston: Beacon Press, 1963.

——. *The Theory of Social and Economic Organization*. Glencoe, Illinois: The Free Press, 1947.

Wendell, Charles. "Five Tracts of Hasan Al-Banna (1906-1949)." *University of California Publications Near Eastern Studies*, (vol. 20), California: University of California Press, 1978.

——. *The Evolution of the Egyptian National Image—From its Origins to Ahmad Lutfi al-Sayyid*. Berkeley, Los Angeles, London: University of California Press, 1972.

Wilson, John. *Introduction to Social Movements*. New York: Basic Books, Inc., 1973.

Wolf, Eric R. *Peasant Wars of the Twentieth Century*. New York, Evanston, and London: Harper and Row Publishers, 1969.

Worsley, Peter. *The Trumpet Shall Sound*. London: MacGibbon & Kee, 1957.

Zakariya, Faud. "Reflections on Arab Tradition and Modernity." *The Jerusalem Quarterly*. No. 10, Winter 1979.

Zwemer, Samuel M. *The Influence of Animism on Islam*. New York: The Macmillan Company, 1920.